FOOD FOR ALL SEASONS

First published in 2016
by Faber & Faber Limited
Bloomsbury House
74–77 Great Russell Street
London WC1B 3DA

Designed, illustrated and typeset by Here Design, London

Printed and bound in Europe by Imago

A CIP record for this book is available from the British Library

ISBN 978–0–571–23590–2

2 4 6 8 10 9 7 5 3 1

FOOD FOR
ALL SEASONS

—

OLIVER ROWE

FABER & FABER

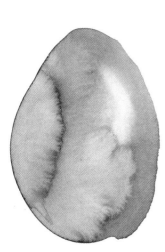

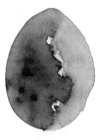

INTRODUCTION

—

Engaging with seasonal food is about engaging with a narrative. At its most basic level this book describes the narrative of a passing year and the seasons as they wax and wane – a personal account of my own journey through the food year and beyond, picking up on what I cook and what captures my attention at various points.

Following the seasons is its own reward. There are social, economic, environmental and dietary benefits to eating seasonally, but more importantly it is the personal benefits, the richness that a sense of understanding the food year brings to life that is most gratifying. There are times of the year when the breadth of produce is more limited, when cooking and eating can seem repetitive, but the overall variety seasonality brings to our lives is always rewarding. It impacts on our diet, our habits and our environment, on both local and global levels. It may be that there has never been a more important time to commit to this engagement – if we are to resolve the growing problem that feeding ourselves presents then surely a good place to begin is at an individual level, finding meaning in and feeling passionate about the food we eat.

Locality has long been an important feature of food for me. This is for a variety of reasons, from reducing road miles and saving energy to connecting with the story behind the food that I eat by being able to comprehend and contextualise its journey and the people that participate in it. But the main reason has always been

—

because it increases my sense of seasonality, pushes me into a deeper engagement with the food seasons – the more local the food you eat, the more seasonal it will be. It was this that inspired me to open Konstam at the Prince Albert in King's Cross in 2006 and to source the ingredients from around London.

Although this book describes a 12-month cycle, it has taken far longer than that to write, and this disrupts any attempt at a simple narrative as the events within it are far from consecutive, and many of the feelings and impressions are disconnected. It is, nonetheless, an attempt to jot down, with the passing of a cooking year, some of the food, thoughts and events that pass through my mind, my life and my kitchen.

The recipes in this book don't always describe complete plates of food. Many of them are elements to be used in combination with each other or with other dishes. Some are barely recipes in any evolved sense of the word, more descriptions of how to cook a dish, and many are little more than a list of possibilities. Mainly this is because cooking, for me, has always been about achieving a familiarity with disparate elements and then letting my creativity pull them together to form dishes, meals and menus appropriate to the context and my resources. No meal is ever the same, even though they can be similar, so it feels wrong for me to be didactic. If the recipes occasionally seem vague it is only because the options are always endless and this vagueness acknowledges the fact. Not only this but it can never be that one way of looking at a specific set of ingredients is the only way, because food is always about change, experimentation and working with what you have. This vagueness is led by a desire to encourage the reader to play with the tools and seasonal palette available to them.

Perhaps because I had no formal training before cooking at Moro in Clerkenwell in 1997, or perhaps just because I love the way food is constantly shifting and evolving, infinitely varied and capricious, I have never felt that being a chef gave me much authority on such a personal and culturally diverse phenomena as food. Cooking is about trying new things, seeing what works and what doesn't – learning for the next time, finding out what works for you. That doesn't mean couching yourself in the comfort of your likes and dislikes – challenge yourself to find ways of understanding and enjoying what lies outside your comfort zone.

And the longer I've worked as a cook the more I've come to understand that it is always about adaptability and improvisation at every level, and often completely on the spot. I've had to cook in fields with only a portable barbecue; tents with trestle tables; tiny kitchens with barely space to rest a plate; as well as in kitchens with wood ovens, charcoal grills, induction hobs and sous vide water baths. I've cooked with the most exquisite of lovingly produced single-farm organic produce, bog-standard veg from the average wholesaler, unknown and mysterious foraged food, and with veg I've picked up at the corner shop. I've cooked with chefs whose experience, creativity and understanding of food cast my own into the darkest of shadows, jobbing chefs with a grudge and a permanent scowl, hard-working cooks who could read my culinary mind, and I've worked shifts with a changing cast of volunteers and part-time staff. While all have their pressures, I've enjoyed each for its own reasons and its own problems solved. Life isn't ideal, food isn't ideal, kitchens aren't ideal and the seasonal food calendar isn't ideal. There are times when you need to improvise and there are times when you can't breathe for choice. Every decision, each experiment or compromise you make in the kitchen takes you on a new journey, and every dish you share with an eager diner or grateful friend makes a new connection – savour every minute of it, as the next one will be completely different.

OCTOBER

—

Squash

Apples

Pears

Pork

Mussels

Medlars

Loquats

Walnuts

*You ought to know that October
is the first spring month.*

Karel Čapek

Not everything starts with a bang, and October escapes
our attention much of the time; in fact, it can be easy to
forget all about it. The fading rays of summer have been
and gone and autumn is well underway, the goodwill and white
noise of Christmas seem a safe distance away and the true cold of
midwinter is still just a bitter edge on an easterly wind. October
strolls into the calendar and gets on with things in a steady and
contemplative way. If May whistles with purpose, October quietly
hums and gets on with a few jobs around the garden.

I've thought long and hard about when the food year starts. It's not
easy to decide exactly when this is because the sequence of planting,
rearing, harvesting and taking to market is a year-round process and
the stages intertwine.

I came to the conclusion that it shouldn't begin with the start of the
calendar year. January is midwinter, and it follows that something
in the middle can't be at the start; in terms of the food year there's
nothing about January that makes me think of a beginning. We do
finally stop thinking about turkey, goose and Christmas pudding
and turn our attention to different foods, but the produce that's
available is essentially the same as before Christmas. Winter is
relatively dormant, and the variety of fruit and vegetables quite
restricted. There are cabbages, stored apples, Jerusalem artichokes,
game, herring and pike but the choice isn't much more extensive.
There is an emotional rebirth in January as we herald the New Year;

it can feel like the start of something new, but the season doesn't change. It's still cold and frosty – even snowy some years – and the trees are bare and forbidding. The ground is cold and hard, making it impossible to plant anything, and there isn't enough light to grow much by. The purple sprouting broccoli is slowly doing its thing and the rhubarb is secretly working away in its candlelit sheds, but by and large there's not much to show for anything. No harvest, no planting. No start, no end.

I considered spring for a while – the buds show on the trees, the daffodils arrive and the lambing season begins. We get new crops too, especially towards the end of the season. But the process of planting and rearing goes some way back; everything that comes to us in the spring has been prepared for previously, so although spring is when we start seeing the fruits of our labour, it doesn't make sense to make it the beginning of the food year.

Summer is when we look for the fruition of our labours. The growing is well underway and it's the finishing touches that matter now, making sure everything is well watered and deciding when to harvest the various crops. This can't be the start of the food year, when we're at our busiest reaping the rewards of a hard year's work.

So, after a great deal of wondering, I decided that it is the conclusion that defines the start. The end of September brings us harvest festival, and this is when we traditionally look at what we've gleaned from the soil. It represents the end point for so many varieties of fruit and vegetables, and from then on we start looking towards the next harvest.

Writing in 1683, the gardener John Reid listed what needed doing in October:

> Gather Winter Fruits. Trench and fallow grounds (mixing with proper soil) to ly over the Winter. Prepare dungs and mannures, mixing and laying them in heaps bottom'd and covered with Earth. Plant Hawthorn Hedges, And all Trees that lose their leaves; Also lay their branches. Prun Roses. Gather seeds of Hassell, Hawthorn, Plan, Ash, Beach,

Oak, Aple, Pear, &c. Cut Strawberries, Artichocks, Asparagus, covering
their beds with dung and Ashes. Earth up Winter Sallades, Herbes,
and Flowers, a little. Plant Cabbage, &c. Plant Tulips, Anemonies,
and other Bulbs. Sow the seed of Bairs-ears, Cowslips, Tulips, &c. Beat
and Roll Gravel and Grass. Finish your last weeding and mowing.
Lay bair leopered Tree Roots and remove what harms them: also delve
and dung such as require it. Drain excessive moisture wherever it be.
Pickle and conserve Fruits. Make Perry and Cyder. You may now safely
remove Bees.

It's a busy time and much of the work is about tidying, finishing off
and lashing things down ready for winter. Reid himself felt that for
the gardener the year began in November, but for me that's too late;
November is well on the way to winter, but October is the month of
transformation. By October the game season is already in full swing,
with pheasant and woodcock joining the party on the first of the
month and with most of the deer still to come. This brings wildness
to the kitchen palette and a richness to the menu, which is only too
welcome as the weather gets cooler.

Another important contributor to our sense of the annual cycle is
the start of the academic year. Until we have children of our own
its significance fades, but it is well learned from a young age and
I think some of this has stayed with me. Coming back to school
after the holidays is an exciting time – absence has softened our
memories of it and we all want to see our friends again. By October
the stories of the summer holidays have all been swapped, and as the
realities of the school year set in, and stretch ahead interminably, so
we hold on to the glow of summer for as long as we can, while the
cold of winter has yet to take hold.

There is no one day – not even harvest festival – when we can put a
wetted finger to the wind, rub a handful of earth between our palms
and, looking to the east, give a sage nod, as if to say, 'This is it –
this is the start of the food year.' It's more subtle than that and the
change is slower, but it comes sometime in early to mid-autumn; I
feel it's in October that the transition from horn of plenty to blank

—

canvas occurs. Maybe it's ushered in by the harvest moon, coming as it does just after the festival. Maybe we really are controlled, as many believe, by the lunar cycle. The Anglo-Saxons called the harvest moon Winterfylleth, which means winter-full, and for them it heralded the start of winter.

There are many reasons to get the food year underway in October, but there is also something whimsical about it; it's a feeling – and it feels right to me. I've always liked the autumn. I love the colours, the darkness of the flavours, the smell of cold rain at night for the first time. If it's been a hot summer the gentle cooling that comes in the autumn can be a welcome relief. Sometimes we get the clear skies of an Indian summer; the sun is lower and the air takes on a different colour and smell. Early rain brings up the loam and any leaves that have already fallen start to go musty. Go anywhere near an apple tree and the pungent scent of windfalls going off rises up to meet you. The leaves still on the trees start to go yellow, orange and gold, clinging on as long as they can before falling in drifts to the ground. I've found that many of my relationships began in the autumn. It's a ripe time and we feel it as much as the land.

Other than the general drop in temperature, October administers the change from dry to wet. When I started my first year of college we had torrents of rain every single day for the first three weeks and everything smelled like old dog. It wasn't the best start but it was typical of October.

There are two genuinely abundant times in the British food calendar, and October is one of them. Most of the root vegetables are as ready as they'll ever be and, if you're lucky, there are still a few tomatoes and runner beans. Courgettes and marrow are available, mature leeks and cabbages really start to kick off, and there are plenty of salads and other greens, including spinach and watercress. There should still be some chard, if not for long, and cavolo nero comes into season soon.

This is the squash season too, and there are copious varieties that thrive in our climate. Butternut squash has become a real feature of British cookery in recent years and is one of my favourite vegetables. It's rich, highly flavoured and, if grown and cooked right, soft and juicy. It's high in magnesium and vitamin A, making it healthy too. Roast butternut is one of the great pleasures of autumn and goes with game, pork, lamb, poultry, grilled oily fish and almost anything else. It makes an excellent gratin and a delicious soup. It stores well, so you can keep eating it for much of the winter, but be careful as the supermarkets will supplement our home-grown crops with squash from every corner of the globe as soon as the UK price becomes too high.

Roast butternut squash and chestnut soup brings together two very seasonal ingredients in a lovely way. Pre-cooked chestnuts are ideal for this recipe, but if you're preparing them yourself you'll need to boil and peel them first. Chestnuts have quite a pervasive flavour, so two handfuls of the prepared kernels to two squash should be plenty.

Soften and cook two or three sliced onions in olive oil until sweet and caramelised. Halfway through cooking add chopped garlic, and fresh thyme leaves shortly afterwards. In the meantime, toss one large or two small peeled, deseeded and roughly chopped butternut squash with salt, pepper and plenty of oil, then roast in a really hot oven, spread out in one layer on a baking tray. Fry a large handful of roughly sliced chestnuts in butter with salt until caramelised and add to the onions. Continue to cook the onions and chestnuts for a few minutes so the flavours mingle.

When the squash is nicely coloured and softened, add it to the onion mixture. Cook together for a minute or two, just cover with water – or chicken stock if there are no vegetarians involved – and bring to a gentle simmer. Cook for 5 or 10 minutes, then blend, using milk to thin to the desired consistency – for me this means runnier than a purée but still unctuous and rich. Bear in mind that the soup will continue to thicken as it sits. Season and then carefully reheat to serve, making sure not to boil. I like to serve it with crispy matchsticks of bacon, more carefully sliced pieces of chestnut fried slowly in butter with salt, then dried and cooled on kitchen paper, and crème fraîche. You can season the crème fraîche with salt and pepper, a little crushed garlic and a bit of oil if you want.

Butternut squash is delicious but I'm also very fond of Crown Prince – a variety of squash with a greenish blue skin and orange flesh similar to that of the butternut. It may not be quite as unctuous but it roasts beautifully and makes a great filling for ravioli, pierogi or similar dishes. Crown Prince, marjoram and Golden Cross – a semi-hard goat's cheese from Lewes, East Sussex – makes a lovely combination for this kind of dish. Roast the squash, mash in the other ingredients with a good knob of butter and then use it as you would any other pasta filling. Make sure you season it well as the filling will have to carry the relative blandness of the pasta.

Spaghetti squash is marvellous too. I've only occasionally seen it on the market in the UK but it's common in North America. The flesh is very unusual – made up of tightly packed strings of squash. They become fragile when roasted but the texture is amazing and I'm surprised we don't see more of it here. I cut it up and roast it with the skin on, but you can roast it whole, then scoop out the insides and use it almost like spaghetti, adding a sauce or just oil and Parmesan. I've used it to stuff pasta too, most often pierogi, a Polish pasta we'll come to later in the book.

It was during October, in 2003, that I bought my café. It was quite a rapid process, in hindsight. I had come back in August from a rather trying period of working in France and was casting about for what to do – still wanting to cook, but not sure in which capacity. My sister's partner saw a little café for sale on King's Cross Road, and I made some enquiries. One thing led to another, and a couple of months later I found myself in possession of the keys to not only the café but the house above it. This was the first real estate I had ever been even close to owning and suddenly I was responsible for five and a half floors of early Victorian bricks and mortar on a busy, dusty and somewhat incongruous road in the arse end of King's Cross. We didn't open the café straight away as there was a lot of work to be done before that, but it was in October that it all began.

I named it Konstam, my grandmother's maiden name, and decked it out with sharing tables, lovely Holophane lights, tongue and groove on the walls and a Gaggia coffee machine. Cork tiles ran all the way down one wall, and over the next few years I collected postcards, old banknotes, interesting objects and interesting photographs, all pinned to it with multi-coloured drawing pins. It was, as *Time Out* quickly dubbed it, cute as a button. I commissioned an artist called Ian Wright to create a drawing pin picture, and ended up with a huge stag – taken from Landseer's *The Monarch of the Glen* – stretching from the skirting boards almost to the ceiling. The counter was set at farmhouse table height and made from one big piece of gorgeous Pembrokeshire oak. The menu was always small – four or five freshly cut sandwiches, four salads, a tart, a frittata, soup, three mains and a pudding or two. I got coffee from Monmouth, bread from Exeter Street Bakery and Breads Etcetera, and *pastéis de Nata* and *bolos de arroz* from Madeira Patisserie in Vauxhall.

I had hoped to open by Christmas, to catch the seasonal rush, but the day before we were set to open the man who came to turn on the gas said he couldn't do it – the meter we'd installed wasn't big enough to cope with the new kitchen equipment. I tried to wangle my way around it as hard as I could, but there was nothing to be done. British Gas told me it would take five-to-ten weeks to get the new meter installed, at no small cost, and so I had to just sit and wait. I remember standing outside on the pavement that night, looking in through the window with all the lights on and dimmed just right, thinking how beautiful it was, and wondering if I would ever be able to open.

I held out, and January rolled around. Eventually they installed the new meter and on the 27th of the month we opened the café. We had a party the night before, and I wrote this about it a couple of years later:

> I remember the launch party with my grandmother and my aunts, my parents, sister, cousins and friends; the people who had helped me make the whole thing happen; a motley collection of staff – all of whom were lovely and willing, but so appalling I had to sack them within a week or two of opening – some neighbours, and quite a few people I'd never met. It looked so great before everyone arrived – with its lovely lights and cork all down one wall, and on the tables some little canapé versions of all the sandwiches that I was going to have on the sandwich menu. Me, some friends and the staff had worked so hard getting it all ready that day and I was covered in grime when everyone was about to arrive. It was still empty when I dashed upstairs to change my clothes, but when I came down it was full and everyone wondering where I was. That left me arriving late at my own party. It'll be like that at my funeral I'm sure.

The next day I had a big group in from Thomas Heatherwick's studio – he was my sister's partner who had spotted the café in the first place, so they were eager to come in and support it – and it wasn't until they'd sat down and ordered their food that I realised I didn't have any proper knives, forks or plates! In all that time it hadn't occurred to me to buy them. I had lovely cups from a reject china shop in Columbia Road, but I'd overlooked cutlery. Fortunately I had thought to order takeaway boxes and wooden knives and forks, but nonetheless I was mortified. I wanted the cutlery to be nice – it may have been a café but you can't beat a good bit of tableware – so as soon as we closed for the day I ran to Habitat and bought some. They cost a bit more than I would have liked, but it was worth it. I can't remember where the plates came from in the end, probably a restaurant supplier the next day, but they were nice too; I didn't want to be ashamed of the dishes I was putting the food on.

Three years later I opened a restaurant on a corner opposite the café, in what used to be a pub called the Prince Albert. After a great deal of thought I decided to call it Konstam at the Prince Albert; I liked the sense of residency it evoked. While I was developing the concept for the restaurant I was starting to think a lot about local food. I'd been inspired by Hugh Fearnley-Whittingstall's early books and realised how these principles tied in with my passion for seasonality and my concerns for the environmental impact of the food chain. The moment I decided to focus on produce that was local to London I started a plan to open with a meal that featured only super-local suppliers. Within seconds of having that thought, however, I realised how much work I'd already put in finding local producers and felt it would be a shame to focus on them for just one meal, so why not make it the first week? It was only micro-seconds before that became two weeks, then six, until eventually I just thought, hell, let's go the whole hog.

My friend Adam Penny owns a production company and when I talked to him about this he thought it was such a good idea that he asked if I wanted to see if anyone might be interested in a programme about the process of looking for the suppliers – something we knew right away would be no mean feat. One thing led to another and eventually we spoke to BBC2. They loved the idea and agreed to make a series around the whole process. This aired as *The Urban Chef* and came out just after the restaurant opened. Filming took around six months and was concurrent with opening the restaurant and running the café, so it was a busy and very stressful time, but one which I recall with great fondness. It's exciting to be part of a big project, and I really enjoyed getting stuck into all these things. Looking back, I'm not sure how it all came together, but it did and I lived to tell the tale.

———

Autumn is a time of abundance and, for me, the kings of the season are the late-ripening orchard fruits – apples, pears and quinces. Their flavours are key to the seasonal menu and they work in both savoury and sweet dishes. Pork and duck go well with them, but they can also be used with other meats and some fish. Orchard fruits ripen at different times throughout the late summer and autumn, even into early winter, so quince – one of my favourite foods – will crop up in the November chapter as they're slower to ripen.

Apples and pears really help to define the autumn, and it feels like there's something almost sage about them – the wise old men of the fruit world. We take them for granted though, especially apples, and it's easy to forget just how great a good one can be: take a bite of a crisp cox or a musty russet and you're transported. The same is true of pears, which have a perfume and eccentricity all their own. Eddie Izzard is absolutely right when he talks about how they can be unripe and hard for days and then, just as you turn your back, they disintegrate into a little puddle in the bottom of the fruit bowl. Catch them at their prime, however, and they really are something else. Pear and prune compote – carefully watched so the pears don't overcook, and left overnight with a fresh bay leaf so the flavours infuse – with a dash of cream is enough to make me weak at the knees.

I came across this apple recipe while running Konstam – simple to prepare, delicious and one I'm very fond of, and not only for the name.

Peasant girl in a veil

Serves 6–8

500g cooking apples such as Bramleys (about 4)
175g caster sugar
1 vanilla pod
150g stale bread in large crumbs
55g butter
200ml double cream

Cut the vanilla pod lengthways, then scrape the seeds out with the tip of a knife and put them in a pan with the apples and 110g of the caster sugar. Heat until the juices run, bring to the boil, then reduce the heat and leave to simmer for 10–15 minutes, or until the apples break up.

Stir the mixture to give a lumpy apple sauce then leave to cool. I think this improves with a day in the fridge, but it can be used as soon as it's cool enough.

Toast the breadcrumbs in a dry frying pan, stirring frequently until they begin to colour. Remove from the pan and melt the butter. Return the breadcrumbs and remaining sugar and continue cooking and stirring so they caramelise slowly and evenly, without burning.

Whip the cream to soft peaks.

In a glass serving bowl, or individual glasses, alternate layers of apple sauce, cream and croutons, finish on the cream but keep some crumbs aside for serving. You can serve it straight away, but letting it rest in the refrigerator for a couple of hours improves it. Serve with the last of the crumbs sprinkled on top.

Pigs don't have an annual breeding cycle in the way that sheep do, so there isn't really a season for them. However, the ingredients they go well with are seasonal, and some of the best of these are harvested in the autumn. Pork and apple is a traditional combination, but pork also goes tremendously well with quince and pear. In fact, it goes well with almost any fruit in any season. Over the years I've paired it with rhubarb, gooseberry, redcurrant, plum, blackberry, elderberry – you name it – but pigs and apples are soul mates of the highest order. On a small scale, pigs are often reared in orchards, roaming freely and living off the windfalls. There are countless recipes for pork and apple, whether it be roasted with apple sauce, combined in a sausage, wrapped in clanger, popped in a pie, braised in a casserole... the list goes on and on.

I've roasted a lot of pork over the years, perhaps more than any other meat. When we ran a Konstam stall at the Green Man Festival in Wales we served pork belly and beetroot remoulade sandwiches to queues of hungry festival-goers throughout a rainy 2008 and a drier, slightly more orderly 2009. Wherever I've been a chef roast pork has been on the menu. Largely because I love it but also because I love the ingredients it goes with, so it gives me a chance to show them off together. One of my favourite things to accompany roast pork is what I call hedgerow sauce, a compote of apples and blackberries or elderberries. Small wild apples are great for this but almost any will do. I like an apple that has a little bit of bite to it – not that I don't like to then sweeten it a great deal – as it affords a volume of flavour that cuts through the rich, fatty pork in the best possible way.

Roast pork belly with hedgerow sauce

Serves 6

½ a good organic, free range, fatty pork belly
Plenty of fine sea salt
4 garlic cloves
½ tsp fennel or dill seed
10 juniper berries
10 white peppercorns
1 tbsp wholegrain mustard
3 onions
2 cooking apples

2 sweet dessert apples, like Jonagold
3 or 4 tbsp sugar
200g blackberries
1 bay leaf
1 cup still, medium cider

First, make the marinade for the pork belly. Crush the garlic in a pestle and mortar with a good pinch of salt, plus the fennel seeds, juniper berries and peppercorns – when you've achieved a smooth paste add the mustard. Then, on a large chopping board, score the skin of the pork belly, just fat deep, with the cuts as close together as you can make them – a very sharp knife is needed, and a Stanley knife is ideal. Turn the belly over, trim excess fat and sinew from the underside and lightly score the meat. Rub the paste all over. Turn the belly back over again and sprinkle a teaspoon of salt over the skin. Rub it in well. Then sprinkle a thin layer of salt over the whole surface of the pork skin, taking care not to leave any bits unsalted. After 25–30 minutes carefully wipe off the salt and any liquid that has been extracted from the skin.

Peel the onions, cut them in half and arrange them (you may not need all of them) cut-side down in the middle of the baking tray so that when you put the pork belly on top of them the uppermost skin side is rounded. This means that in the oven the juices will run off the pork instead of pooling and softening the skin.

Preheat the oven to 250°C. Put the pork in the middle of the oven – there should be some room for hot air to circulate over the top of the skin. Turn the tray every 15 minutes or so. If the juices on the bottom of the tray are starting to burn, pour a litre or so of water into the tray. Be careful as this will produce a lot of steam. Replenish if it boils dry. When the skin is crispy and bubbly (about 45 minutes) turn the oven down to 160°C and cook for another 30–45 minutes. The pork is done when the rib bones can be pulled easily from the flesh. You may need to top up the water in the tray every now and again, but don't open the oven door too much as the oven needs to be blisteringly hot, at least for the first part.

While the pork is cooking, peel, quarter and core the apples then cut them into chunks – smaller ones for the dessert apples, larger for the cookers. Put them in a large saucepan with a dash of water, the bay leaf and the sugar. The amount of sugar depends on taste and the sharpness of the fruit. I like it with a sweet edge to it, but you may prefer it sharper. Start with less and add more later if you like. Cook until the cooking apples have started breaking down and the dessert apples are soft, then add the blackberries, bring up to a simmer and remove from the heat. I like it when the blackberries aren't too soft and broken up. This is the point to add more sugar if you feel it isn't sweet enough.

When the pork is cooked remove from the oven, taking care not to spill any liquid. Take the pork from the tray and leave to rest, loosely covered with foil for a good 10–15 minutes. Pour the juices from the tray into a jug and pour off the fat – you can reserve this as it makes excellent dripping. Sieve the remaining juices. Put the tray, with the onions still on it, over a high heat on the hob. When it's sizzling and any bits stuck to the pan are starting to colour, deglaze it with the cider – again, this will produce a lot of steam and there is a chance the alcohol will ignite, so be careful. Cook hard for 30 seconds or so to make sure all the alcohol has evaporated and then add the cooking juices. If you don't have much of these you can add more cider, some chicken stock or water. Scrape all the bits off the pan and transfer to a small saucepan. Reduce until slightly thickened and check the seasoning. Strain again to remove the onions.

When the gravy is ready, slice the pork into finger-thick slices straight across and place in a big serving dish. A breadknife is good for cutting through the crispy skin. Arrange on a tray and serve with the gravy and the hedgerow sauce. This goes really well with Sunday trimmings, or the celeriac gratin on page 56.

I like cooking with cider, and in 2013 I was lucky enough to watch and take part in a communal pressing using a 600-year-old cider press in Dorset. The apples are first minced up and then built into a block by four people with a handmade straw wall before a huge, one-tonne piece of wood is lowered on top of the whole thing and the juice is slowly squeezed out. The fermentation is kicked off by natural yeast in the straw and surrounding air, and the end result is unlike any cider you're likely to have come across, full of farmyard flavours and punchy with it.

You can use cider in place of wine in almost all recipes, and one I like is for mussels, another inhabitant of October and the months to come. We are blessed with fantastic mussels along the coast of the British Isles, and when rope-grown they are among the most sustainable of seafood. This dish is very simple but must be cooked quickly to make sure the mussels are at their most tender.

Steamed mussels with cider, cream, garlic and thyme

Serves 4 as a main course or 6–8 as a starter
2kg mussels
4 garlic cloves
1 tbsp olive oil or butter
1 cup cider
½ cup cream
4 sprigs thyme
2 sprigs parsley
Salt and pepper

Pick through the mussels and remove any beards they may have with a sharp tug, and discard any that are open or don't close or respond when tapped. Give them a good rinse but don't leave them submerged in water. Drain thoroughly.

Finely chop the garlic. Gently heat the oil in a large saucepan and add the garlic. Fry for a couple of seconds and then turn up the heat. At the first sign the garlic is starting to take on colour, add the mussels and the cider – put the lid on and give them a good shake. Keep the heat high for 30 seconds or so, and add the cream and the thyme. Turn down the heat to medium and cook for a few minutes, shaking vigorously once or twice.

The mussels should be done when they open, although large ones may take a second or two more. It's important not to overcook them as they will turn rubbery. When they're nearly all open (there are always a few that won't), tip them into a colander with a bowl underneath to reserve the liquid. Return the liquid to the saucepan and reduce rapidly until slightly thickened. Check the seasoning – mussels give out a fair amount of salt so you may not need much.

Roughly chop the parsley. Put the mussels in a big bowl and when the juice is ready pour it on top, scatter the parsley over them and serve with lots of crusty bread and butter.

There is another orchard fruit that ripens in the autumn months, one we don't see very much, but it's this archaic quality that makes them exotic in their own particular way. Medlars are a strange fruit. They look odd, like a small, round pear with an inverted bottom, and they consist mainly of pips with not a great deal of flesh. The few times they've come into my possession I've found them difficult to get to grips with – unusable until very ripe, and even then they don't give you much to work with. They taste slightly spiced and a little muddy.

Finding myself with a bag of them, back when I was running the restaurant, I dug out a rather vague Old English recipe for medlar cheese, similar to membrillo, but when I attempted it the result was unimpressive. Since then I've found a recipe for medlar jelly, which has been stuck under a magnet on my fridge for several years in the hope I come across them again. You could be forgiven for wondering why I mention them at all. Well, I wouldn't if I hadn't recently visited one of the Turkish shops on Green Lanes in North London, where I came across a plum-sized yellow fruit with a slightly bruised skin. I was surprised to see a sign in the box describing them as medlars. I asked in the shop and they confirmed that this is what they called them. This happened in April rather than October, so I was somewhat confused. Obviously, I bought some and did a little research before I tried them. They turned out to be loquats, and a different matter altogether. The skin is a little tough, so you're well advised to peel them, but underneath is an incredible fruit with an extraordinary flavour.

Like the English medlar they must be very ripe before eating, which is why they seem bruised. They are also full of large pips but with much more flesh and a very unusual taste. There is a hint of dryness or astringency, like quinces, and a delicious balance of sweet and sour. The texture is similar to a slightly under-ripe apricot. My research also showed why they're called medlars: they're both part of the cherry family, and share the same oversized black pips, but apart from that they're quite different. Both have an edge to them but loquats are much more succulent and giving.

Medlar jelly

2kg ripe medlars
Preserving sugar
Lemons

Peel and roughly chop the medlars. Put them, stones and all, into a pan and just about cover with water. Simmer until the flesh is soft. Tip into a jelly bag over a bowl and leave overnight. Measure the juice and put in a pan with 450g of sugar and the juice of 1 lemon to each pint. Add a few strips of pared lemon rind and heat slowly until the sugar has dissolved. Boil rapidly until the jelly sets when tested. Strain and pour into sterilised jars.

Loquat, red onion, fennel and feta salad

Serves 4 as a starter or side

3 loquats

1 head of fennel

1 red onion

100g feta

2 tbsp white wine vinegar – ideally Moscatel or Chardonnay

8 tbsp olive oil

1 tsp Dijon mustard

½ bunch dill

2 sprigs flat-leaf parsley

Salt and pepper

Peel the thin skin of the loquats and cut them into sixths. Peel and thinly slice the red onion in half moons. Break them up and place in a mixing bowl with the loquats. Trim and thinly shave the fennel. Add this to the bowl.

In a separate bowl, season the vinegar and mustard with salt so the flavours are nicely balanced. Add the olive oil – you may need more, but the dressing should be punchy without catching unpleasantly on the back of the throat. You can add a tiny bit of honey if using a standard white wine vinegar, and a little squeeze of lemon juice if you like. Check the dressing on a piece of the fennel to make sure it's doing its job properly, adding oil, salt or vinegar if needed.

Pick, wash and dry the parsley, add this (whole) to the bowl with the rest of the salad ingredients. Chop the dill and add this with the dressing to the salad. Toss well, double-check seasoning and serve.

October is the tail end of the fennel season in the UK, another of the vegetables we'll never be able to rely on as a natural crop. A great deal of the fennel we use here, especially outside the summer months, will be grown under glass in Holland or Spain. During the season it's mostly French or Italian. Its aniseed flavour doesn't suit every palate, but converts are diehards. We get the name from the Old English words *fenel* or *fenyl*, which comes from the Latin *foeniculum*. There are two main types of fennel: one only produces stems and foliage and is used mainly as a herb, and Florentine fennel, which produces the large pale green bulbs. It's very versatile and can be eaten raw or cooked, roasted, braised, grilled or steamed. It's quite high in vitamin C but doesn't have a particularly high nutritional value aside from that.

Fennel has a natural affinity with pork – a combination found time after time in Italian cooking, both in vegetable and seed form – but it also goes well with fish, beef and chicken. Aniseed is traditionally associated with sweet dishes in this country, but it can also be a useful bridging flavour to bring sweet and savoury together.

I use fennel seed a lot in my cooking – it's one of my base flavours. It brings a freshness to certain dishes as well as a complex hidden warmth and spice. I almost always use it in pork rubs, whether expressing a southern or northern European palate, and it often features in my chicken marinades. My favourite of these is fennel seed, crushed garlic, white wine, lemon zest and olive oil. And an anchovy or two and some rosemary doesn't hurt. The ingredients combine to help preserve the chicken too, so you get a really deep marinade if you leave it in the fridge for a day or two before cooking.

One of the most common types of walnut tree is the English walnut, but you don't see them often here. They grow well in our climate and soil, but you'd be hard pushed to find English-grown walnuts in the shops. I wish it were easier, so maybe I should just grow a tree of my own, as I do like cooking with them. They go well in salads – a great combination with beetroot and goat's cheese, or pear and Roquefort. One of the best kinds of walnut is pickled. They look like tiny wrinkled black brains, but they have an old-world taste – very gentlemanly. One of my favourite things is a seared ox tongue sandwich with pickled walnut and beetroot remoulade.

Pickled walnut and beetroot remoulade

This is more of a condiment, and as well as seared ox tongue sandwiches it's also great with lots of cold cuts. It's a very simple recipe if you've got your mayonnaise technique already sorted out. If you haven't, it's time to get it under your belt.

For the beetroot:
2 large beetroot
1 tbsp sugar
1 tbsp sea salt
100ml red wine vinegar

For the mayonnaise:
2 egg yolks
A pinch of salt
250ml sunflower or other flavourless oil
1 tsp wholegrain mustard
2 tbsp white wine vinegar or lemon juice

Additional:
1 tbsp crème fraîche
A touch of fresh horseradish
4 or 5 pickled walnuts

Put the beetroots in a saucepan to fit. Cover with cold water and add the sugar, salt and vinegar. Bring to a simmer and cook until the beetroot slides off the end of a small sharp knife inserted into the flesh. Remove from heat and leave to cool in the cooking liquid. When still warm, but cool enough to handle, slide the peel off with your fingers. This should be easy if the beetroot is cooked enough, but you may need a small knife to help with any stubborn bits.

To make the mayonnaise, put the egg yolks in a mixing bowl and beat with a whisk for a minute or two. Add the salt and whisk a little more. Continue whisking and start pouring the oil, one drop at a time or in a very thin stream – if you add the oil too fast the mayonnaise might split. Once you've achieved an emulsion you can start to add it a little more quickly, but patience pays off at this point. If you see droplets of oil on the surface of the mayonnaise, stop pouring and just whisk for a few seconds – you can whisk in a couple of drops of water if you're worried. When all the oil is incorporated, add the vinegar and mustard. Check for seasoning and acidity. Although this mayonnaise is geared up for this recipe, the basics work whether you want to add a different mustard or acid, garlic, tarragon, capers or whatever you like.

Once the beetroots are cool, grate them on the coarse side of a box grater and put them in a mixing bowl. Add the mayonnaise, crème fraîche and horseradish, and mix. Pickled walnuts are very fragile, so gently cut them in half and then into cubes if you can. Fold them into the rest of the mixture – don't stir too vigorously as it's good not to break them up too much.

As I reach the end of October I realise two things: that my thoughts are dominated by fruit, and that October seems an evocative and nostalgic time. Many of the vegetables around now are covered in chapters on either side with their growing season extending across the month and beyond, so it's the fruits that stand out as fleeting and noteworthy. As for the wistfulness, maybe this is to do with the sense of change and the feel-good factors: the weather is still fairly mild in the afterglow of summer, the flavours are homely, and the trees get stuck into the year's seasonal trump card as the leaves undergo their dramatic transformation. Overall, it's not such a bad time. November is a different matter though, a month none of us look forward to quite so much.

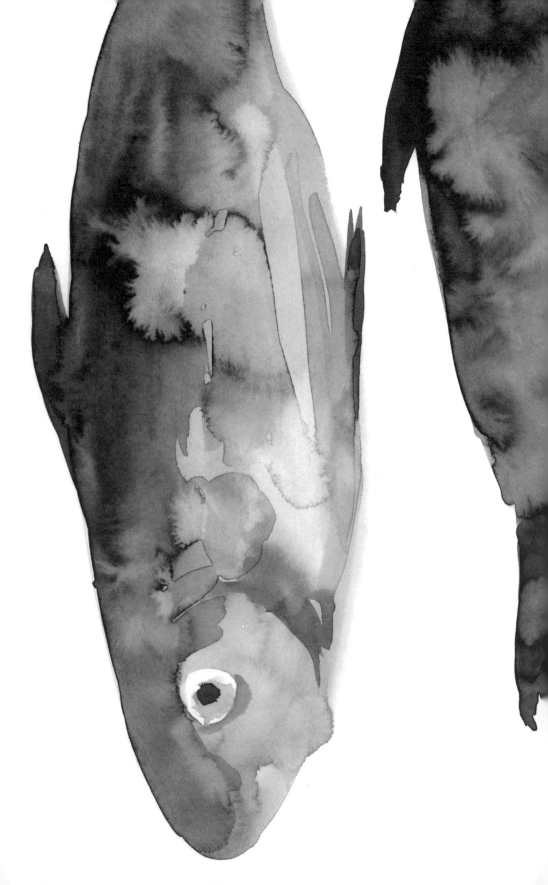

NOVEMBER

—

Mulled wine

Toffee apples

Quince

Rabbit

Herring

Rosehips

Celeriac

Kale

All in November's soaking mist
We stand and prune the naked tree,
While all our love and interest
Seem quenched in the blue-nosed misery.

Ruth Pitter, 'The Diehards' (1941)

November creeps. Dark comes early and melancholy catches up with us. Desolate and vagrant cold settles in like a squatter, unwanted and unwelcome. Undercover, winter slides near, etching itself on the landscape, a cloud passing the sun. Bright days punctuate the gloom to deceive us, making us believe that all is crisp and well, but all the while the leaf mould thickens, slowly rotting down in the edges of the garden, slippery on flagstones and harbouring decay.

I like the look and feel in the mouth of the word November, and have always felt it should be held in respect. It ushers in the winter, a stark, transitional month, the business end of autumn. The key events in November – Bonfire Night and Remembrance Day – set a maudlin tone. In Mexico the 2nd is the Day of the Dead, so we're not alone in feeling its morbidity.

Bonfire Night means standing out in the cold, so break out the mulled wine. Despite its sweetness I didn't really like the yearly sip of mulled wine we were allowed when we were children, but these days I have to be wary of its sneaky drinkability and deceptive alcohol content. Mrs Beeton's recipe from 1838 has extensive directions regarding the pan required and lovely instructions on how to make the drink to taste.

To Mull Wine

Ingredients: to every pint of wine allow 1 large cupful of water, and sugar and spice to taste.

Mode: It's very difficult to give the exact proportions of ingredients like sugar and spice, as what quantity might suit one person would be to another quite distasteful.

Boil the spice in the water until the flavour is extracted, then add the wine and sugar, and bring the whole to the boiling-point, then serve with strips of crisp dry toast, or with biscuits. The spices usually used for mulled wine are cloves, grated nutmeg, and cinnamon or mace. Any kind of wine may be mulled, but port and claret are those usually selected for the purpose; and the latter requires a very large proportion of sugar. The vessel that the wine is boiled in must be delicately clean, and should be kept exclusively for the purpose. Small tin warmers may be purchased for a trifle, which are more suitable than saucepans, as, if the latter are not scrupulously clean, they will spoil the wine, by imparting to it a very disagreeable flavour. These warmers should be used for no other purposes.

I like recipes that encourage the reader to use their own judgment, and I personally make mulled wine by eye. I do this with varying degrees of success, but it generally gets better as the years go by, and definitely better after each cup. The Germans drink it by the bucket-load all winter long, with street vendors selling Glühwein in little cups to chase away the Berlin winters. You get mulled wine in some form or another all over the colder parts of Europe, from Norway to the north of Italy, from the UK to Moldova. The recipes differ a little but they're generally pretty constant – wine (usually red), spices such as cinnamon, nutmeg, mace and cloves, the odd bay leaf, usually orange or lemon and sugar. Below is my version.

Mulled wine

The amount of sugar below is a guideline only and it should be added according to taste and the acidity of the wine. Start with less and add more if needed. More wine and sugar can be added to top up as the evening progresses.

2 bottles red wine

About 200g sugar

2 bay leaves

1 small sprig thyme

Orange zest – 2 strips

Lemon zest – 1 strip

1 cinnamon stick

4 cloves

2 blades of mace

5 white peppercorns

Combine all the ingredients in a pan and bring to a simmer. Allow to cook very gently for 10–15 minutes, but don't let it boil, then turn it off and let it infuse for as long as you can wait before drinking – at least half an hour. Reheat as needed during the evening, but never boil.

The traditional sweet things to keep the children happy on Bonfire Night are toffee apples and cinder toffee. It struck me that the two might well be combined to increase the distractive powers of each. Cinder toffee is the honeycomb candy at the heart of a Crunchie bar and it's made by explosively adding bicarbonate of soda to hot caramel. First, you make the honeycomb and then break it up and roll the just cooling toffee apple in it to produce a rare and fearsome confection. You can add chocolate flakes to the mix or crushed nuts too if you like – hazelnuts are ideal. Pears work well as an alternative to apples.

This recipe assumes you have a sugar thermometer or temperature probe. They're cheap and useful, especially the little digital ones, but if you don't have one then you want the colour of both caramels only a little darker than Scotch whisky. Bear in mind that the caramel will cook in its own heat for a minute or two after it comes off the hob.

There is always a bit of toffee left over, and if you want to use it for something else you can pour it into a flat, greased tray to solidify. This is easily cracked out and reheated or eaten as it is. Scattering nuts over the surface while it's still melted will give you a simple praline.

Always be careful with caramel – this is a massively fun recipe but hot sugar burns are no joke, so take care with little hands and fingers.

Cinder toffee apples

For the cinder toffee:

75g golden caster sugar

2 tbsp golden syrup

1 level tsp bicarbonate of soda

For the toffee apple:

4 small eating apples, Cox's and Pink Lady® are both nice in different ways

250g Demerara sugar

75g golden syrup

1 tsp cider vinegar

150ml water

4 lolly sticks

First, make the cinder toffee. Grease a small, high-sided baking tray. Put the sugar and golden syrup into a scrupulously clean medium saucepan and add a couple of tablespoons of water. Over a medium heat and without stirring, cook until it reaches 140°C and then remove from the heat. Immediately whisk in the bicarbonate of soda and pour out into the tray. Leave to cool completely.

When the cinder toffee is cool, make the toffee apples. Bring a pan of water to the boil and dunk the apples into it for 30 seconds. Lift them out and cool them in a bowl of cold water. Put all the other ingredients in a large heavy-bottomed saucepan over a low heat and swirl until all the sugar is dissolved. Increase the heat and bring to the boil. Cook until the temperature reaches 140°C (about 10 to 15 minutes). Make sure you use a large pan as it bubbles up a great deal during this stage.

While this is cooking, crush half the cinder toffee into chocolate-drop-sized pieces. Save the rest for a rainy day in an airtight tin with a piece of dry kitchen towel stuffed into the top. It goes chewy after a day or two, so don't hold back too much. Put the crushed toffee into a wide flat-bottomed plate. Skewer the apples on the lolly sticks.

Turn off the heat and let the bubbles subside, then submerge and roll the apples in the toffee, using the sticks to hold on to, coating as much of the surface as you can. Let any excess drip back into the pan.

When the toffee on the apple has cooled a bit but is still soft, roll the sides of the apple in the cinder toffee, pressing in a little bit, but not too much, and leaving the top free. Set with the sticks facing up on parchment to cool.

The garden undergoes another transformation in November. There's still a lot to do at this time of the year – mulching, pruning, sweeping, bringing plants in – a general battening down of the proverbial hatches.

Things really start to change in the kitchen too. The transition from late summer and autumn produce to the sparser fare of winter is underway. One of the consolations November brings is quince; these beautiful greenish-yellow fruit with their downy skin have a flavour that falls somewhere between that of apples and pears, but it also has a floral element all its own. It's very tart when raw and, rather perversely, I like the drying of the mouth you get when you eat them before they're cooked. The texture can be grainy until you cook them thoroughly, so it's the norm to process them first – bottling, stewing, jamming or jellying – before using them in a preferred dish or spread on toast.

Quinces have a slightly citrus and more aromatic, earthy taste
than pears. In Latin they're called *Cotoneum malum* or sometimes
melimelum, and it's from this that marmalade derives its name.
Quince is the principal ingredient in membrillo – the sweet, firm
orange jelly that the Spanish, French, Italians and Portuguese eat
with cheese. I tried to make it once and was up half the night
burning my forearms every time it bubbled and spat up a gobbet of
superheated quince lava onto the soft skin on the inside of my arms.
After all that licking of wounds and not inconsiderable expense, the
membrillo that came out of it wasn't quite as good as I'd hoped. I'd
overcooked it, so the flavour became a little caramelised. It did keep
well though – I was using it as a syrup some three years later.

Although it can sometimes be hard to distinguish all the different
memories that food evokes, quinces take me to one place and one
place only: my grandmother's house, and her pantry in particular. It
was a tiny cupboard room at the end of the kitchen, tacked on the
end of the house, and a little colder than the rest of it. Outside was
a huge holm oak that spread its shade over this part of the house
and garden, so the outside walls of the pantry were protected from
the sun. The pantry had a smell all its own, of brown bread and
slightly overripe fruit.

The garden was long, with a big mulberry tree that had fallen over
on its side years ago, and a shed with all my grandfather's gardening
tools. This was another place with an extraordinary smell – twine,
grass clippings, lawnmower oil and old wood. They had more
than one quince tree over the years, which would produce so many
quinces that the jars of jam and jelly would last all year.

It's this kind of food memory that led me to become a chef.
Flavour, like scent, is extremely evocative and so food is laden with
associations, which we can go on to share with others. For instance,
and I'm not sure why, but writing about this has jogged a memory
of tasting figs warm off a tree in Greece at the age of 16, and being

given them by an Italian farmer from a tree in his field when I was 14. These sensory echoes are powerful and they take a long time to fade.

I love using quince to make tarte Tatin, a dish traditionally made with apples and, as the story goes, accidentally invented in 1889 by the Tatin sisters in their eponymous hotel in Lamotte-Beuvron, France. It's made by caramelising the fruit, then putting the pastry on top and baking it, turning it over only when it's out of the oven. Because it's on the top, the pastry comes out very light and the apples very moist. It can be made with shortcrust or puff pastry, but I always grate sweet pastry on top. This gives a light crumbly texture with a satisfyingly moist bit where it's in contact with the fruit.

Quince tarte Tatin

Normally I'd cook the fruit in a tarte Tatin from raw, but quinces take a bit too long so I poach them first. The poaching liquid will be delicious and makes an excellent cordial or fruit syrup for the marmalade puddings on page 109. The tradition is to use puff pastry for tarte Tatin, or rolled sweet pastry, but I grate sweet pastry on top of the fruit. Puff pastry is very time-consuming to make but it's nice to have the lightness, so this technique gives you a bit of both elements. Of course, if you want to make your own puff pastry then go for it, but you can buy good quality puff pastry, so feel free to use that if you want to save time.

For the quinces:
3 medium quinces
1 lemon
1 litre water
600g sugar
1 cinnamon stick
1 vanilla pod
1 bay leaf
Lemon zest – 1 strip
Orange zest – 1 strip

For the pastry:
225g flour
150g cold butter
115g icing sugar
2 egg yolks

To bake:
115g butter
115g caster sugar

Put the flour, butter and icing sugar into a food processor. Blitz until a rough crumb consistency is achieved. Add the yolks and work just long enough to bring it together to form a dough. Remove from the processor, form into a fat, flattened disc, wrap in cling film and freeze.

Peel and quarter the quinces. As you're preparing them, put the fruit into a bowl of cold water with the juice of a whole lemon squeezed into it. Then place in a saucepan with the water, sugar, bay, vanilla, cinnamon and zests. Bring to a boil, reduce the heat and simmer until the quinces are tender. Remove from the heat and fish out the quinces with a slotted spoon. At this point it's ideal to let them cool in the fridge as it firms them up and makes them easier to handle, but if you don't have time just let them cool until you can handle them. Cut out the cores and slice the pieces lengthwise into thin-ish slices. You can put the slices back in the poaching liquid, and everything can be made well in advance to this point.

Preheat the oven to 220°C. In a 10-inch ovenproof frying pan or tart tin (not the sort with a removable base), preferably non-stick, melt the butter with the caster sugar. Cook until lightly caramelised and remove from the heat. Place the quince slices in a tight-fitting layer over the bottom of the pan. Remember that the underside is the side that will be on top.

Remove the pastry from the freezer and, using the coarse side of a cheese grater, grate the pastry with long steady strokes over the quinces until it forms an even layer at least 1 inch thick. Tidy the edges but do not press down. Put the tart in the oven, turn the heat down to 200°C and bake until the pastry is golden brown – about 20–30 minutes.

Remove from the oven, run a knife around the edge and turn out carefully onto a large plate, board or other flat serving dish. Remember to give the bottom of the pan a few sharp taps all around before lifting it off to loosen any stuck bits of quince. Leave to rest and cool for a few minutes before serving. This is delicious with the lavender ice cream on page 275.

You can buy farm-reared rabbit all year round, but wild rabbits are plumpest from July through to December, so this is a great time of year to eat them. Rabbit is a very lean meat and can be difficult to cook well – I've had many an overcooked, dry rabbit stew in my time – but it has a great flavour, like slightly gamey chicken, so it's worth a few goes if you don't master it the first time. I'm not a big hunter, but I've been out looking for rabbit a couple of times. The first was on the Isle of Eigg, part of the Inner Hebrides, off the west coast of Scotland, when I was sailing around the islands with the Cape Farewell project in 2011. We were a group of 14 artists and scientists (lord knows where a chef fits into that Venn diagram!) sailing on a lovely boat called *Song of the Whale*, which spends most of its time researching whalesong and had been chartered for the trip. Cape Farewell works to bring together these disparate disciplines to create new dialogues around climate change, and this trip focused on looking at peripheral communities, the kind that will be hit earliest and hardest by small changes in the climate, not only here but globally. We stopped off at Eigg in particular because its then 65 residents had joined up with the Highland Council and the Scottish Wildlife Trust in 1997 and successfully bought the island as a community in a bid to be free of difficult and absent landlords. We were shown around the island and later we cooked a big barbecue for the inhabitants, but before that we went rabbit hunting. I was taken around the lanes and through the fields, shooting fruitlessly for some time, but I did eventually get one in my sights and managed to hit it clean through the heart, if I remember correctly.

The rabbit recipe below was one I developed when I was the head chef at a restaurant near Hammersmith called Maquis. It pairs the rabbit with braised chicory, one of my very favourite foods. Chicory, or endive, is a winter salad in season from November to March, and I love it in all its forms. I mention some salads later in the book which include it, and I also like serving it as an hors d'oeuvre, sliced lengthwise into quarters or sixths and accompanied with mustardy vinaigrette to dip it in. It's delicious braised or roasted, and the rich butteryness and sharp notes go well with the bacon in the rabbit dish below. The Italians serve wild chicory with fava bean purée, something that works just as well with almost any greens, but braised endive or grilled radicchio would be good replacements.

Rabbit with bacon, mustard, cider and braised chicory

This is a slightly more complicated recipe than many others in this book, with two cooking techniques for different parts of the rabbit. The saddle of a rabbit is very tender and lean and suits the slightly faster fat-led cooking that it gets in the oven, leaving it tender on the inside and coloured on the outside. The legs benefit from a slower method, so that the sinews are broken down very gently. The recipe also assumes some butchery skills – ask your butcher to do these parts for you if you don't feel up to the task.

It's very easy to overcook rabbit, leaving it dry and underwhelming. Keep an eye on it as it cooks and remember that the last bit of cooking will happen while it's resting. This dish is great with mashed potato.

Serves 4
1 large rabbit
4 slices of pancetta or streaky bacon
Olive oil
2 tsp fresh thyme leaves
95g butter
1 onion
7 garlic cloves
1 tbsp wholegrain mustard
1 cup cider
1 cup chicken stock
4 heads of chicory

A handful of parsley or chervil leaves
Salt and pepper

You'll also need:
Butcher's twine

Take the legs off the rabbit and set aside. Remove the ribcage section and the tail section from the saddle. Leave the 2 fillets attached to the spine, but carefully trim the outer layer of sinew around them, taking care not to remove too much of the meat. Cut the saddle crosswise into 3 or 4 equal chunks.

Purée 5 of the garlic cloves and add 2 teaspoons of chopped thyme leaves. Rub the 8 pieces of rabbit with this paste. Wrap the pieces of bacon around the saddle sections and tie in place with butcher's twine. Chill all pieces and leave to marinate for at least an hour, or overnight if possible.

Dice the onion and remaining garlic and set aside separately. Rub the marinade off the legs. Season and brown them in a frying pan with olive oil, then tip out the fat and deglaze the pan with the cider.

Preheat the oven to 180°C. Cut the chicory into quarters length-wise. Place in a baking tray big enough to hold them in one layer and dot with 75g of the butter. Season, cover with tin foil and place in the oven. After 20–30 minutes, or when the chicory has started to soften, remove the foil and cook until lightly caramelised. Remove from the oven.

Heat 20g of butter in a medium saucepan over a medium heat. When it's melted, add the diced onion and cook for about 15 minutes, stirring often. When they start to go translucent and golden brown add the garlic and remaining thyme leaves. Cook until the garlic starts to smell creamy and has the merest hint of gold, then add the cider and the mustard. Cook on high for a minute and add the stock and the rabbit legs. Cover and turn down as low as you can. Gently simmer for 10 minutes or so, then check the rabbit – it should be firm with just a touch of spring. If

you have a temperature probe, the internal heat it needs to reach
is just over 70°C, but it will do the last 5 degrees on its own.
This takes about 20 minutes in total. The front legs will cook in
about 10 minutes, so remove them earlier. When done, remove the
other 2 legs from the pan and set them all aside to rest, covered in
foil. Reduce the sauce until it starts to thicken – like very lightly
whipped double cream. Check seasoning.

Meanwhile, season and brown the saddle pieces, on the bacon sides
too. Place on a baking tray and cook in the oven until just done.
This takes 10–15 minutes. Remove from the oven and leave to
rest with the legs for a few minutes. If the legs need warming at
this point, do so very gently in the sauce. Serve a piece of leg and a
piece of saddle per person with the chicory and the sauce. Sprinkle
chopped parsley or chervil fronds on top. The legs aren't all the
same size so there may be some squabbling.

Herring prosper in late autumn and winter, along with sprat. We
don't eat them as much here as they do in Scandinavia and other
parts of northern Europe, at least not as herring anyway. Pickled
herring is delicious, but I can't recall ever having seen a truly
British version. Our most common form of herring goes by another
name, but only after it's been smoked. Naturally, I'm talking
about kippers, which are spatchcocked, cold-smoked herring, the
breakfast of champions and one of the best hangover cures I've ever
encountered. When they're hot-smoked they're left whole and these
are called bloaters, again delicious and absolutely great in a picnic
or served with a radish, a piece of toast and a spot of remoulade.

The first bloater I had was when I visited Forman's, the big smokery
that used to be located in the middle of what is now the Olympic
Park in East London. I was able to catch some herring from the
Thames and then took them to Forman's, where they turned them
into the most fantastic bloaters you can imagine – plump, moist

and bursting with flavour. Herring, like many oily fish, have quite a lot of flavour and so they stand up well to pickling or smoking – the high oil content stops them from drying out. They are fantastic eaten fresh too, and this is a recipe I've played around with and used in various forms over the years.

Herring in oatmeal with orange zest

Serves 4 as a starter
4 large herring, cleaned and gutted but left whole
100g plain flour
2 eggs
150g rolled oats
Salt and pepper
Butter for frying
1 orange
A dash of red wine vinegar
½ tsp wholegrain mustard
2 tbsp extra virgin olive oil
250g washed rocket

Put the flour in a bowl and add nearly all the orange zest. Break the eggs into another bowl and lightly whisk. Season the oats in a third bowl.

Dredge the fish, first in the flour, then the egg, and finally the oats. Melt the butter in a heavy-bottomed frying pan over a medium flame and fry until just done and golden brown.

Meanwhile, make a dressing with the mustard, vinegar and olive oil, and use it to dress the rocket at the last minute.

Serve the fish with a squeeze of orange juice from the zested orange and some fresh zest scattered on top.

My cycle ride to and from school through Queen Mary's Rose Garden in Regent's Park used to provide me with a double dose of guilty pleasure. The first was illicitly cycling in the park, so I would always be on the lookout for park-keepers. The second was the heady scent of the roses. As a schoolboy it really wasn't done to get quite as excited about the smell of roses as I did. I used to pedal furiously through the park – predictably late – only slowing down as I sped through the rose garden, filling my nostrils with the heady scent from the impressive array lining my way. Most of the roses bloomed in May and June, the days of summer's early sun, and the chore of going to school was made a great deal easier because of it.

It never seems long before the rose petals fall, and when they do the rosehips start to form. They continue to ripen throughout the summer and into autumn. The reason they've made their way into this chapter is because it's traditional to harvest rosehips after the first frost, which in London and the south-east usually comes in early November. The frost softens them and they sweeten, making them easier to handle and fuller-flavoured.

Rosehips are well known as a source of itching powder – the little hairs packed inside them can be irritating in the extreme if caught up in the cloth of a shirt. But rosehip syrup was also a traditional food supplement, fed to children alongside the dreaded cod liver oil. As it happens, this is no old wives' tale as they are higher in vitamin C than almost any other foodstuff. Rosehips have a flavour like the smell of an overripe apple wrapped in honey, and a syrup made with them is a good winter cordial. They are also a superb flavouring for ice cream, milkshakes or winter Kir.

Rosehip and lemon syrup

This can be made without the lemon. Just omit the stage with the lemon zest and go straight to adding the sugar after reducing.

1kg rosehips, washed and chopped
Zest of 1 large, unwaxed lemon, if using
1.2kg caster sugar
20g citric acid

Rinse, drain, pick through and chop the rosehips – you can do this by hand or in a food processor. There's no need to top and tail them first.

Bring 2 litres of water to the boil in a large pan. Add the rosehips, return to the boil, remove from the heat, cover and leave to infuse for half an hour, stirring occasionally.

Strain the mixture well through a jelly bag or a colander lined with muslin. Reserve the strained juice and place in the fridge.

Bring 1 more litre of water to the boil in the same pan and add the strained rosehip pulp. Repeat as before, this time leaving to strain for longer, overnight if possible. Reserve the strained juice and discard the pulp.

Clean the pan and combine the two batches of strained juice. Bring to the boil and reduce by half. Remove from the heat. Put the lemon zest in a bowl and pour over the hot juice. Leave to steep for an hour.

Strain through a sieve to remove the lemon. Add the sugar and citric acid, and stir until dissolved. Return to the stove, bring to the boil and boil hard for 5 minutes, then pour into sterilised bottles and seal.

As root vegetables become more and more available year round, the part of the year when you find celeriac on the menu in many restaurants becomes longer and longer. And it's true that you only need a spell of cold weather to make you want to dig into a celeriac, but I like to keep it to the autumn and winter. Although its season can start in late summer, November is when it's in full swing. Not long ago celeriac was the bogeyman vegetable that confused anyone with a veg box – the last to go and often a subject of debate. People are more used to it now and have found more ways to use it – this is unsurprising as it's a very versatile ingredient. Obviously it can be mashed like a swede, dressed with lashings of melted butter, a dash of milk and a generous pinch of salt, but it can be used in all sorts of other ways. Fantastic roasted and great in stews and casseroles, its flavour also marries nicely with apple, and these two with pork are heavenly. Remoulade, a raw shredded salad mixed with crème fraîche or mayonnaise, is most traditionally made with celeriac.

Celeriac is a variety of wild celery originating in the Mediterranean; it is carefully cultivated for its bulbous, aromatic rootstock. Celeriac is pretty ugly and a peeler isn't the tool to tackle it with. You need a sharp knife to shear off the skin and rootstock, but once this is done you'll find creamy aromatic flesh that cries out to be cooked.

Celeriac soup is one of my favourites, but it's difficult to get absolutely spot-on. It needs very few other ingredients as there is a natural complexity to the flavour of the celeriac itself. Sweat down and lightly caramelise some onions in olive oil with a touch of garlic added after the onions have started to colour. Add a bay leaf and a sprinkling of fresh thyme, cook this for a minute or two and then add the peeled and diced celeriac. I like to give it a moment frying gently together in the pan before I add the stock or water. Cook it until the celeriac is tender and then blitz it all up. If you can remember, it's not a bad idea to take out the bay leaf – I often forget, so I wouldn't worry about it too much. Blend to a really smooth consistency with a good splosh of milk to thin, and then serve with a spot of crème fraîche and – a tip I learned from the gifted Rose Carrarini during my stint at the Rose Bakery – a few crushed roasted hazelnuts. If you get it absolutely right celeriac soup should have a hint of truffle about it. Something earthy and ripe is released from what is, on the face of it, a very humble root vegetable and suddenly the whole thing becomes unctuous and sexy in a way you wouldn't necessarily imagine.

I love celeriac gratin. It's quite laborious but worth the effort. Once cooked it will keep for days in the fridge – in fact, it only gets better, so don't feel you have to stuff yourself if there are leftovers.

Celeriac gratin

Serves 6–8

1kg celeriac

1.5kg potatoes

2 large white onions

1 garlic clove

2 cloves

10 black peppercorns

2 bay leaves

1 sprig thyme

1 carrot

1 celery stick

1 leek

A few fennel seeds

1 pint double cream

½ pint milk

A good knob of butter, plus more for greasing

Salt and pepper

Preheat the oven to 180°C. Infuse the milk and cream in a saucepan with 1 onion, roughly sliced, the carrot, peeled and roughly chopped, the celery stick, roughly chopped, the garlic clove, bay leaves, cloves, peppercorns, fennel seeds, leek, chopped and washed, and the thyme. Bring it gently to a simmer and leave it to cool with all the ingredients in. Check that the cream hasn't caught a little on the bottom of the pan; if it has, transfer it to another container to cool.

Melt the butter and fry the other onion, thinly sliced, until sweet and golden brown. Peel and thinly slice the potatoes and celeriac – do this on a mandolin if you have one, to make sure they are of even thickness but not paper-thin – 3 or 4mm is good.

Butter a baking dish large enough to fit all the potato and celeriac, then place them carefully in alternate layers starting with potato and finishing with potato, with the onions and salt and pepper scattered between the layers throughout. When you've layered the last of the vegetables you can scatter a spot of raw sliced onion if you have some left over. Pour the infused cream over the top until it just moistens the top layer but doesn't cover it. You can top up with fresh cream or milk if you don't quite have enough.

Cover with foil and place in the middle of the oven. Cook for about an hour, or until the celeriac is getting tender, then remove the foil and allow to cook until golden brown on top. If it doesn't brown but the vegetables are cooked, pop it under the grill for a minute or two to colour.

It's best to leave gratins to rest and set before serving. They're delicious straight from the oven, but even better if you let them cool and warm them again later.

Food trends come and go, but eating goes beyond the mere need to sustain life: it's embedded in culture and therefore becomes entwined in the mores, values and aspirations of the time. Tea and coffee, ice cream, pasta, pineapples, chocolate – these are some long-lived examples of foods that were once considered all the rage. More recently we can look back to aspic, fondue, prawn cocktail, blancmange, sundried tomatoes and balsamic reductions. They caught the collective imagination due to a sense of the exotic, but it isn't always 'otherness' that brings a foodstuff to the cultural fore.

One item of winter produce is of a very humble nature yet has gained a significant following over the last few years. Perhaps it's this humility that chimes with something in the hearts and minds of many. Kale may be standing on the shoulders of its brother cavolo nero, which had a similar popularity some time back, but it's currently the go-to greens for anyone who knows anything, and justly so – it's healthy and tastes good. There are several types of kale and the most common is curly kale, the one found limply shredded in bags in the supermarket. I've also cooked with Russian kale, which starts off a lovely purple but turns a deep green like curly kale when cooked.

In the last few years kale has become something of a phenomenon with recipes from kale lasagne and kale stir-fry to kale and grapefruit salad and, of course, kale chips. The latter have long been a firm favourite of the kale crowd and are made by dehydrating the leaves. They have a texture similar to potato crisps, but are clearly a lot healthier. Kale is also easy to grow – one of the reasons it's been the hipster's staple for so long.

I must confess I'm in the kale camp. I wouldn't say I dote on it as much as some but am always very happy when I find it on my fork. As is my wont, I like to treat it with respect and serve it simply. One of my favourite recipes is to blanch it, toss it with lemon dressing and sprinkle it with toasted pumpkin seeds – nice as a side dish or even as a zingy, earthy starter. This recipe works with cavolo nero and Russian kale too. In fact, it works with almost any brassica – Savoy and spring greens are also great like this. You can add chopped chilli or replace the pumpkin seeds with all manner of nuts and other crunchy things. The acid in the dressing can similarly be swapped with your vinegar of choice – sherry vinegar and balsamic are particularly good. This dressing should be made on the day of use. Lemon juice loses the freshness of its flavour with time: it may last a day, but is best when just squeezed.

Lemon-dressed kale with pumpkin seeds

Serves 4
500g kale
1 lemon
4–6 tbsp extra virgin olive oil

75g pumpkin seeds
Fine salt
Maldon salt

First, toss the pumpkin seeds with a good pinch of salt and a few drops of oil and tip into a baking tray to toast for about 8 minutes at 180°C. Check them after 5 minutes to see if they've started to colour; if so, take them out early. Put them on a plate to cool.

Squeeze the lemon into a medium mixing bowl and season with the Maldon salt. The salt will balance the acidity of the lemon. When you feel a good balance has been achieved, add the olive oil. There should be enough oil to stop the lemon catching on the back of your throat, but there should still be a nice brightness to the flavour.

Pick through the kale, discarding any brown bits and cutting off the ends of the stalks, including any tough bits of leaf. You can slice it, but I like the shape of the leaves so much that I keep them whole, especially if they're young and tender. Bring a pan of well-salted water to the boil and blanch the kale in it. It should be tender – not crunchy and not soft. Drain it and toss it in the lemon dressing. Arrange it on a plate and sprinkle the pumpkin seeds on top.

So November draws to a close. By this time most of us are looking towards Christmas and the tail end of the month can easily slip away. By now the produce has started to settle into a wintery rhythm and the changes come more slowly as the weather gets sharper and the ground gets harder.

DECEMBER

—

Oranges

Spices

Saffron

Mustard

Turkey

Goose

Venison

Guineafowl

Potatoes

Roast vegetables

Chestnuts

Brussels sprouts

Cider

Eggnog

Bread sauce

Red cabbage

*It is December, and nobody
asked if I was ready.*

Sarah Kay

Soft, deep drifts of billowing snow; stark black trees and
red-breasted robins; log fires and damp mittens; snowballs,
snowflakes and icicles. The images of December are finally
here, but negotiating our way to the New Year can be a challenge.

Despite the cold and the steadily harsher conditions, there is
still a lot of produce available by the time we get to the back-
end of the calendar year. Celeriac and kale are still with us and
Jerusalem artichokes are gearing up. Everything we associate with
our Christmas meal is abundant, and there are always apples and
pears – quinces too, if you know the right person. Many think that
December is when it gets hard to source seasonally, but the worst
time is some way off. Cabbages and leeks are still easy to come by
and swedes are plentiful.

There's no escaping the fact that December is dominated by
Christmas. We all say it comes earlier every year, and I recently
saw a shop advertising its Christmas range as far ahead as August.
As a specifically Christian celebration it's occurred on the 25th
of December since the 4th century, when it was introduced as a
substitute for the pagan solstice celebrations based on the solar
cycles. In Europe and many other parts of the world it's easily the
most important festive day in the calendar, and it casts its shadow
across the whole of the month. Not that this is necessarily a bad
thing. There are some real positives about Christmas. It's a time for

families to get together and air their grievances, which some might see as therapeutic, and the economy gets a massive boost too.

And while I have very fond memories of spending time with family members I don't often see, sitting around the living room watching Bond movies or *Star Wars*, I also remember some blistering rows – and Christmas shopping can shoot my blood pressure off the chart. The insidious commercialisation of Christmas can be wearing, too – not that I remember a time when it wasn't exploited, but it did use to feel a bit more home-made. By that I don't just mean decorations or cards, but more that it didn't feel like such a shared cultural event, slightly homogenised and experienced in the same way by all and sundry. It used to feel a bit more intimate. But maybe that's just down to me not being nine anymore. They say that the loss of innocence is represented by no longer believing in Father Christmas, but I think it's one step further than that: it's coming to understand the sheer effort involved in making it seem like he exists.

The thing I really love about Christmas is the food. It isn't just Christmas dinner, it's the wealth of produce around this time. I like that it isn't until around the 28th that I start to feel a twinge of guilt that I'm on my third stuffing, red cabbage and camembert sandwich and it's not yet lunchtime. It's a rare point in the year when we really let ourselves enjoy our food and end up sitting on the couch, looking down at the bulbous entity that has taken the space once assigned to our bellies, top buttons discreetly eased undone, and actually feel pleased with ourselves. Christmas dinner is an achievement and takes a great deal of organising, so when it's finally over and the last roast potato has been politely enquired about and met a sticky end lathered in gravy, there's a profound sense of relief. I also love that it's the one meal of the year that makes us truly European: everyone is obsessed with food. People talk about how they've cooked this, or used the old family recipe for that. And everything on the Christmas plate is seasonal by definition. It's the one genuine celebration of seasonal fare.

The food of Christmas starts in small ways. Dads across the globe might say that it begins in the middle of the night with a sneaky mince pie and a small glass of brandy or port en route to the chimney, or at the foot of their children's beds as the stockings are filled for the morning. It's the stockings themselves that provide the next instalment – nuts, chocolate money and satsumas were ever present in our house on Christmas Eve. Remember trying to peel an orange aged five? The faff, the pith, the general mess? But satsumas were brilliant, with a puffy peel that almost came off in one piece, hardly any pith except for an easily extricated spur through the middle, and segments that came apart with ease. They would always disappear very quickly. The chocolate coins, however, would go more slowly, halfway between food and toy – a fiscal asset to be spent wisely. I'm not sure if we ate many of the Brazil nuts at eight in the morning, but they still seemed to make it there every year, along with a smattering of walnuts, hazelnuts and almonds.

In hindsight, it seems our Christmas stockings may have been a bit culturally confused because the traditional toe-piece of a Christmas stocking is an orange. Oranges are supposed to represent gold in this context, tracing back to a story of St Nicholas tossing bags or balls of gold to children at Christmas. This symbol of opulence would almost certainly have been enhanced by the high price oranges used to command. I also suspect that citrus fruits just coming into season, coinciding with the lack of fresh and readily available produce during the winter months, will have encouraged the orange's adoption into the canon of Christmas traditions.

Oranges originally came from Asia and were introduced to Europe through Italian and Portuguese traders in the 15th and 16th centuries. There was a bitter Persian variety documented in Italy in the 11th century, but it was only used for medicinal purposes.

Orange flavours still crop up in botanicals and bitters — there's something sharp and cleansing about the flavour, especially the zest. We'll look at Seville oranges in January, since it's where they belong as an ingredient, but this festive aspect of the orange means it gets to straddle two months.

A recipe we spent a lot of time on at Konstam combines the familiar taste of orange with the aromatic flavour of Earl Grey tea, a pairing that arose from the palette of flavours we had available to us, including Earl Grey tea from Tregothnan in Cornwall. The orange is set in a jelly floated across the top of a cream pudding. Both are made with gelatin, but one is rich and the other bright. The flavours marry perfectly and the two soft but dramatically different textures set each other off beautifully.

The reason it took so long to get right is that the two elements must be the right consistency or the whole thing jars — both must be only just set — and getting them right wasn't easy, especially as the gelatin responds to the acidity of the oranges, which differs all the time. Earl Grey gets its distinctive flavour from the addition of oil extracted from the skin of bergamot, a fruit grown mainly in Calabria on the Ionian Sea and known variously as a sweet lemon or a sour orange, depending on who you ask. Although the Earl Grey notes are much more floral, it's pleasing that there is a citrus continuity throughout the dessert.

Tregothnan Estate in Cornwall is, to my knowledge, the only tea grower in the UK. Although we were supplied coffee from Monmouth coffee roasters in Borough Market, blurring our local sourcing rules to allow a fairly traded produce from abroad, it was very exciting to discover that we could provide delicious tea without contradicting our remit quite so much. Tregothnan's Earl Grey is particularly good.

One of my most striking memories as a chef came one evening at the restaurant when a man sitting at the table next to the open kitchen paused halfway through his dessert and looked over at me with a tear in his eye. He was enjoying it so much it made him cry. It's probably the biggest compliment I've ever been paid as a cook.

Earl Grey and orange cream pudding

Serves 4
475ml double cream
50ml whole milk
200g sugar
1½ gelatin leaves
2 Earl Grey teabags
Juice of 3 oranges, about 210ml

Combine half the sugar, 350ml of the cream and all the milk in a pan with the tea bags. Gently bring to a simmer, squeezing the tea bags well into the cream mixture, and then remove from the heat. Leave to infuse for 10–15 minutes. Strain.

In the meantime, soak one of the gelatin leaves in cold water for 5 minutes and then dissolve it in the cream mixture while still warm. Set aside to cool.

When the cream mixture is completely cool, whisk the remaining cream into soft peaks and gently fold in. Pour into ramekins, wiping any drips from around the edges, and put in the fridge to set.

Soak the remaining half-leaf of gelatin in cold water for 5 minutes. Put the orange juice and the rest of the sugar in a saucepan and heat until the sugar is dissolved. Remove from the heat and dissolve the gelatin in it.

When the cream has set, pour the cool orange syrup over the top, cover each one with cling film and leave in the fridge to set again.

Smells are very evocative – and the Christmas period is packed
full of them – but, to me, the scent of pomanders (oranges
studded with cloves) is perhaps the most magical of the season.
The combination of the opulent orange and priceless spices must
have been a truly heady one in days gone by. London, my port of
choice, had a significant role to play in the spice trade, and the East
India Company, the huge commercial operation that administered
British trade interests in Asia and beyond, was based here. Spices,
and especially black pepper, were an extremely important part of
the British economy and led our drive to dominate the seas. The
rewards reaped in this endeavour would be traded at a price that
gave spices great social significance. Gentlemen were known to keep
their pepper in small bags about their person, and the cuisine of this
period would often feature ostentatious quantities.

Not all spices were imported; the most valuable of all, saffron,
was produced domestically in reasonable quantities. Saffron is the
harvested stigma of the saffron crocus (*Crocus sativus*). Each flower
yields only three such stigma and just 12 grammes of saffron are
produced for every kilo of flowers. The saffron harvest only lasts two
short weeks in the autumn and is a very labour-intensive process.
Ideally the saffron is picked in the morning, when the flowers are
freshest, but in practice it's often necessary to keep going day and
night. Because of the small yield and the intense effort required,
the price of saffron is very high, often higher by weight than that of
gold. Saffron Walden in Essex is named after the flourishing saffron
industry of the 14th century, which was centred in Norfolk and
Suffolk but also present in many parts of the south-east. Supposedly
curing almost everything, including cancer, it was in great demand
for its medicinal properties during the Black Death and would have
been grown extensively throughout that dark chapter of our history.
There is only one grower left in the UK today, in Wales. It's fairly
easy to cultivate your own saffron and end up with a relatively
high-quality product for your culinary or curative requirements.

It wasn't until I started working at Moro, in the late 1990s, that I really encountered saffron; it was there that I learned about its pervasive and exotic flavour. Saffron is well known for its vibrant colour but its taste, which is often overlooked in this country, brings a touch of hay and honey to dishes.

Saffron isn't the only spice we can grow in the UK. Mustard has been grown here in substantial quantities for centuries, and somewhere between 1,500 and 2,000 tonnes are still produced each year. Colman's, a household name and a brand that has been on the go for about two hundred years, is still made with English mustard seed, although only about 50 per cent, the rest coming from Canada, the world's largest mustard producer by far. When I was a child, bright yellow fields of mustard were a common sight, especially in East Anglia, but now most of the yellow crops you see dotting the countryside are oilseed rape. Mustard-growing in the UK would have petered out entirely only a few years ago but for the establishment of the English Mustard Growers Co-operative, which was formed as a response to both the dwindling viability of mustard-growing and the Unilever takeover of Colman's. The company is now pushing the growers to step up their production so they can make Colman's from 100 per cent English mustard again.

Tiptree, another well-known brand, makes preserves of all kinds, most famously jams, but they make a small range of mustards too, using varying degrees of English and Canadian mustard seed. They also produce an East Anglian mustard for Waitrose, which uses only seed from that area. It's rare that large companies invest in local products in this way, as it doesn't always represent the cheapest option when global trade structures can offer alternatives from overseas, but it's heart-warming when it does happen.

Spices are a key element in cooking the world over, from the pepper that graces our tables to the exorbitant saffron. Perhaps more than any other ingredient, spices tell stories of shared cultures and the movement of people around the globe. Cinnamon used in southern Spain is a remnant of the Moorish occupation, and chilli was unknown in India until Vasco da Gama landed there in the late 15th century. The ongoing push of the Portuguese Empire into other parts of Asia took the chilli with it, and to this day it is an integral part of the cuisines in the region. Until then heat was attained through the use of pepper, and Keralan dishes still maintain that tradition.

Using spices well is the hallmark of a good cook and one should never be heavy-handed with them, but it wasn't until I visited India myself that I learned not to be intimidated by them. Seeing how heady blends of punchy flavours could be intertwined to balance and enhance each other was an education. Creating these powerful blends still requires subtlety though, including a sensitive understanding of timing and masterful control of cooking heat.

At various times at Konstam we used fennel seed, dill seed and celery seed all grown in or around London. When the plants have flowered, the seed pods are left to dry and then the spice is harvested. Harvesting like this can be difficult in England – our climate and the changeable weather makes sizeable production a tricky proposition, but on a domestic or experimental scale it's easy and fun. Simply let the plant in question go to seed, and when it looks like it's dying cut it and hang it in bunches until thoroughly dried before stripping off the seeds and storing them in a jam jar. Likewise, dried pulses are difficult crops and restrictively pricey because, like spices, they need to be left on the plant to dry. I know of a grower in Cambridgeshire who produces borlotti beans, and at Konstam we occasionally received batches of cannellini beans from Mill Hill, but again these were the result of passionate experimentation rather than serious agricultural staples in development.

At Christmas we go through oodles of mincemeat – laced with mostly nutmeg, cinnamon, ginger and allspice – but these days it bears little resemblance to the original, which was largely made of beef or mutton and has only in later years come to mean a sweet filling for mince pies. Although it no longer contains meat it should still be made with suet. Mincemeat was a classic example of a sumptuous dish where the spices either showed off the ostentatious palette of the kitchen producing it or masked the flavour of the dubious nature of the meat being used.

A lovely dish that has spices at the heart of it is pilaf. There's a knack to making a good pilaf, but it's traditionally a feast dish so it's perfect for this time of year. Pilafs and other similar rice dishes are found in all areas of the world but mainly in the Middle East, the Caucasus, Afghanistan, India, Pakistan and Bangladesh. They go by many related names, including pilau, pilav, plov and pulao. A pilaf is made by adding rice and water to a pot in which spices have been fried in butter or ghee, then more water is added and a close-fitting lid put on top. All the water is soaked up by the rice and often the base is allowed to go crispy. I first learned to cook them at Moro, but I make them at home quite a lot and find the buttery spices and the fluffy rice a great source of comfort. I like to use black cardamom in my pilafs, as I love the smokiness it brings, along with the aromatic quality you'd expect of green cardamom. Incidentally, in many countries rice is harvested late in the calendar year. Although this has no real effect on the product we use, it's nice to know it fits with our seasonal brief.

Black cardamom and onion pilaf

This is a basic pilaf recipe and many different spices or more substantial ingredients can be substituted or added. This may affect the cooking times and quantities a little, but once you've made it a few times you should be able to gauge this fairly accurately in advance.

Serves 4
280g white basmati rice
2 onions
2 tbsp olive oil
Salt
50g butter
3 or 4 black cardamom pods, crushed
1 cinnamon stick
Lemon zest – 2 strips
A pinch of saffron (optional)

Slice the onions crosswise and fry in a saucepan with the olive oil and a pinch of salt until soft and well caramelised. Tip into a sieve over a bowl to drain off excess oil

Rinse the rice in 3 changes of water and set aside to drain thoroughly. Meanwhile, melt the butter in a medium pan with a close-fitting lid over a medium heat, then add the spices. Cook and gently fry until the butter starts to caramelise and the spices smell aromatic. Add the rice, a couple of good pinches of salt and the lemon zest and stir well to mix. Increase the heat, then add 560ml of boiling water. Spread a piece of dampened, crumpled parchment over the surface of the water and put the lid on. Cook on a high heat for 5 minutes then lower the heat and cook for another 10.

Remove from the heat and leave to stand for 10 minutes without taking the lid off. Remove the lid and check the rice is done. If not, add another 100ml of boiling water and put back on the heat for another 5 minutes. Remove from the heat and let stand a little bit longer before testing again. The rice grains should be tender but not too soft. Check for seasoning and gently fold in the onions and any extra seasoning required.

All this talk of spices leads me back to the clove and the wonderful decorations it becomes part of at Christmas. A pomander is made by painstakingly piercing the orange skin with little clove stalks, then hanging it up with ribbon for the orange to dry out and emit its exotic aroma. It combines two sensually harmonious ingredients and symbols of domestic opulence to produce a scent that lies, for me at least, at the very heart of Christmas.

My memory suggests that once the chaos of Christmas morning stockings was over we were often starved of a proper breakfast to conserve our appetite for the feast ahead. So by the time we got to our Christmas lunch we were ravenous and desperate for roast potatoes and gravy. I'm not sure this wasn't a foolhardy decision as tempers would inevitably fray, and no doubt the empty stomachs of the children in the Rowe family contributed to the particular emotional maelstrom of excitement, expectation and general stress that only comes around once a year.

The meat of choice for Christmas lunch is still turkey, although goose has made a dent in its domination in recent years. Indigenous to the Americas, turkeys were brought to Europe by the Spanish and introduced to the UK in the 16th century by the English navigator William Strickland. For many years the turkey conceded the Christmas table to the more popular beef and goose, but in the 20th century it came to the fore as the nation's choice, in part due to a significant fall in price as a result of improved farming and disease control and the influence of American culture, especially film.

It's certainly not my favourite meat, and I rarely cook with it at any other time of year, but I like its place on our festive table. Having said that, the fuller flavour of goose makes for a delicious alternative – which reminds me of one Christmas at my cousin's house when I was charged with the task of roasting the bird. We were a bit pushed for time, so I didn't have a chance to make a stuffing. The goose took longer to cook than I thought, and everyone was seated at the kitchen table waiting for their dinner before it was ready. The table was near the cooker and I was sitting next to it, periodically checking on the goose. It was while I was peeking inside the cavity that I saw an unidentified object, so I poked in the tongs and had a feel around. There was definitely something in there but I couldn't figure out what it was. I gave it a tug but it wouldn't budge, so I gave it a firmer tug and it still wouldn't shift. I finally gave it a hefty pull and suddenly out came a plastic bag full of giblets and associated juices. Unfortunately, most of the liquid contents of the bag sprayed all over the assembled guests. I was mortified – not only because I'd just sprayed everyone with hot bloody cooking juice, but also because, having been a chef for some years by then, I hadn't remembered to take the giblets out in the first place, or made a stuffing to put in their place!

Turkey and goose are by no means the only meat around in December. Venison is in season, rabbit is abundant and guineafowl are plump and in their prime. Slightly richer than chicken, guineafowl make an excellent alternative to turkey. The only drawback is that they're quite small, so you may need several of them. I can eat half a guineafowl without blinking but, then again, I am quite greedy. The fallow, red and roe deer seasons are in full swing for the whole month and, as always, muntjac deer is available. For anyone looking for a richer meat to adorn their festive table, venison surely rules. Much lower in fat than a lot of meats, venison has to be cooked carefully as it can end up tough or dry: rather a waste of a lovely, and usually expensive, piece of meat.

Despite having been a chef for many years now, the preparation and cooking of family Christmas meals has only recently started falling to me, and the reason for this is simple: December in a restaurant kitchen can be pretty hellish; it's the busiest time of the year and the hours are excruciatingly long. By the time I get to Christmas Day all I can do is fall into bed, exhausted by my recent travails and the stressful last-minute shop for presents. My mother has always been very mindful of this and not relied too heavily on my labour for this all-encompassing and emotionally charged meal. However, it has always been down to me to make the gravy.

I wouldn't go so far as to say I have a tried and tested recipe written on parchment which I dust off each year to produce a gravy of superlative sophistication, more that I throw in a bit of whatever I can lay my hands on, in judicious quantities, and tweak it until it's just right. I like a drop of port in my Christmas gravy, but wine, brandy, sherry and cider have all found their way in at various times. For this sort of gravy I always stir flour into the roasting pan with the gunk and cook it for a few minutes before adding liquid, as opposed to a more cheffy jus-type sauce. I like the viscosity of this kind of gravy and its homely flavour, though I do like to use good, home-made chicken stock as well as the wine to bolster the flavour.

My favourite part of the Christmas meal is the roast potatoes, and it's always these I return to 15 minutes after I've finished my second massive helping. There is no doubt that the best technique for roasting potatoes is to parboil, fluff them up and season before tipping them into a blistering hot baking tray with lashings of shimmering fat. Many say that duck fat is irreplaceable in this role, but I often use either a combination of olive oil and butter, or rapeseed oil on its own. The latter enhances the yellowy hues of the end product in a very appealing way.

Rapeseed has the advantage of being easily grown in the UK and is therefore an excellent local product. It has a nutty, buttery taste with less cholesterol and a higher burning point than olive oil. At Konstam we used rapeseed oil from Suffolk, not only because it was very high quality but it also helped keep us to our local remit. Olive oil has greater subtlety and variety of flavour, and is superior as a finishing oil, but I feel there are environmental, commercial and cultural considerations that mean we should endorse local ingredients, which should in turn encourage producers to develop them and their flavours. To that end there is a burgeoning number of rapeseed oils available on the market, and in the matter of roasting potatoes, rapeseed oil is a strong contender.

All manner of vegetables are delicious roasted, but it's easy to get it wrong – I know I haven't quite achieved the result I was looking for on many occasions. If it does go awry it's always disappointing – anaemic and mushy or burned and inedible. Getting it right can create a stunning contribution to a dish composed of very humble ingredients, and Christmas is a perfect time to put that into practice.

Roast vegetables

Toss the vegetables with ingredients such as crushed garlic, thyme, rosemary, spices, seasoning and a good slug of oil in a big bowl rather than on the baking tray – it's one more thing to wash up but it's worth it as the vegetables get evenly coated with the oil and seasoning. Spread the veg out on the baking tray and then drizzle any oil left in the bowl evenly over the top – use a little extra if none is left in the bowl. I often use parchment underneath the vegetables as it makes the washing-up afterwards a lot easier.

Arrange the vegetables in only one layer on the baking tray. This way the heat can get to them from all sides and they don't steam each other, which means they colour properly and don't turn to mush before they've caramelised.

Turn and agitate. Always make sure you move the vegetables around at least three times. The first time should be done fairly soon after putting them in the oven. Then do it twice more, a bit more carefully so they don't break up. Turning the baking tray to minimise the effect of hotspots in the oven is a good idea too.

Have the oven on full heat, at least to start – it'll keep you on your toes, but it's the only way to get lovely, sweet and caramelised roast vegetables. Dare to get some colour. Let your vegetables take on golden brown colouring; let them get soft with chewy, crispy exteriors. You can always turn the heat down if they're cooking too fast.

Some veg, like fennel, endive or beetroot, can be covered with foil for the first part of cooking. Fennel can be started with some white wine and endive with lots of butter. Remove the foil at the end to colour.

As I said, potatoes need parboiling, steaming after draining and fluffing before being carefully tipped into a preheated tray with a good layer of almost smoking oil. Watch out for splashes. Start with parsnips and work your way up to butternut squash. You should cut out the hearts of parsnips if you want to get a really tender result.

In the café we used to roast parsnips, carrots and celeriac, then toss them with a wholegrain mustard and cider vinegar dressing to make a salad that people couldn't get enough of – we went through bowls of it when it was on the menu. I was a real stickler back then and we used to make it fresh each day, but now I'd say that the veg will last perfectly well in a fridge for a day or two before being dressed, especially if refreshed in a hot oven before use.

As mentioned at the beginning of this chapter, it's a myth that there isn't much fresh produce in the winter. Admittedly, it's not quite the abundance of different crops we see from late spring through to autumn, but it isn't until further down the line that things start to get seriously tight. Many of the root vegetables we've been enjoying for a few months, such as beetroots and carrots, are still around, if coming to an end, and there are still leeks and cauliflowers. Parsnips are nearly at their best and Jerusalem artichokes are starting. Some of the healthiest crops come into play around now, such as kale and Savoy cabbages, both fantastic sources of iron, and watercress is beginning to show its face.

Chestnuts are a winter treat and amazing roasted in a pan on an open fire – one with holes is best to let the smoke and flames get through to the nuts for that burned-sweet flavour. When I was little I remember being half-fascinated and half-scared by the sooty-faced men with the fiery oil drums who used to sell delicious but too-hot-to-eat chestnuts in paper bags during the cold midwinter. There is an Italian dessert called Montebianco – Mont Blanc in French, after the mountain on the Franco-Italian border – which is, in the general tradition of dishes involving fresh chestnuts, painstaking to make but results in a gorgeous heap of squiggly sweet chestnut paste covered in softly whipped cream and caramelised violets. It's especially appealing to children, but I recommend a test run before presenting it to the family. It also makes a good alternative to Christmas pudding. You can do all sorts of nice things with deep-fried chestnut purée too – squeezed like churros into hot oil, dusted in sugar and eaten while still warm.

One of the freshest crops at this time of year is also one of the most controversial in the seasonal calendar, a real love-them-or-hate-them food. Obviously I'm talking about Brussels sprouts. The customary cooking method in Britain is to boil the hell out of them. But if you boil them you need to do it right – too quick and they're crunchy and bitter, too long and they're dull and unpleasant. Get it just right – vibrant green and tender – and they're sweet and delicious.

In recent years I've learned a few tricks. My friend Luke Matthews, who used to work with me at Konstam, pulls the leaves off to make lovely little salads, which I think he learned when he was doing an internship at Noma a few years ago. In this form they're rather beautiful, if a little painstaking, with a lovely shape and texture. While I was doing my internship at Chez Panisse in Berkeley, California, in the winter of 2012, I came across a couple of other great ways of preparing them. The one I've reproduced most successfully is simply to deep fry them – I saw this done as party food at Boot and Shoe in Oakland. This is a really delicious way of cooking them, the outer leaves crispy and sweet and the centre crunchy and full of flavour. I like them best served with a goat's cheese dressing and a few black chilli flakes, but a dollop of crème fraîche and some parsley will do just fine.

Deep-fried Brussels sprouts with goat's cheese dressing and black chilli flakes

I've only found these flakes in one or two shops in East London. They're sweet and not excessively spicy, but the moist red ones available in Turkish shops will do if you can't find the black ones. This dressing is good with just about any brassica from spring greens and kale to sprouting broccoli and cima di rapa.

Serves 4
30–35 Brussels sprouts
4 tbsp soft, full-flavoured goat's cheese
1 tbsp olive oil
½ tsp grain mustard
A good dash of milk
Salt
Black chilli flakes
2 sprigs parsley
Oil for deep-frying

Prep the sprouts by trimming the bottom, removing the coarse or damaged outer leaves and crossing both ends with a knife – the top should be scored almost halfway down. If they need washing make sure they're well dried before frying.

Mash or blitz the goat's cheese with the olive oil and mustard. Add milk until a thick drizzling consistency is achieved. Season with salt to taste – fried food takes a lot of seasoning so make sure that the flavours come through really well.

Heat the oil to 170°C using a thermometer if you have one. Otherwise, a crouton of bread turning golden brown in a little over a minute will indicate a good temperature, but make sure it's no hotter than that. Deep-fry the sprouts until the outside few layers of leaves are golden brown but the inside is still green. You can shallow fry them if you like, or roast them, but for optimum crispiness deep-frying is best.

Drain and tip onto kitchen paper and leave, preferably in a warm place, for a minute or two. Season with fine salt. While the sprouts are resting, wash and chop the parsley, then arrange the sprouts on a big plate, drizzle the dressing on top and sprinkle with chilli flakes and parsley. Serve while warm.

Another way I saw sprouts cooked in California was in a gratin, at Bar Jules, Jessica Boncutter's restaurant in San Francisco. Doused in cream, topped in breadcrumbs and baked in the oven in individual dishes, they were fantastic – I remember fighting over the last ones with a friend who was sitting opposite me.

It isn't just the food that makes Christmas what it is, the drinks are a huge part of it too. They're usually warming and alcoholic in a bid to fortify the bones against the creeping cold of winter. It may be more traditional to drink mulled wine after carol singing, for which you can look back to the recipe in November, but mulled cider has been making a comeback in recent years. It's an age-old drink made pretty much the same way as mulled wine but with a little less sugar. Mulled cider is drunk at all sorts of occasions over the winter, but it often replaces the somewhat archaic wassail, which goes hand in hand with the ceremony of wassailing, the blessing of the apple trees; counter intuitively, it's traditionally made with beer or, more properly, mead.

Cider is more historically appropriate than wine or fruit juice, though sherry will do just as well if mead isn't available. Wassail is supposed to be topped with pieces of toast – something Mrs Beeton nods to in her recipe for mulled wine – to be eaten as sops. Sops are one of my favourite things, pieces of bread soaked in liquid and eaten with whatever they're sponging up. One of the very best is thickly buttered toast steeped in leek and potato soup.

Although we don't drink it very often, eggnog has its own place in the popular traditions of Christmas. Its roots are firmly British, but these days it's most commonly drunk in North America. For years I had a low-level curiosity as to what it actually was, but I never asked as it seemed to be one of those things that everyone else knew about and I was mildly embarrassed that I didn't. Then I was given some a few years ago and realised just why it goes down so well at Christmas. Eggnog has its origins in posset and consists of eggs beaten with milk or cream, sugar and brandy, Madeira or sherry. It's incredibly rich and most of us would be ill-advised to get drunk on it for fear of an instant coronary. That said, it tastes divine and fits with the general sense of indulgence at this time of the year.

Eggnog

This recipe makes enough for 8 or 9 small glasses, or 4 to 6 very generous ones. You can try different alcohols and mixes, such as bourbon and Madeira, or a darker sherry such as Oloroso or even Pedro Ximénez, but the dark rum and Manzanilla sherry in my recipe make for a warming and complex combination.

3 very fresh eggs
350ml milk
150ml single cream
150ml dark rum
50ml Manzanilla sherry
105g caster sugar
1 cinnamon stick
Nutmeg

Combine the milk, cream, cinnamon and nutmeg in a saucepan and bring to the boil. Take off the heat, leave to cool and remove the cinnamon.

Separate the eggs, and whisk together the yolks and 75g of the sugar. Retain the whites. Stir the cool milk and cream mixture into the beaten yolks. Add the two alcohols and refrigerate until required. It will keep well in the fridge for two or three days.

To serve, whisk the egg whites with the remaining sugar until they form stiff peaks, then fold into the eggnog. Serve with a delicate scrape of nutmeg on top.

The weeks from mid-November to Christmas are full on in the restaurant trade, but the work involved stretches back months. It's amazing how early the bookings start to come in, especially for office outings. By the time you get to August the requests for the Christmas menu are getting more frequent, and with all the day-to-day work involved in running a restaurant only a really organised chef can have it ready this far in advance. At Konstam it was often well into September or October by the time my Christmas menu was done and dusted. As it gets closer the work the managers have to do starts to ramp up as they try to keep on top of all the bookings and special requirements.

Naturally, people want to make changes to the menu you've created, so you tend to spend a lot of time trying to work out how to accommodate everyone. It's not just the big parties that make things hairy; the sheer volume of bookings starts to increase as Christmas approaches, and the workload increases with it. It's always just at the point when everyone is working their hardest and the hours are taking their toll that a bout of colds spreads through the team and people start to get ratty and feel overstretched. Each day becomes a mountain to climb and, inevitably, there are moments when something gives – a temper flares, a course goes out cold, a customer waits for their meal, or a booking gets overlooked – there are any number of things that can go wrong and most of them, at some point, do.

By the week before Christmas everyone is run ragged. If you've ever had the misfortune of running out of petrol on the motorway you'll know how it feels heading into that last week. There is no more fuel left but you just hope the momentum of the vehicle will get you along the slip road and into the petrol station before you come to a halt. One year I had to dismiss my two most senior staff members over the weekend leading up to this last week – that was a particularly difficult time for me and the rest of the team.

All in all, Christmas for a chef can feel a bit out of sync – you sometimes feel you're watching it go by like a fish in its bowl. Nonetheless, in the midst of it all there is always time to sit down with tired colleagues or understanding friends, drink a glass or three of wine and make good cheer until the early hours of the morning. It may not be wise and many a yuletide hangover has added to the general exhaustion, but you need those moments to reconnect with the world and to understand what you're doing it all for. It helps you to keep cooking delicious food and to put the love into each plate you send out.

Eventually we get to Christmas Day and the organised chaos begins. From the stockings and the bird-basting to the table laying, gravy pouring, present unwrapping, and bloated TV-watching, the whirlwind finally blows itself out, one last glass of wine is drunk and everyone lollops off to bed.

We don't traditionally make bread sauce in my family but, partly because of the lovely bread we had at Konstam and partly because I like it, I've cooked it a great deal myself. I feel we can't be done with the festivities until I've included a recipe for this and one other side dish I feel is a highlight of the Christmas meal – red cabbage. My mum makes great red cabbage, having learned it from my grandmother's housekeeper, Lore, a German woman who worked for her from the age of 22 until she retired in 2004 at 75. By this time they were both pretty unsteady on their feet, and my grandmother passed away a few years later. Lore cooked for four generations of my family on my mother's side and had a profound influence on her cooking and mine. Unfortunately, I didn't take down her recipe for red cabbage but my mum's is reproduced below. It's quite a simple recipe but you can jazz it up if you like. I often add a variety of ingredients, including chopped or grated apple, orange zest, cinnamon, cloves, nutmeg, red wine, port, brandy or cider.

Red cabbage

This keeps very well in the fridge for 2 or 3 days, so can be cooked well in advance. The flavours develop with time so it's best made ahead.

Serves 6
1 red cabbage
75g butter
1 onion
1 cinnamon stick
4 cloves
Zest of ½ an orange
1 eating apple
100ml red wine or cider vinegar
1 tbsp honey

Slice the onion and fry it in half the butter with a good pinch of salt in a big pan with a lid until soft and golden brown, stirring occasionally. While it's cooking, discard any old leaves from the cabbage, cut it in half and remove the core. Shred it thinly, grate the apple and when the onion is ready add these to the pan with the rest of the ingredients. Stir well and put the lid on. Cook, stirring occasionally, for about an hour or until meltingly tender. Be careful not to let it get mushy. Remove from the heat and stir in the rest of the butter.

Bread sauce

Serves 4
1 pint of milk
½ onion
2 bay leaves

5 whole black peppercorns
A few parsley stalks
1 blade of mace
100g breadcrumbs
100g butter
A few scrapes of nutmeg
4 tbsp cream
Salt and pepper

Add the bay, onion, peppercorns, parsley stalks and mace to the milk in a saucepan, bring to the boil, then remove from the heat and leave to infuse. I often make this the day before and leave it in the fridge overnight with all the aromatics in it.

Strain the liquid and return to the saucepan. Bring it to a simmer. Add the breadcrumbs in a steady stream whilst whisking and cook, whisking occasionally, until incorporated and smooth. Add the butter, cream and nutmeg. Season and add extra milk if too thick, or cook a little longer if too thin.

I rather like the part of December that comes after Christmas. It's one of the few times that London empties out and a degree of peace descends on the city. It can feel a bit lonely and eerie as the white noise of Christmas fades and you become aware of the cold silence of winter. This is the time for turkey, Brie and cranberry sandwiches, sitting on the sofa, reflecting on what the hell happened over the last couple of weeks and wondering what's to come. This musing continues for a few days and then you realise New Year's Eve is almost upon you and you haven't worked out who you're going to spend it with or where. The phone calls begin, the texts start flowing and another bout of chaos begins.

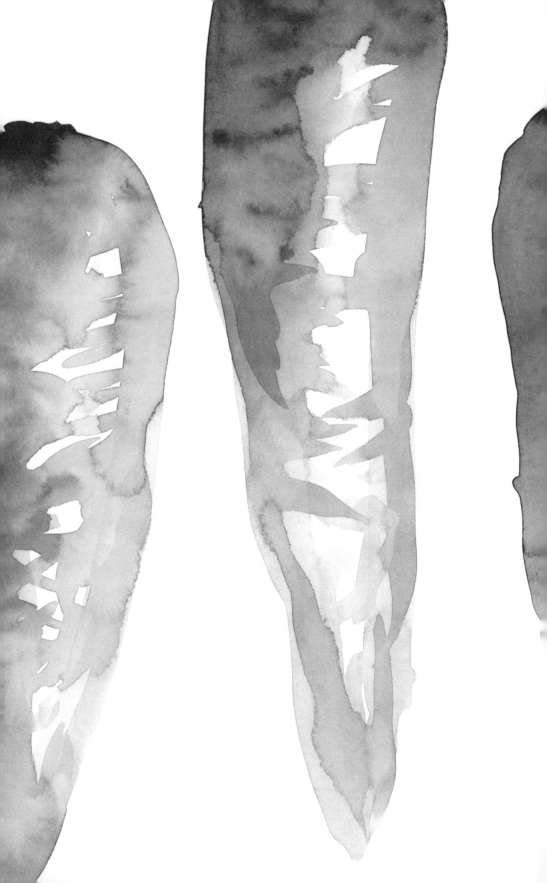

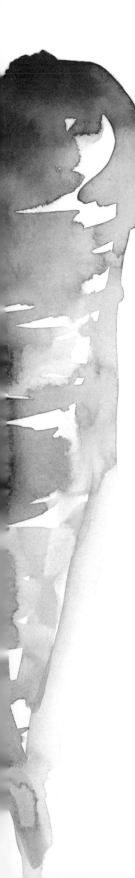

JANUARY

—

Cocktails

Spirits

Beer

Parsnips

Jerusalem artichokes

Seville oranges

Blood oranges

Beetroot

Chocolate

Somerset brandy

Swede

Haggis

Persimmons

Cauliflower

Every man should be born again on the first day
of January. Start with a fresh page. Take up
one hole more in the buckle if necessary, or let
down one, according to circumstances; but on the
first day of January let every man gird himself
once more, with his face to the front, and take
no interest in the things that were and are past.

Henry Ward Beecher

Despite giving the beginning of the food year to October, I can't deny January its place in our souls. It's the beginning of the calendar year and this gives it an unassailable gravitas which months like March and October can only dream of.

It should be noted that January hasn't always been the first month of the year, and even now in many countries the year still starts at the end of March. This is largely a result of the change from the Julian calendar to the Gregorian. The Julian calendar was used by the Romans from 45 BC by decree of Julius Caesar and endured until 1582 when it was supplanted by the one we use now, introduced by Pope Gregory XIII. The old calendar year was too short by just under 11 minutes, which meant that the spring equinox, by which we calculate the date of Easter, was getting earlier and earlier. By the time the change was made the equinox was ten days out of sync. The Gregorian calendar inserted leap years to ensure that the calendar stayed in sync with the celestial bodies. It also confirmed 1 January as the start of the year, instead of 25 March.

Although the Gregorian is the internationally accepted civil calendar, there are still many people around the world who observe variations depending on nationality, culture and religion. Even now in the UK the fact that our fiscal year starts near the spring equinox is a hangover from when the year used to begin. Knowing that so many different cultures celebrate the New Year at such different times gives me comfort when contemplating the eccentricity of my own seasonal year.

The portal to January, New Year's Eve, is a celebration of hedonistic consumption, but along with the general debauchery many traditions and customs have developed over the years in different countries – from plate smashing in Denmark to the lowering of a large ball in New York City's Times Square – but my favourite is the German tradition of watching a British TV comedy sketch called 'Dinner for One'. It started life as a skit doing the rounds of the music hall circuit, but in 1963 a German television station recorded it, with the performance in English. It only has two characters, an elderly upper-class woman and her butler, who gets increasingly drunk during his efforts to impersonate her four deceased friends as he serves and then is required to consume the toasts for each guest throughout a four-course meal. I first became aware of it when I was in Berlin for the New Year in 2000, and I love the fact that it's almost unheard of over here despite its overseas fame, being broadcast each year in Norway, Sweden and Denmark, too.

All good New Year's Eves should start with, and go on to include, several cocktails. My favourite changes over time, but one that continues to endure is the Negroni. It's made from equal measures of gin, Campari and sweet vermouth. It sounds simple but the various permutations of gins and vermouths are endless. You can age the three together or switch the Campari for other bitters or aromatics; play with the brand, type and colour of the vermouth, or try different gins, of which there are thousands. All in all, there are many ways a bartender can personalise it, so I recommend sampling it in as many different establishments as you can. My friend, and trusty bartender, Julian de Feral makes the best Negroni I know, and has this to say about it:

> Cocktail lore has always maintained that the exuberant and slightly wild Count Camillo Negroni is responsible for asking a bartender to slip a little gin into his Milano Torino in around 1920. The Milano Torino gets its name from the cities that respectively produce its two ingredients, Campari and Martini Rosso. Certainly the story would make sense as this bon vivant was renowned for his hard drinking and had travelled to England several times, where he was no doubt introduced to gin.
>
> Recent evidence suggests that it might have been a milder-mannered relative who was responsible for the Negroni's creation, and despite the many hot-blooded protests from Italian bartenders the world over, the theory originates from the Negroni family itself. In the end, which Negroni created the Negroni is by the by. The important thing is that nine out of ten cocktail cats would happily refer to it as their favourite cocktail, and there is something distinctly classy about the connoisseur who orders a Negroni before dinner.
>
> I find great comfort in a drink as simple as three ingredients in equal measures: the herbaceous, floral and piney notes in gin complement and harmonise with the botanicals in the vermouth, and the botanicals in the vermouth do likewise with the bitters. Like old, mutually respectful friends, they never interrupt each other, nor try to dominate the conversation.
>
> But how to make it? When I'm at home I just build it in a rocks glass, equal proportions of gin, sweet vermouth and Campari. One could rightly point out that the proportions depend entirely on the gin. Indeed, if using 'new world' gins, which pack a lighter botanical punch, it would make sense to increase the proportion of gin. But I would say don't use a juniper-heavy one like Tanqueray Export, Plymouth or Junipero. Besides, if we're getting particular, and we are, who says you're using Campari and Martini Rosso anyway? Why not use the exalted Carpano Antica Formula vermouth, one of many different vermouths out there. Campari has its substitutes too, such as its lighter and fairer cousin Aperol, or why not court controversy and let a Frenchie in – the gentian and orange-heavy Amer Picon can certainly compete with Campari where dryness and intensity are concerned.

What all this says about the Negroni is that, like any classic cocktail, it's great for tinkering with and tweaking. However, as much as I like to play, I always come back to equal measures – and that means equal, none of this roundabouts or by-eye nonsense. If you don't possess a jigger use an egg cup or an espresso cup.

Finally, the method. As I mentioned, at home I build the drink directly into the glass, with the lightest ingredient going in first: gin, vermouth then bitters. It's a good idea to keep your glassware frozen, and it's also important to pay attention to the ice; cubes made in dinky little trays can be unsatisfactory as they melt and dilute in a heartbeat, and it takes pretty much a whole tray for a decent-sized Negroni. To make a Negroni that you can really take your time over – aperitivos are not to be rushed affairs – why not make your own block ice? This isn't nearly as daunting as it sounds. Fill a Tupperware box several inches deep and wide with water. After a bit of practice, hand-chipping off a couple of chunks for your drink will come naturally. It pays to invest in a good ice pick, but I simply use a large, solid serving spoon.

The traditional Negroni garnish is a slice of orange, but you can also include an orange twist for added aroma, or an orange wedge so your guests have the choice of squeezing a little juice in if they find the drink too full-on. The Italians are said to have an aversion to lemon, lime or any other citrus in a Campari-based drink, claiming that it impairs the flavour and jars with the components, but I have found no evidence of this.

Although the Negroni would have been an appropriate cocktail for Konstam – once we'd sourced an independent, local gin – I don't think we ever served them. We didn't run a full cocktail list as the bar was too small, and once we'd arranged all our wines and a few spirits there wasn't much space for the many different spirits and mixers required. This meant that many great cocktails passed us by. We did, however, make our own version of Bloody Mary.

We decided to put this on the menu soon after we started doing Sunday brunch, as nothing comes closer to sorting out a hangover. We weren't able to source local tomato juice, and rarely even tomatoes, but we did source local vodka, and added local celery seed and local horseradish to spice it up. I wanted to give our Bloody Mary something of an Eastern European flavour, so we stirred in a pinch of ground caraway seed for a little Konstam twist. The flavours work beautifully together and many a customer's ropey Sunday morning was given a good kick-start because of them.

Drinks can pose a few problems when you're sourcing locally since many of the spirits we take for granted are overseas imports. Certain spirits produced in the UK are only now becoming financially viable, due to the increase in support and publicity for local producers. Obviously whisky is an easy one, and there are thousands of beers and ciders with all sorts of regional variations. London is now home to countless independent breweries, but when I first opened Konstam we didn't have a great deal of choice. Meantime Brewing Company wasn't the huge business it is now, and I was an early subscriber to their bottled beer. Back then they were still brewing in a lock-up near Charlton Athletic football ground, before they moved to the Greenwich brewery in 2010. Their award-winning London Porter was always a favourite, so much so that I developed an ice cream made with it. Part of the reason for coming up with the recipe was that I missed the Malaga raisin ice cream at Moro, a long-standing favourite, and I wanted to find local ingredients to try and replicate it.

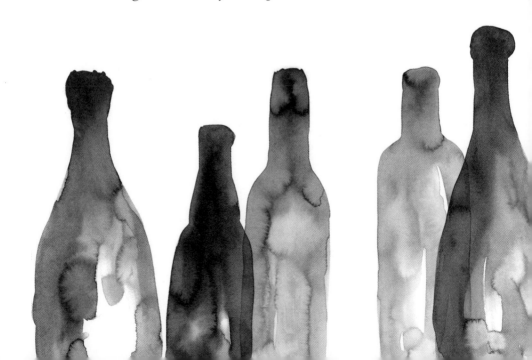

London Porter ice cream

Makes 1 litre of ice cream

Syrup:

125ml of Meantime London Porter beer

40g soft light brown sugar

40g currants

Base:

375ml double cream

375ml whole milk

7 medium egg yolks

100g soft dark brown sugar

60g golden caster sugar

40g Demerara sugar

First make the syrup. Combine the ingredients in a saucepan and bring to the boil for about 6 or 7 minutes to reduce by a third. Set aside to cool and then place in the fridge.

To make the base, cream the yolks with all the sugars until well combined. Slowly bring the milk and cream to the boil then remove from the heat. Gently stir (not whisk) 1 large ladleful of the hot cream mixture into the eggs, then another, then slowly pour in the rest while continuing to stir gently. Return to a low heat and, stirring continuously, heat until the mixture thickens enough to coat the back of a large metal spoon – about 10–12 minutes.

Transfer to a large plastic or metal container and leave to cool, with cling film covering the surface – this will prevent a skin forming.

Churn the base (but not the syrup) according to the instructions for your ice cream machine.

To make without an ice cream machine, chill the base over an ice bath until cool, then place in the freezer. When it starts to freeze around the edges, whisk to churn – an electric whisk is ideal for this. Put it back in the freezer and repeat every half an hour until it freezes fully. This will take about 3 hours, depending on your freezer. It may turn out a little icier than the machine-made ice cream, but it will still be very good.

If using a machine, drizzle three-quarters of the syrup and currants between basting-spoonfuls of churned ice cream base, then freeze. If using a whisk and elbow grease, fold the syrup into the ice cream after the last whisk. Be careful to leave big streaks of it running through the ice cream. Use the remaining syrup to drizzle over the ice cream as you serve it.

We now also have a burgeoning British vodka industry, a no-brainer since we grow all the required ingredients and have a fair bit of know-how when it comes to distilling. This means it's becoming increasingly possible to put together a locally sourced drinks list featuring outstanding seasonal cocktails.

So January starts with a bang, then it's all hangovers and good intentions, but by the end of the month we're starting to feel the strain of winter and everyone is feeling the pinch after the extravagances of the last few weeks. The food year keeps on turning and the frost is unaware of our excesses. Although we're generally unenthusiastic about the cold there are several vegetables that thrive on it. They use sugar as antifreeze and produce more of it in response to a good hard frost. The sugar acts to depress the freezing point of the water in the plant cells, enabling them to survive through the winter.

Any gardener worth their salt will tell you that parsnips are best after the first hard frost, and although this can happen any time from the autumn on, down in the south-east we can't rely on it until the depths of winter. This makes them an ideal January crop. Parsnips can appear unassuming but they're delicious when cooked the right way. Parsnip soup sounds uninspiring, but add a few apples and it takes on a new dimension. I remember my mum making it for a dinner party many years ago, and I can still taste the perfect balance of sweet and savoury. I've made it countless times since then, but only occasionally getting that ratio just right.

Parsnip and apple soup with gin

I like my soups quite simple, so the fewer ingredients the better, but there needs to be a bridge between the parsnip and the apple, so make sure to get enough sweetness from the mirepoix – the celery, onion and carrot combination that goes in at the start. My mum adds some lemon zest at the end, too, which doesn't sharpen it, just brightens the flavours.

Serves 4
2 tbsp olive oil
2 onions
2 carrots
3 celery sticks
2–3 garlic cloves
2 fresh bay leaves
1 sprig thyme
4 medium parsnips
1 white potato
1 Bramley apple
1 eating apple
Vegetable stock (optional)
Zest of half a lemon (optional)
Salt and freshly ground black pepper
4 tsp crème fraîche
A few sprigs of chervil or parsley
4 shots of good gin

Peel and dice the onion and carrot. Wash, trim and dice the celery. Heat the olive oil in a medium saucepan, add the onion, carrot, celery, bay, thyme and a good pinch of salt – this will help soften the vegetables as well as providing seasoning. Cook the vegetables quite gently for 5 minutes, then add the peeled and chopped garlic and cook them all together until softened and light golden brown.

In the meantime, peel, quarter and core the parsnip, dice and add to the vegetables in the pan. Peel and dice the potato and add to the pan. Leave to cook together over a medium heat for a few minutes – and make sure there is enough oil in the pan to prevent the vegetables from sticking. Peel, quarter, core and dice the apples. Add these to the pan, stir and cook for a minute or two then cover with stock or water and bring to a gentle simmer. Cook until the parsnip and potato are both soft and the apples have broken down.

Remove from heat and blitz in a blender until smooth. If too thick – and this is always a matter of taste – thin with a little extra stock, water or milk. Season well, and add lemon zest, if using.

To serve, add a teaspoon of crème fraîche on top of each bowl, a twist of black pepper and a drizzle of olive oil. Chervil looks so nice as whole leaves, so just arrange these on top or sprinkle over some chopped parsley. Accompany with a shot-glass of very cold gin.

There isn't a great difference between the produce available in December and January, partly due to a general slowing of the rate of growth at this time of year. However, there are a few changes. Although Jerusalem artichokes are available at the end of the year, they really come into their own as the New Year swings around. They're native to North America and were cultivated by Native Americans long before the arrival of Europeans. These artichokes belong to the genus *Helianthus*, the same as the sunflower, and it's from this that they get their name. Early Italian settlers named them *girasole*, the Italian word for sunflower, derived, like the French word for sunflower, *tournesol*, from the flowers' habit of rotating over the course of the day to follow the sun. In time *girasole* evolved into 'Jerusalem' in general usage. They taste a bit like regular artichokes, but despite both being part of the Asteraceae (daisy) family they are very different species. One similarity, beyond their taste, is that they both store inulin instead of starch, but Jerusalem artichokes do so in unusually high quantities, such that our digestive system finds it difficult to process. It's well known that they can cause spectacular bouts of wind and sometimes great discomfort. Simply made, a smooth Jerusalem artichoke soup topped with lightly toasted crushed walnuts, a dollop of crème fraîche and a drizzle of good olive oil is gastronomic heaven, but unfortunately I rarely indulge these days as for me it means a very unsettled night's sleep.

Jerusalem artichoke soup with crispy breadcrumbs and goat's cheese

Serves 4
2 tbsp olive oil
2 onions
3 celery sticks
2–3 garlic cloves
2 fresh bay leaves
1 sprig thyme
About 500g Jerusalem artichokes
Vegetable stock (optional)
Salt and freshly ground black pepper
2 or 3 slices of sourdough bread
50g crumbly goat's cheese

Peel and dice the onion. Wash, trim and dice the celery. Heat the olive oil in a medium saucepan, add the onion, celery, bay, thyme and a good pinch of salt to help soften the vegetables. Cook gently for 5 minutes or so. Add the peeled and chopped garlic and cook together until light golden brown.

While the other vegetables are cooking, scrub and roughly chop the Jerusalem artichokes. They often have grit stuck in their nooks and crannies so it's important to soak them a bit first and scrub them carefully. You can peel them, but I prefer not to as you lose some of the lovely, earthy flavour. Add to the vegetables in the pan. Cook together for a few minutes, then cover with stock or water and bring to a gentle simmer. Cook until the artichokes are very tender, about 20 minutes.

While the soup is cooking, pick the bread into irregular crumbs, the size of a large pea, and toss in a bowl with a tablespoon of oil and a pinch of salt. Spread out on a baking tray and roast in the oven at 160°C until golden brown.

When it is ready, remove the soup from the heat and blitz until smooth. If you like you can thin it a little at this point with more stock, water or a dash of milk, and a splash of extra olive oil will help make it richer if you feel it's lacking. Season well. If you want your soup to be really smooth you can pass it through a sieve, using the back of a ladle to help it on its way.

To serve, pour into bowls and drizzle with olive oil. Crumble the goat's cheese over the top and sprinkle with a few breadcrumbs. A little bit of good balsamic, pomegranate molasses, chilli flakes, paprika, toasted ground cumin, black onion seed, toasted crushed walnuts – any of these can be sprinkled or drizzled in moderation. Crème fraîche or yoghurt are great instead of goat's cheese – it all comes down to taste and experimentation.

~~~

Roasted Jerusalem artichokes are also great – they are high in fructose, which caramelises as the artichokes roast, giving a wonderfully sweet result. Fructose browns at a lower temperature than glucose or sucrose, so you don't need to roast them at quite as high a heat as many other vegetables. If you get it right they end up almost like candy and go really well with most meat or fish. I like to show them off and usually serve them as a salad with roast garlic cloves and home-cured bacon. This recipe can be easily adapted for vegetarians by omitting the bacon.

Roast Jerusalem artichoke, roast garlic, walnut and bacon salad

The individual ingredients for this salad take a little while to prepare, but can all be prepared in advance and assembled at the last minute.

Serves 4
400g Jerusalem artichokes
15 garlic cloves, unpeeled
1 bay leaf
⅓ glass of wine
⅓ glass of red wine vinegar
Cold-pressed rapeseed oil or olive oil
1 tsp Dijon mustard
1 tsp honey
3 rashers of streaky bacon
50g walnuts, very lightly roasted
1 small frisée
Salt and freshly ground black pepper
1 small bunch of parsley
½ bunch of chives

Put the wine and the vinegar into a small saucepan with 3 garlic cloves and the bay leaf and reduce by two-thirds. Remove the bay and whizz in a food processor or blender, adding the mustard, honey, seasoning, and 3 or 4 times the amount of reduction in oil. This is to taste and should be just dilute enough that the dressing doesn't catch the back of the throat.

Soak the artichokes in cold water for half an hour, then scrub carefully, making sure to dislodge any grit. You can peel them but you'll lose some of the flavour. Leave whole if small, or cut in halves or quarters, lengthwise, if bigger.

Heat the oven to 180°C. Toss the artichokes in a bowl with salt and oil and spread out on a baking tray. Roast until soft and caramelised – about 30 minutes. Remove from the tray and spread out on parchment while still hot – the caramelised sugar that comes out of them will harden and stick them to the tray like glue if they cool too much.

Turn the oven down to 160°C. Toss the remaining 12 cloves of garlic in a little oil and a pinch of salt and spread out on a tray. Roast until nutty, caramelised and sweet – about 25 minutes. Pop the cloves out of their skins as soon as they're cool enough to handle, trying not to squash them. Set aside to cool.

Heat the walnuts in the 160°C oven for 8–10 minutes, until lightly toasted but not coloured. Set aside to cool.

Matchstick the bacon and fry quickly in a hot frying pan with a teaspoon of oil. It should take on a little colour but not go too crispy – I like a mixture of sweet, juicy bacon and crispy bacon. Lay out on kitchen paper to drain and cool.

Lay the frisée on its front with the stalk pointing up on a chopping board, remove any damaged leaves from the back and trim the darker green parts with a very sharp knife – like you're giving it a haircut. Lift it up by the stalk and cut the leaves off the stem into a big bowl or sink of cold water – gently separate and leave to crisp for 15 minutes. Pick the parsley into the water and the chives too – snipped into 1-inch lengths. Drain in a colander and dry in a salad spinner, handling gently all the time.

To assemble the salad, carefully toss together all the ingredients (except the leaves, dressing and walnuts) in a frying pan until hot through. Place the leaves in a large bowl with the warm ingredients and a couple of tablespoons of dressing, then toss and arrange on the plates. Break the walnuts with your hands over each salad and drizzle a little extra dressing on top. Serve immediately.

When I first started writing this book, back in 2006, it was quite a shock to the system. I hadn't really written anything formally for some time, though I've always been a bit of a scribbler – the odd page or two in a notebook or a few recipes here and there. Having said that, I once copied my Konstam menus and recipes from one hard disk to another and it came to nearly 300 megabytes of data, so obviously I am required to tap at the old keys a fair bit.

However, nothing I'd written in the 11 years since my degree was of any significant length, so when I decided to write a book I had to get used to the idea, alongside thinking hard about the form I wanted it to take. My initial feeling, once I'd decided to follow the food year, was to write it like a diary – to follow the year as it passed and include food-related events as they unfolded at the café and restaurant. In the end this didn't work, partly because it was hard to find the time to write entries on a sufficiently regular basis, but mainly because the book eventually stretched over a number of years and I found myself layering year onto year, rewriting over and over, disrupting its logical chronology. So I started again and went for a more general approach. I was able to use a lot of the material I'd initially written, but I had to change the structure a great deal.

I mention this because we're focusing on January – and the first January after I opened Konstam at the Prince Albert was an eventful one for me. As I was writing this chapter I reread what I'd written the first time round, and I feel it captured something of the time – the dual narrative of both running the restaurant and working with seasonal food, how they intertwine and become one.

> The night before going back to the restaurant after the Christmas break I went to my parents for supper and found it incredibly difficult to talk about work. Trying to run a business like the café, which runs on exceptionally tight margins, and an untested one like the restaurant means that money is always elusive – even when it's coming in. There's tremendous pressure on cash flow, so talking about finances can very quickly bring to the surface fears that I spend a fair bit of time choosing not to examine too closely outside of work. Looking into the immediate future and not really having a clear idea at a particular moment how exactly you're going to get yourself out of a predicament that threatens to draw to a close everything you've poured your heart and soul into for

several years can really knock the wind out of your sails. If I get a bad letter from the bank in the morning or someone asks me some pertinent questions, I'll walk around all day with a little madness kicking around inside, wanting to shout 'I don't know' when anyone asks me anything. Then you get to the end of the day and you can walk a little taller because it's one more day you survived, one more time when you pushed on through. Very soon after taking on the café, I learned that when I wasn't working I had to find a way of switching off, especially with the café directly beneath my flat. If I walked around in a cloud of stress, sniping at people and letting my frustrations out willy-nilly, then it was very hard to keep people onside. So I learned to put a layer of myself over the fear to protect others and preserve my own down-time. Now I'm generally more able to relax when I need to, but being resistant to talking about work can be a symptom of that.

Christmas's brief hibernation means that the first day back is a massive effort of will. Taking a break means that restarting involves a tremendous amount of work. Just getting the body back into motion after sitting on a sofa for the best part of a week (followed by a few beverages on New Year's Eve) can take quite a bit of doing. The restaurant is cold, which saps the energy, and there is very little ready to use, so a lot of preparation is needed for that first service. Having a little time off also means my mind is always in a very different place, so my head needs a bit of cranking up too. It helped a little that I came in with my sous-chef yesterday for a few hours to do a recce and a stock take, so we knew what we needed to do and felt pretty organised. My normal suppliers for the restaurant were still away for their Christmas break so last night I ordered herbs, salads and a couple of other essentials from the vegetable supplier we use in the café. But today, when it got to nine o'clock and there was still no delivery, I telephoned to find out what was wrong and was told that our account had been suspended over the Christmas holidays – we owed them money which we couldn't pay. Because the veg didn't arrive we couldn't open the café that day. To make matters worse, my mother was in hospital that morning, so it was extremely difficult to keep my mind focused on the matter at hand. You could say it was a fairly stressful day all round.

We got through our prep in the restaurant though, and had five people in for lunch. That may not sound like very many, but we were expecting to be entirely empty, so it still meant a fair bit of running around. On top of that, we had 35 covers in the evening. That was pretty good considering we didn't have any bookings at all when we were sitting down for coffee at 8.30 in the morning and going over the menu.

Although it was a pretty busy day, some nice things came out of it food-wise. I really enjoyed putting out some of the dishes on the new menu – grilled mackerel with horseradish cream and baby leeks; sea bass with potato and roast Jerusalem artichoke salad; braised duck leg with red cabbage, roast potatoes and quince jelly; lamb with caper, onion and parsley sauce. We haven't managed to get entirely into the swing of the January produce but it felt like we would get there.

Before we broke for Christmas, we bedded the restaurant down and put everything we thought would last in the fridge. Some of the produce survived surprisingly well, which is great, but we needed to use it up and that kept us tied in with December and our Christmas menu. I made some delicious rillettes just before the break, which improved with a couple of week's storage and went beautifully with the pickled cauliflower we made in the summer. The braised duck legs had only got better too – snuggled together under their layer of fat while we were away. Despite the glance back at last month, what was most exciting was the sense that the year had turned, and we were cooking different dishes, with slightly different produce to that which had run through December. Because of Christmas we'd been cooking essentially the same menu for several weeks, so the change felt like opening the windows in a stuffy room. Looking back, it's easy to see how draining December was, so to come out of it and start enjoying the cooking at the start of the new year was a good feeling.

January finds us counting our food pennies. We're not yet bankrupt for produce, but we're trying to make it stretch through to the end of April. At this point the question is fruit. Once the comfort zone of the summer and the abundance of autumn are left behind, the orchard gets very bare, the apples are off the trees, the quinces are quinced and the pears are pared. Everything sweet to eat is in storage, laid out on hay in a barn or a garage, covered with two layers of newspaper; or bottled and standing on one of our big shelves in the restaurant. Unless we can make these supplies last, there's very little until late May, when gooseberries, one of my favourite things, will hopefully start to pour through the Dartford Tunnel from Toby Williams at Stanhill Farm. Garden rhubarb should start in March, of course, and that will be very exciting, but I'm a bit worried that the dessert menu will become one-dimensional – rhubarb sorbet; rhubarb ice cream; rhubarb tart; rhubarb crumble; rhubarb surprise. Then, of course, there's June with strawberries and July with cherries. By then you're about to be engulfed by a waterfall of fruit. The task then is to find a use for everything that comes your way, and, believe me, this year we'll be bottling like crazy.

As you read in October's chapter, it was in January 2004 that I opened Konstam Café. However, not all was well when we opened again after Christmas at the beginning of 2007. We'd recently lost our chef to maternity leave, so I was working shifts at both places – my workload was pretty excruciating and keeping focused on all the things I had to manage was very stressful, so I didn't realise at first quite how bad things were. It hadn't been making enough money for a little while, but over the break, what with holiday pay and Christmas bills to meet, things had reached tipping point. This next section was written a short while later. It shows just how hard it is to manage one business, let alone two, especially if you set yourself additional challenges like sourcing produce from around London, and there can be a personal toll to pay if things go wrong. I poured my heart into the café and am still very proud of it, in some ways more than I am of the restaurant; I often see friends and old customers I got to know and I can tell by the warmth in their voices when we talk about it that the café meant something to them, too.

I closed my café last week. It's taken me ten days to write about it. Basically, it wasn't making enough money so I had been subsidising it for some time out of my earnings from other sources, and eventually I couldn't carry on. Economies of scale were to blame, and to some extent location. We didn't have enough seats or an efficient enough take-away system to support the wages of an experienced and skilled chef. We had some great cooks along the way who put in a lot of hard work, but in the end it needed someone who had a really special touch with food, a lot of enthusiasm, and an eye on the long term – a Konstam touch – and that doesn't come cheaply.

I gave a great deal to the café. There was copious sweat and not a little blood, undoubtedly money and, especially right at the end, after the last day of trading, after I had finished my shift at the Prince Albert and after I was safely in the café with the door locked, lots of tears.

For some reason the downstairs storeroom hit me hardest – full of things to cook, with a low cupboard door I'd banged my head on countless times, and a forlorn bag of dried limes I'd had from the start and meant to but never used.

I drank a bottle of Chapel Down vintage brut and, chain-smoking, painstakingly took down all the postcards that filled the cork-covered wall running down one side. They weren't all addressed to me, some were just collected somewhere along the line, but they all had meaning and they all connected to someone – people I'd forgotten, people I'd loved, people I'd met only once, people on holiday, people at home. And not just postcards: there were photos, printouts, a couple of adverts that had made it on there for some reason or other, even though I was always very strict about those – I was adamant that I didn't want it to end up a free-for-all community board. There were some real oddities too: a photo of one of our sandwiches (taken in the café) that was left, without explanation, on a table one day; the Pope plaque donated to me (of Jewish heritage) by the Muslim man from the shop around the corner where I used to buy a newspaper every day; the postcard from a Spanish man who I waved at while cleaning the window, and, to top it all, the card from my recently deceased great-aunt wishing me luck after the launch party three years earlier – I'd forgotten she'd sent it to me and it really knocked me sideways. Reading all these cards and remembering all the stories behind them, I think I only then fully understood what it was that made it special, why I and other people had found something a little bit irreplaceable in that space.

I still have all these mementos in a big envelope stashed away somewhere. I like to think that one day I'll put them into a big scrapbook, but I'm not sure I'll ever have the stomach.

It stands to reason that as the British seasons don't correspond to the seasons elsewhere, crops are harvested at different times all over the world. This can make eating seasonally a little complicated, but it's worth learning a little bit about when the best produce will be available and from where. It will always be better quality and cheaper than produce grown out of season. Naturally, I don't mean food grown here and available in its own season, but produce that is specific to other places and which we can't produce here. Whilst this also applies to more everyday produce, such as fennel and artichokes, the ingredient I have in mind at this time of the year is the annual crop of oranges from Seville.

Seville oranges are very seasonal, and as they're the main ingredient in marmalade they have a quintessential Britishness that I find alluring. You can tell from the taste of marmalade that Seville oranges are incredibly tart; their juice has a dryness similar to that of raw quince. The word 'marmalade' has a distinguished and complicated etymology that stretches back thousands of years, through Greek, Latin, French and Portuguese (see November and the discussion of the word 'quince'). There's a story about its origin which claims that Mary Queen of Scots used it as a medicine for an upset stomach while crossing the Channel, and asserts that this led to a garbling of the words 'Marie malade', the French for 'sick Mary'. Although this makes a nice story it's almost certainly untrue.

Marmalade needs few ingredients, so recipes always bear a close resemblance, but that doesn't mean they're all as good as each other. A photographer friend of mine, Richard Smith, is a passionate marmalade connoisseur and makes a batch every year without fail. His recipe, when executed with an experienced hand, produces a superlative marmalade.

Marmalade

Makes 3.5kg
1 kilo of Seville oranges
2 kilos of sugar
2 litres of water
2 lemons

Juice the oranges and lemons. Strain the juice, setting it to one side and reserving the pips and other strainings. Scrape the halved rinds free of excess pith, again reserving the pith. Discard the lemon peel.

Finely shred the rind and put it in a large saucepan with the water and the juice. Tie the pith and the juice strainings together in a piece of muslin. Submerge this in the pan, tying the bag to the saucepan handle to retrieve easily.

Slowly bring the mixture to the boil, reduce heat and simmer gently for 2 hours. Stir occasionally and give the muslin bag a squeeze every now and again, extracting the maximum amount of precious pectin from the pith and pips.

After 2 hours add the sugar and continue to simmer until the marmalade reaches 105°C. At this point it should be ready for decanting into sterilised jam jars or Kilner preserving jars. Fill to within a centimetre of the top of the jar and close while still hot.

I met Richard through an even older friend, Emma Miles. Emma is a fantastic cook and runs a café called Clerkenwell Kitchen, where they make lovely food with produce sourced along lines very close to my heart. They close on Saturdays, and one of the best batches of marmalade we made was in their kitchen. We became a factory that day and churned out kilos of delicious, sticky marmalade. Marmalade-making has always been a group activity for me, and one year I had my mum chopping orange peel for hours in the café. When we made it at the Clerkenwell Kitchen we had this book's very own editor, Walter Donohue, toiling up to his elbows in pith as we strove to make a mammoth batch of Richard's marvellous marmalade.

We didn't initially serve breakfast at the restaurant, so we had to find an appropriately yummy use for all the marmalade we'd made. We ended up developing little marmalade desserts which were like mini upside-down cakes – the hot, runny marmalade would gloop all over the steaming pudding as you turned it over and pulled off the dariole mould just before serving. Because of our open kitchen this was always done in full view, and as soon as one person ordered it we'd get a steady stream of orders as other diners saw them being served.

Marmalade pudding

Serves 8

100g butter

125g caster sugar

2 eggs

175g self-raising flour

175ml crème fraîche

2 tbsp fruit syrup – for this I usually use some liquid from a compote, or a drizzle from whatever bottled fruit I have kicking around. Cordial will work too

1 jar of marmalade

Preheat the oven to 200°C. Butter 8 dariole moulds or ramekins, and put 1–2 tablespoons of marmalade into the bottom of each one.

Cube the butter and let it soften a little, then cream it with the sugar until pale and fluffy. Mix in the eggs one at a time. Gently fold in the flour until fully incorporated, then mix in the crème fraîche and fruit syrup. Spoon the mixture into the moulds on top of the marmalade, about two-thirds of the way up the mould.

Place the moulds in a generous baking tray and add 1 inch of boiling water. Put in the oven, reduce the heat to 170°C and bake for 35–40 minutes, until risen and golden brown, and a skewer comes out clean. Remove from the oven, score round the edges with the tip of a small knife, and turn out onto serving plates. Serve immediately with ice cream or double cream.

Blood oranges are in season now too. Their stunning colour makes any plate look good, and they have a tremendous amount of flavour, sharp and sweet in equal quantities. I was once served them in a salad with beetroot and red onion by a friend in New York, and I've used this set of flavours in several dishes over the years. Like the taste of elderberries, there's something dark and lurking that is almost unsettling; it's delicious but in a way that isn't entirely pleasurable. As a cook there are so few times when you're allowed to create something that doesn't have pleasure entirely wrapped up in it, and I find this dish fascinating and rather liberating.

Beetroot and blood orange salad

Serves 4–6
4 or 5 medium beetroot
Red wine vinegar
Salt
Sugar
2 blood oranges
1 small red onion
Olive oil
Wholegrain mustard
Fresh marjoram

Boil the washed but unpeeled beetroot with a very healthy splash of vinegar, a handful of fine salt and a handful of sugar. When they're tender allow them to cool enough to handle and then rub the skin off – it should come off very easily, unless the beetroot are a bit old or they're not cooked enough. Either cook them a bit more or use a peeler.

Make the dressing with 1 tablespoon of vinegar, 1 teaspoon of mustard, a pinch of salt and 4 or 5 tablespoons of oil. Slice the beetroots and toss them in the dressing. Using a small sharp knife remove the peel from the oranges and slice them crosswise and the same thickness as the beetroot. Peel the red onion and slice into thin half-moons.

Arrange the beetroot on the plate, interwoven with the oranges, separate the red onion and scatter on top, then drizzle the remaining dressing from the bottom of the bowl you dressed the beetroot in. Finally, scatter a few fresh marjoram leaves on top.

This dish works well on its own, or with roast pork or grilled pigeon breast. Beetroot cooked like this can be used in many different ways. When sliced very thin, preferably on a mandolin, it takes on a silky texture and is superb when dressed and served as a salad. For a relish to go with fish, finely dice the beetroot and a red onion, and then dress with toasted sesame oil, light soy or fish sauce, toasted white and black sesame seeds and a touch of rice wine vinegar.

As my career has been much more focused on savoury food, I don't cook with chocolate very much. I have a passing understanding of it but I don't have the deep feelings that a good pastry chef will have for it. Working with chocolate, as with most cooking relating to desserts, is a combination of art, science and alchemy, and I'm happy to leave it to the experts and sit back and enjoy the fruits of their labour. This means my repertoire is limited, but there is one particular chocolate cake recipe I keep coming back to. At Konstam we didn't allow ourselves chocolate as it wasn't local (I allowed coffee and lemons, but not chocolate. Go figure). This recipe originates from my days in Hammersmith at Maquis.

I mention it at this point for two reasons: one is that it contains orange zest, but more importantly because the ingredients include

Armagnac, although you could easily make it with Somerset apple brandy. Somerset has been awarded an appellation contrôlée and can only be made in the county. We served apple brandy made by the Somerset Cider Brandy Company, the same people who make lovely cider under the banner Burrow Hill, which we also used to sell. I've drunk quite a lot of their apple brandy over the years, and although the younger ones have a certain amount of vigour to them, the longer-matured ones are worth savouring.

Chocolate, almond and Armagnac (or Somerset) cake

250g chocolate (70 per cent cocoa)
325g unsalted butter
150g blanched almonds
3 tbsp Armagnac (or Somerset apple brandy)
Zest of 2 oranges
8 eggs
250g icing sugar
Crème fraîche and icing sugar to serve

Preheat the oven to 200°C. Butter and line the bottom and sides of a 10-inch spring-form cake tin with baking parchment, making a collar inside the tin that protrudes 2 or 3 inches above the top.

Blitz the almonds in a food processor. They should be mostly as fine as ground almonds, but take out a couple of handfuls while they're still a little coarser, then blitz the remainder again.

Combine the chocolate, butter, Armagnac, almonds and orange zest in a bowl over a saucepan of very gently simmering water. Do not stir. When the chocolate and butter have completely melted remove from heat, stir to combine and set aside to cool to blood temperature.

While this mixture is cooling, separate the eggs and whisk the yolks with half the sugar until pale and fluffy. Add this to the chocolate mixture and lightly mix.

In a very clean glass or metal bowl, starting slowly, whisk the egg whites (using an electric whisk) with the remaining sugar until they have a sheen and form stiff peaks.

Carefully fold the whisked egg whites into the chocolate mixture, pour into the lined spring-form tin and put in the centre of the oven, turning it down to 180°C immediately.

Bake for about 35–40 minutes, or until a skewer inserted into the cake comes out clean. It should still be wobbly but not molten.

Allow to cool completely. Remove from the tin, dust with a little icing sugar and serve with a big dollop of crème fraîche.

While we're on the subject of seasonal fruit from abroad, I've noticed in recent years that in early January many of the Asian and Turkish shops in London stock up on a soft red fruit that the British don't seem to get particularly excited about. These are persimmons, and although there are lots of varieties there are two main types – astringent and non-astringent. The astringent ones, often called hachiya, are eye-wateringly tart until they reach full ripeness, at which point they turn to nectar and their jelly-like flesh is one of the most delicious things I know, so soft you can scoop it out with a spoon. The non-astringent varieties, fuyu, can be eaten while firm and less ripe. Both are good but I prefer the decadence of the hachiya.

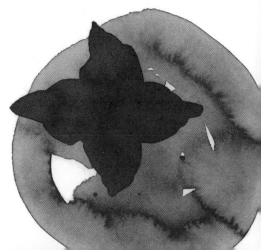

One of the reasons I mention them is that during my internship at Chez Panisse they were in full swing and both types featured on the menu in a variety of ways. During the winter restaurants across the San Francisco Bay Area use them in any number of dishes – salads, mains and, of course, desserts. They're mostly grown in China, Japan and Korea but also in California, and one variety, called the date-plum, has been grown in Britain since 1629. They're high in beta-carotenoids and have a slightly vegetal taste reminiscent of tomatoes. It's the kind of fruit, like a ripe peach or pear, that's impossible to eat without spilling the juice down your front, but the flavour makes you feel such behaviour is entirely acceptable.

Persimmon, hazelnut, goat's cheese and chicory salad

Serves 4

2 ripe persimmon
½ small red onion
3 tbsp crumbly, creamy goat's cheese
35g toasted hazelnuts
1 tsp Dijon mustard
1.5 tbsp sweet, red wine vinegar
4 or 5 tbsp good extra virgin olive oil
2 heads chicory
big handful chervil
1 sprig mint
Maldon sea salt
Pepper

Make a dressing in your salad bowl by mixing the mustard and vinegar, and seasoning it with salt and pepper. Then add the oil and check for acidity, adding more oil and salt, if necessary.

Either slice the chicory across in generous 1 cm strips or pull off the leaves and slice them in half. Finely dice the onion and roughly chop the mint and nearly all the chervil. Put all of these into the bowl with the dressing. Scatter the goat's cheese on top.

Gently peel the persimmons and cut them into wedges. Toss the salad with the persimmon. Crush the hazelnuts and sprinkle on top. Scatter with the remaining chervil and serve.

Whilst January is surprisingly abundant, there is a sorry lack of home-grown fruit. Apples, pears and quinces should have lasted this long if stored well, but it's all a bit thin on the ground. If we're lucky, the raspberry or gooseberry harvests come early and begin in May, but we're pretty much devoid of native fruit until June. However, there is a gleam of light in the darkness.

Although rhubarb isn't technically a fruit, we mostly treat it as one. If you're being strictly local and live in the South, you'll have to wait until the weather breaks in March or April, when it will grow very nicely in the average garden, but in the North – in the 'Rhubarb Triangle' formed in Yorkshire by Wakefield, Morley and Rothwell – the forced rhubarb is well underway by now. This early rhubarb is grown in the dark in long, low sheds and harvested by candlelight. The darkness inhibits its chlorophyll production, removing the green colour from the stems, making the pink brighter and more vibrant. Forced rhubarb is taller, pinker and more tender than the later-harvested, garden variety. You can achieve the same results on a domestic scale by using terracotta cloches.

Although the forced rhubarb season begins in earnest in January – its arrival is an exciting part of the winter food landscape – its peak season comes later, so the bulk of my rhubarb thoughts and recipes can be found in the March chapter when the garden variety takes off.

The humble cauliflower often gets overlooked and is rarely seen as a highlight of the food year. Personally, I think this is a shame. It's a well-known fact that if you cover anything with enough cheese sauce it will taste good, but my mum really does make the best cauliflower cheese ever. Cauliflower cheese is genius, but it's a far more versatile vegetable than this one dish suggests. I've always loved the way they cook it in India, and this influence is clear in the recipe below. I developed it as a salad at the café and it was very popular, adding a touch of richness and warmth in the winter months.

Cauliflower with brown butter and pine nuts

This works either as a warming lunch dish with rice, as part of a spread, or with fish, chicken or lamb.

Serves 4
2 tbsp raisins
1 small red onion
1 cauliflower
50g butter
½ tsp turmeric
1 small red chilli
A handful of pine nuts
2–3 sprigs parsley, mint or coriander (or all three)
A little nutmeg
Salt and freshly ground pepper

Pour boiling water and a pinch of salt over the raisins and leave them to soak for 10 minutes, then drain.

Dice the onion, deseed and finely chop the chilli, and pick through and roughly chop the herbs. Break the cauliflower into bite-sized florets and blanch in plenty of salted, boiling water until just tender – about 3 minutes. Drain and leave to steam for a minute or so.

In a large frying pan or wide saucepan heat the butter until it melts. Throw in the pine nuts and continue to cook. When they start to brown and the butter starts to caramelise (be careful if the base of your pan is dark as this makes it hard to spot), turn up the heat and throw in the red onion and turmeric. Sizzle for a couple of seconds, then throw in the cauliflower, chilli, a scrape or 2 of nutmeg, and finally the herbs. Season, toss until the cauliflower is evenly coated with the butter, and serve.

Roast cauliflower is terrific too. Break off all the florets and toss them in a bowl with salt, pepper and oil, and spread out on a baking tray. Fifteen minutes at 180°c, or just enough time to get a bit of colour and you've got a very easy and quick addition to Sunday lunch.

Roast cauliflower also makes a great soup. Caramelise some onions while you're roasting the cauliflower, add a large pinch of coriander seed and cook for a few minutes, add some water then blitz everything with a bit of milk, or cream if you're feeling decadent. I like its simplicity, but you can add a lot to this recipe if you want.

Yotam Ottolenghi has a nice recipe for deep-fried cauliflower salad with tahini, spring onions, pomegranate molasses and mint. Luke Matthews – my former sous chef at Konstam – makes a great version of it at the Hoxton Beach Café.

Pickled cauliflower is particularly good when laced with sliced onion and a few coriander seeds. It's possibly one of the easiest pickles to make, and goes very well with rillettes, charcuterie and all manner of terrines and pâtés.

Pickled cauliflower

This is a simple pickling recipe, and fills a 1-litre Kilner jar. The basic technique and the pickling liquor can be used for a broad range of vegetables.

1 large cauliflower
250ml white wine or cider vinegar
250ml water

250ml sugar

1 tbsp coriander, cumin, caraway or fennel seeds (or a mixture)

1 large onion

Cut the cauliflower into smallish florets no bigger than a walnut. Blanch in salted, boiling water – 1 minute or so should be enough. Refresh immediately in cold water and drain. Put the cauliflower into a sterilised Kilner jar.

Slice the onion finely, then make a pickling liquid by bringing the vinegar, sugar, spices and water to a boil. Put the sliced onion in and bring back to the boil. Pour the boiling liquid and onions over the cauliflower and fill to about a centimetre from the top of the jar. Seal immediately. This will keep for several weeks or months, if stored in the fridge.

Another modest vegetable that doesn't get much attention after Christmas south of the Scottish border is the swede, or neeps as the Scots call them. It can be nice roasted, but it's truly delicious when mashed. Peel it, cube, boil, drain and steam, and then mash it with lots of goat's butter and salt and it's incredibly moreish. Neeps and tatties, when both swede and potato are mashed together, is the traditional accompaniment to haggis on Burns Night – along with a fair bit of single malt and readings from the work of Scotland's premier bard. It's also one of very few dishes that celebrates this overlooked vegetable. I love haggis, in its natural state and also as an ingredient to use in other recipes. Haggis Scotch eggs are great – and we'll come to them later – but I love haggis on toast too. Mashed with crème fraîche, cheddar cheese, mustard and chopped parsley, it makes the perfect topping for a meaty rarebit. Simply toast the bread on one side and spread the haggis mix on the other, then put it back under the grill on a baking sheet until bubbling and a bit crispy on top. Make sure to spread the haggis all over the bread so it doesn't burn. By now we are into the depths of winter.

At the start of the month it felt like there was very little produce around, but we've realised there are still many good things to eat, though it's clear there is less variety and supplies are dwindling. In a way this is the start of the good times in the seasonal food calendar, the times that make us appreciate everything that comes along, yet make us yearn for the wealth of produce later in the year.

FEBRUARY

—

Beetroot

Preserving

Lardo

Chicken livers

Brines

Sprat

Salt

Salmon

Fish

Purple sprouting broccoli

Pancakes

Stock

My entire cooking career has been geared up to menus that change with the seasons, so I thought I knew what that meant. However, it was only in the first winter after opening Konstam at the Prince Albert, when we were faced with such a restricted palette, that I really came to understand that from December there is no 'blink and you miss it' produce – the food landscape starts to change much more slowly. In the summer and autumn it's like a high-speed train, new fruit and vegetables come and go very quickly, and some have such short seasons that you need to be on your guard or they'll pass you by. As winter draws on, even if it hasn't been a particularly cold one, the rate of change drops steadily from train to car to moped to bike to jog and finally to a gentle stroll. Nearly all the fresh produce is that which stores well, or can survive the cold ground – and this doesn't lead to a great deal of variety.

There are a few ways you can tackle this, but the easiest, and perhaps most important, is to stick to what is seasonally available. Many of the foods around at this time contain valuable micro-nutrients which some of the better-known 'healthier' fruit and veg don't contain. Beetroot, for example, is an excellent source of magnesium, potassium, vitamin C, betaine, nitrates and boron; parsnips also provide potassium, along with manganese and folate. Cabbages, especially Savoy, are a good source of iron, and you find dietary fibre all over the place at this time of year.

—

Our genetic make-up is particular to our climate, resources and
cultural practices. For instance, in parts of the world where dairy
forms little or no part of the diet there are high levels of lactose
intolerance. This is because the lactose digesting enzyme lactase
disappears after weaning. Our bodies are used to making the best of
what is available, and if we ignore the range of produce the year has
to offer we run the risk of missing out on vital nutrients. Although
I haven't found any medical studies to support the theory that our
body's nutritional system works on an annual basis, discussions on
the subject with various health industry professionals suggest that it
isn't too far-fetched. For this reason alone keeping in tune with the
steady march of produce year-round makes a lot of sense.

Focusing on available produce also discourages growing it out
of season, which returns us to the environmental implications I
mentioned in earlier chapters. Another advantage of rolling with
the seasonal punches is that it pushes you to be more resourceful.
Not only will you need to be more creative – the 'what to do with
the parsnips today' syndrome – you'll also need to think about ways
to extend the life of produce available at other times of the year.
Some fruit and vegetables, like apples and beetroot, are very happy
if stored correctly and will last most of the winter and beyond;
this affects the taste very little, although quality will naturally
deteriorate. Others need preserving, which takes several forms and
can be used for meat and fish too.

One of the simplest and most common ways of preserving is
jamming. This is an excellent and relatively easy way to get year-
round pleasure from summer and late spring fruit. A general rule
of thumb is equal amounts of sugar to fruit then cook until the
mixture reaches setting point, which I always test with a stack of
small plates in the fridge. Place a teaspoonful of the mixture onto
a cold plate, put it back in the fridge for a minute or two and if it's
formed a thin rubbery skin then it's ready. Some fruits have higher

levels of pectin than others and will form jam more easily. Rhubarb has almost no pectin, so it's difficult to make good jam with, whereas plums have a much higher content and make a nicely set jam quite easily. You can add pectin to the sugar, but there are other ways around it, such as combining fruit higher in pectin with those with a lower content, or by suspending a muslin bag of apple cores (the pips are very high in pectin) in the jam while it cooks.

When we opened Konstam it was in April so we were very aware of the shortage of vegetables in the late winter and early spring. Accordingly, as soon as fruit became abundant we bottled and jammed a lot that first summer. It put us in good stead for the following winter; we had some nice bottled gooseberries that lasted all the way to February, when we created a dessert to use them in. Bottling is good but can be a little less reliable than jamming. To a large extent how well it keeps depends on how well you've sterilised your jars and equipment. This is easy enough at home when working on a small scale, but when you're working with 15 three-litre clip-jars and many kilos of fruit it can be a bit more hit and miss with more of the produce spoiling. Jamming is easier because the large amounts of sugar help preserve the fruit and make it less volatile. The thicker texture also means it's more impenetrable to air.

Pickling is quite easy and a great way to preserve vegetables. Chutneys are delicious but making them just right is complicated by the fact that the flavour develops over time and it can take months before you know how it's turned out. For this reason it can take years to become a really good chutney-maker. The same is true of pickling, but to a lesser extent as the flavours are more stable and you need less time to see how you've done.

With meat and fish the main methods of preserving are drying and brining or salting. Smoking is not sufficiently preservative as a long-term method when used alone, but it does add a wonderful flavour.

Bacteria need three things to thrive: heat, oxygen and water. Natural preserving techniques are nearly all concerned with inhibiting the growth of harmful bacteria by reducing or preventing their access to one or more of these. Freezers make it too cold for them to multiply, so they remain dormant in the food and at levels our bodies can cope with. Drying works by removing the moisture, thereby preventing bacteria from growing.

Preserving actions often happen in conjunction with each other, so it's not as easy to tell what's going on as you might think. Much of the time, fermentation is one of the key processes. Organisms in certain fermentation processes produce lactic acid, which creates a hostile environment and prevents the growth of bacteria. It's this acid that gives the sharpness to pickled cucumbers and sauerkraut. You can ferment almost anything – vegetables, meat and fish. In Norway they make *rakfisk*, fermented herring, in Iceland they make *skata* – putrified skate – and the Romans used to make a fish-gut condiment called *garum*. Ketchup started its life as a fermented fish-gut sauce called *kôe-chiap* from China, which made its way west via Indonesia and Malaysia where it was known as *kecap*.

A lot of cured meat products also undergo a fermentation process that helps prevent spoilage. Some meat-curing methods, particularly those used in the US and northern and Eastern Europe, rely on a faster fermentation process to prevent bacteria and will have a more sour flavour. Cured meat products from the south of Europe take place at a higher temperature, and air-drying is a more significant element in the process.

Alcohol is a by-product of fermentation and its end result is highly prized. The process is controlled very closely, and much of the science and skill of winemaking relies on a vintner's mastery of this process. In this case it's the alcohol that primarily creates a hostile environment, with malic and lactic acids produced later by the fermentation. Malic acid imparts a green apple flavour, and further fermentation will lead to a more honeyed taste. Wines in cooler regions tend to be higher in malic acid, and it's this that gives English wine its distinctive zest. The delicate balance of flavours in wine means that although the acidity and alcohol prevent it from being harmful, once a bottle is opened exposure to air will cause the compounds to change: the carefully curated layers of flavour will start to break down and the taste of the wine will deteriorate.

Salting reduces the moisture content of the food being preserved, but it also creates an environment that is hostile to bacteria in a more direct sense. Osmosis is the process whereby the semi-permeable walls of a cell will seek to balance high external concentrations of a solute, such as salt, by allowing a flow of water from inside the cell. What this essentially means is that salt has the effect of dehydrating living and dead cells. This affects the cells of the food but also the cells of the bacteria, either killing them or making them dormant. Yoghurt and cheese-making preserve milk and cream by encouraging good bacteria to the point where they prevent the growth of bad bacteria. Yoghurt's additional secret weapon is the releasing of acid as a waste product of the bacteria's respiratory process, which means the yoghurt slowly becomes more and more acidic until the bacterial content balances out and bad bacteria are even more inhibited. This is why the vinegary brine of a pickled cucumber or beetroot will keep it preserved over a long period.

Fat is impermeable to air, so a layer of oil, butter or goose fat will prevent it reaching cooked food and thereby slow down its decay. This is the technique used in potted shrimp and most pâtés. Antipasti can be kept for a long time by being bottled in olive oil. Vacuum-packing is a more modern approach to the same method, and is now very popular in restaurant kitchens as relatively small, cheap and powerful vacuum-packing equipment is becoming more available. Big kitchens often have blast-chillers and sometimes drying ovens, which are both useful in the fight to preserve food.

The preserving of meat and fish by salting is more than just a practical method; the subtleties of the process are an art form that produces lovely foods such as salamis, bacons, hams, anchovies and gravadlax. Most of these are possible to make domestically with a few items of equipment and a certain amount of know-how. Prosciutto-style hams are a bit more difficult but can be achieved if you have a cool, dry cellar. One of my favourite salted products is lardo. This is made with thick slabs of pig's back fat cured in huge marble basins packed with salt and herbs. Colonnata in Tuscany – a village in the area of Carrara, where the famous marble is quarried – is well known for it, but it's found all over Europe in some form or another. The fat is sliced like ham and laid on hot toast or bread. I love it melted gently on almost anything warm, and it goes with eggs almost as well as bacon. One delicious way to use it is to lay a few slices on top of a halved baked potato, then return it to the oven and bake until the lardo is golden brown and crispy, the liquid fat having rendered into the potato. It makes a very good, rich carbonara, too.

Over the years I've salt-cured many types of meat and fish. At Konstam we got our pork from Stockings Farm near Amersham, run by Keith and Liz Bennett. Their meat is consistently excellent – I've worked with them for nearly a decade and have visited the farm on many occasions. Keith still does nearly all the deliveries himself, and it's always a pleasure to stop and have a catch-up whenever he makes a run. We had a good process in place at Konstam whereby we would receive six to eight of Keith's fresh pork bellies each week. The ones we were cooking fresh would get used in the first few days, but the bellies for bacon we would brine for a week, hang for a week and then send some of them back to Keith, who would slice, vac-pack and redeliver them. The brined bellies we didn't send back were either served as boiled bacon or kept hanging for pancetta. The rasher bacon came out very well once we'd got our heads around it, and when we started doing Sunday brunch it made a very special fry-up. The pancetta would get used in lots of different dishes, but perhaps the most regular was a chicken liver and bacon pâté made with livers from free-range chickens (reared just north of London by S.J. Frederick and Sons) and our own cured pork. It was usually cooked with a good slosh of Somerset apple brandy.

Chicken liver pâté

This was a Konstam favourite and one we served many times. It should be smooth, light and very rich. Serve with toast and pickle. I love it with the pickled courgette on page 313.

Makes 1 whole terrine or 10–12 individual ramekins
225g chicken livers
2 onions
A good pinch of fresh thyme
2 garlic cloves
3 medium slices of bacon or pancetta
150ml double cream
275g butter
Extra butter to top

Dice and fry the bacon in a little oil until browned, then add the finely chopped onions, garlic and thyme and sweat until golden and soft.

Heat 150g of the butter and cream until the butter is melted, then set aside.

In a small frying pan melt 25g of butter and sear the chicken livers until medium-rare. Remove from the pan. They will finish cooking in their own heat. If you're worried you can cook them a little more, but the pâté is much nicer when the livers are still a little pink.

While the livers and onions are still warm, put them in a blender with the cream and butter mixture and purée finely – you may need to push it down with a ladle if it's too thick.

Pass through a fine sieve or chinois while still warm and liquid, and check the seasoning – remember that the flavours will be a little muted when cold. Pour it into a terrine lined with cling film, or individual ramekins, and tap the sides to level. Wipe the edges and put in the fridge to set. Melt or clarify some butter, 100g should do it, and cover the pâté with a thin layer to seal. I pour it on and then tip most of it off, leaving a very thin layer. Clarifying the butter will help it keep longer and the butter will be smoother when cold.

Brines

Below are two recipes for salt brines, one for ox tongue and one for pork belly. These should be enough for 1 whole belly or a couple of whole ox tongues, so for smaller cuts you may want to scale it down a little. The important thing is the ratio of water to salt and sugar; the other ingredients you can play with and add or subtract at will.

Pork brine:	*Tongue brine:*
2.5 litres water	2.5 litres water
0.5kg salt	0.5kg salt
250g sugar	350g sugar
250g honey or brown sugar	1 cup vinegar
10g saltpetre	10g saltpetre
1 tbsp juniper berries	1 tbsp juniper berries
2 tbsp whole black peppercorns	2 tbsp whole black peppercorns
1 tbsp fennel seeds	1 tbsp fennel seeds
4 garlic cloves, halved	
5 bay leaves	

Bring all ingredients to a boil and cool completely before submerging the meat. Keep in the fridge while curing.

If you're in a hurry and want to cut the cooling time, use half the stated quantity of water, bring to a boil, then add the remainder in ice to help cool and dilute the mixture.

Tongue needs 7–10 days in brine; unboned pork belly for bacon needs 1 week, but less with the bones out; pork loin (boned, skin on) for grilling or roasting needs 48 hours; pork chops need only 1–2 hours.

The brine can be used 2 or 3 times before it becomes too dilute to inhibit decay. Any sign of thickening, sliminess, cloudiness or bad odour and it must be discarded.

One of the most traditional dishes in Sweden is a very simple gratin called Jansson's frestelse, which means Jansson's temptation. It's made with sprat which have been salted like anchovies. To make this dish, cut potatoes into matchsticks, layer them with sprat (rinsed of salt and deboned), then nearly cover with cream infused with thyme, bay, onion and black pepper. Bake in the oven at 180°C until the potatoes are soft and the top is coloured, then allow it to cool a touch so the cream and the potatoes stiffen a little. I think it's even better made a day ahead and then warmed up so the flavours have time to develop and mingle.

There are several explanations for its name but my favourite is that Jansson was a devout orthodox preacher to whom all pleasures of the flesh were forbidden, but one day he was discovered stuffing himself on this simple dish. The curiosity of this story is that it wasn't lust or money that tipped him over the edge and made him renege on his godly oaths, but this unprepossessing dish of potato, sprat and cream. Many purists would say you can't improve on something so classic, and I would be inclined to agree with them, but you can tinker with it. In the past I've substituted a third of the potato with beetroot and it came out very well. I'm not saying it's better – there isn't quite as much starch so it's a tad looser – but it tastes lovely and it looks good too.

As a truly Scandinavian speciality ready-salted sprat isn't easy to find in the UK, but it's pretty easy to make and great to cook with.

Buy very fresh sprat, gut and clean them, pack them in layers in coarse salt in Tupperware with a tight-fitting lid. Put salt in the bottom first, between each layer and then another layer on top, and leave them in the back of the fridge for a month or two. The sprat season runs through the winter, so if you salt them in December by the time February comes around you should be ready to go.

Salt is essential to the very existence of life and has shaped the modern world in ways that are easily overlooked, yet we strive to expunge it from our diet and frown upon those who are liberal with it. While we shouldn't ignore that it can cause your arteries to harden and your heart to pack in, on the other hand, life should be enjoyed and well-seasoned food is an elemental part of that. I would rather live a slightly shorter life full of rich and wonderful flavours than live to be 115 having eaten an interminable number of drab and lifeless meals. In general, it's the highly processed, shop-bought food we need to be especially careful about. A diet of food cooked at home with a controllable amount of salt to achieve a reasonable level of flavour won't be harmful. I once compared the seasoning of a mayonnaise I'd made myself (and thought was pretty punchy) with a jar of Hellmann's – I had to add two or three times as much seasoning to get it to the same level as the stuff in the jar. I was amazed to find out how highly seasoned some products are without us even noticing.

The significance of salt in the days before refrigeration was such that the salt trade was of paramount importance. Sites where it was mined and areas naturally suitable for extracting it from seawater wielded tremendous power. The incredible trading force of Venice in the 13th century was based in no small part on its domination of the Mediterranean salt trade, being located on the shallow and therefore more highly saline Adriatic. The US and Canada both have vast seams of rock salt, and Liverpool's prominence in the 19th century was kick-started by its role as conduit for the great quantities of salt mined in Cheshire. The trade in salted food influenced the huge success of the fishing industries of Scandinavia and the east coast of North America, based on the herring and cod-rich North Sea and Atlantic.

Although we are no longer a world power in the salt industry, production continues in Cheshire, at Middlewich, by British Salt (the company that markets Saxa), and there are several artisan salt works around Britain. The best known of these, and an internationally renowned brand, comes from Maldon in Essex. It was very exciting for me to visit the salt works there a few years ago; throughout my cheffing career I've used the lovely, flaky salt crystals they produce from the brackish waters of the salt marshes. Watching the timeless method of raking crystals out of slowly evaporated water and then standing in front of huge piles of it was an experience I enjoyed tremendously.

Some people say they can't tell the difference between salts, and I must admit I've taken and failed a taste test, but that doesn't stop me believing that good salt does make a difference to food. I find the taste of Maldon, and other good sea salts, to be slightly sweeter, leaving less of a chemical tang on the back of the throat than highly refined table salts. Up to 3 per cent of table salt is made up of anti-caking agents such as magnesium carbonate and sodium silicoaluminate, and it's this absence that makes the flavour of artisan salts so superior. Maldon isn't the only artisan salt in Britain – Halen Môn from Wales and Cornish Sea Salt are also very high quality, but I feel a stronger connection to Maldon because of its ongoing role in my career and its geographical location, which means it's a local source. Whatever variety you use, salt remains the very essence of cooking, culture, commerce and life itself.

In what may seem like an interruption – although I hope the thread will become apparent in due course – I want to talk a little bit more about fish, starting with salmon. There is something very romantic about wild salmon – unfortunately, less so with farmed salmon, though they do grow in some pretty amazing settings. Their wild cousins, however, are renowned for the globe-spanning journeys they undertake, returning to mate in the spot where they themselves were spawned. Unforgettable images spring to mind of salmon leaping up rapids or dodging the claws of huge bears, as well as treasured memories of dining on their glorious orange-pink flesh. I could eat smoked salmon all day, and I also love it served raw, revelling in the oiliness of the meat. The oh-so-simple *unagi nigiri* – a sliver of raw fish on a finger of sticky rice – when made with good salmon is one of my favourite sushi dishes.

While most of the salmon we eat is farmed, and along with sea-caught salmon is available all year round, river-caught salmon is seasonal and comes at a hefty premium. The season starts on the majority of British rivers on 1 February, and there is a minor scrabble among the top London restaurants to be the first to have it on their menu.

Salmon and many other oily fish are well known for their high levels of vitamin D and omega-3, key elements of our diet as the human body is unable to synthesise them. They are essential to growth in young children and prevent a variety of conditions and diseases. For these and other health-related reasons, and because it's so good to eat, we are consuming more and more fish. This, however, is hugely problematic – there is already great pressure on the planet's fish stocks and many feel that the fishing industry and the governments that control it aren't doing nearly enough to combat this. It's fair to say that over the past 30–40 years there has been a global assault on fish populations from several angles.

One of the main factors is the technological development that allows fishing on a far greater scale than ever before. We now have an unprecedented level of access to all parts of the ocean, thereby exerting overwhelming pressure on crucial and very delicate biosystems. This is exacerbated by the fact that regulations have failed to respond quickly enough to the rate at which this technology has developed. Fishing quotas are vital to the industry but their distribution often seems to bear little relation to the welfare or even the availability of fish. The cogs of international politics turn slowly, and a long-term view of how best to manage quotas is only recently being discussed at the necessary level.

An increase in disease spread by the proximity of fish farms to wild populations is also a major problem, but perhaps more important than any of these factors is that the financial and political pressures on fishermen lead to obstructions in selling what is known as 'by-catch' – accounting for up to 50 per cent of all fish caught – and as a result it goes straight back, dead or dying, into the sea. A great deal of work has been done in recent years by organisations such as the Marine Stewardship Council and the Marine Conservation Society to put in place sustainability certifications and raise public awareness of the situation – helping us make better informed decisions when purchasing fish. Likewise, many chefs and restaurateurs have used their public profiles to bring attention to the plight of global fish populations, but the demands we place on our oceans are still too high.

Salmon is the world's most farmed species, constituting a worldwide industry worth billions. Aquaculture, or fish-farming, has been documented in China as far back as 2000 BC, and was practised in Italy by the Etruscans from 500 BC. It now represents 46 per cent of the global fish market. Farming might seem an effective solution to the depletion of fish stocks, but it's far more complicated than that. One of the most significant obstacles is that most of the fish we eat are carnivores, meaning we still have to catch wild fish to feed farmed fish. Estimates vary, but it takes approximately three kilos of caught wild fish to produce one kilo of farmed salmon. There are plant-based feeds under development, but our land-based crops are already under a lot of pressure and the effect of such a massive change in diet for such a significant fish population is not known and therefore extremely worrying.

Fish farms can have a grave impact on their immediate environment too. The faecal waste produced by salmon farming can extensively harm the surrounding area, and shrimp farming is especially destructive, leading to destruction of mangrove swamps, rendering useless vast tracts of agricultural land and causing widespread outbreaks of disease due to the artificial spread of pathogens. Catching wild shrimp causes terrible damage to coral reefs around the world, making it a dish to steer clear of.

Added to this, we're still left with the unavoidable fact of a globally rising population that needs to be fed. Fish are the largest sector in animal agriculture, and while the debate over how best to farm them continues, we are placing a greater and greater burden on our natural reserves. The cost to the environment isn't the only thing creating global anxiety. The fishing industry is heavily subsidised and if we deplete the fish stocks more than they can recover then the livelihoods of the millions who depend on it will be destroyed.

Though the situation is pretty grim, public awareness is increasing and this will hopefully lead to a change in consumer behaviour. There are fish species that have less environmental impact than others. Farmed molluscs, oysters, cockles and mussels feed on nutrients that are naturally plentiful in seawater, and they usually cause very little damage and in some cases can even be beneficial.

The following are, for now, in a reasonably sustainable state: pollock, coley, gurnard, herring, sardines, squid, red mullet, lemon sole and skipjack tuna; farmed turbot, halibut and rainbow trout (sea trout go in and out of season but when not spawning can be a good choice). Although there are concerns about poorly managed, open-pen and sea-farmed tilapia, it's the only non-mollusc to get top sustainability ratings. The tilapia is very versatile as it lives in a wide range of habitats and will happily exist on a vegetarian diet. This means that organic and closed-system farming has in this instance been successful.

The long list of threatened fish changes over time, but it's no coincidence that it includes many of our favourites: Atlantic cod and salmon, haddock, skate, wild bass, halibut, grey mullet, monkfish, rock salmon, sturgeon, bluefin tuna, plaice, whiting, dogfish, sharks of all types, all the skates and most of the rays (North Sea thornback, starry and spotted ray seem to be rallying, but be cautious). King scallops are on the endangered list too, unfortunately.

Mention scallops and it's difficult to avoid the topic of dredging. I talked about this with Guy Grieve of the Ethical Shellfish Company on Mull, having had the privilege of tasting his incredible dived scallops when I was working there with Cape Farewell. Guy's description of the damage dredging causes to vast swathes of the seabed left me somewhat distraught. Those doing the dredging claim that it takes place in a controlled and regulated fashion, but I couldn't help but be alarmed, and empathise with how distressing it must be to witness it first-hand.

On the whole, the depletion of global fish stocks is a sobering topic and one that needs each of us to do our bit where we can. Although it sometimes feels like we're powerless in the face of the political and economic forces that contribute to these problems, we can make a difference if we vote with our feet and wallets, whether shopping or eating out.

At Konstam we committed ourselves to local produce, and that meant local fish too. We looked at various ways of sourcing it from the waters in and around London, and although there were some interesting high points, like crayfish from the canals and trout from Syon Park, it was always troublesome and erratic. Eventually I rang the best fish supplier I knew – Ben Woodcraft at Ben's Fish, based on Mersea Island, Essex. I asked him if he would only sell us fish that came in from day boats (smaller vessels which are always out and back in a day), and he was perfectly happy with this. We would call each afternoon to see what they had. The shorter boat journeys meant a fresher catch, and with Ben being the only supplier I know who delivers in the evening the fish caught that day, it meant we really were getting incredibly fresh fish.

Many fish can be cured, but salmon lends itself to it superbly. In Sweden they do it with dill to make gravadlax, but the recipe I use most often has beetroot and citrus peel.

Beetroot-cured salmon (or trout)

Serves 6–8, depending on its place in the meal and the size of the fillet

½ side of responsibly sourced salmon, or 1 whole sea trout fillet, skin on

2 medium raw beetroot

300g caster sugar

175g coarse salt

1 tbsp juniper berries

Zest of 1 lemon

Zest of 2 oranges

Lay the salmon, skin-side down, on a board and brush your hand along it. If you feel any little pin bones remove them with tweezers or your fingers.

Grate the beetroot – there's no need to peel them, just give them a good wash first. Bash the juniper berries and mix with the beetroot and all the other ingredients to make the cure.

Put half the cure into the bottom of a non-reactive dish and place the salmon on top, skin-side up, then scatter the rest of the cure over the top. Cover with cling film and weigh down gently with a board and a couple of tins. Put in the fridge for 24 hours, then turn the salmon over, re-cover, weigh down again and leave for another 24 hours.

To serve, remove the salmon from the dish, brush off the marinade and dry it with kitchen paper. Slice into thin slivers and serve. I like it with dill and horseradish crème fraîche.

On a local level there is more seafood resident in London and its surrounding waters than you might think. It's claimed that salmon can be found the length of the Thames, and bass as far up river as Greenwich. There are fishing lakes in Walthamstow and Syon Park, and eels under London Bridge. I've heard rumours of little Chinese crabs thriving on the banks of various waterways, and in recent years there has been an invasion of signal crayfish from across the Atlantic. Having escaped from farms in the 1970s these aggressive and omnivorous crustacea have decimated native white-clawed crayfish populations and can be found in waterways across Britain. Though unwelcome, once cooked they taste great and have become a rich resource for those in the know.

If you're prepared to go further downstream to the mouth of the Thames you'll find herring, dab, cod, bass, plaice, sole, mackerel, skate, mullet (grey and red) – I've been out on the river with fishermen and caught a hundred stone of sprat in one day. Oysters used to be dirt cheap and were a staple food in East London. Although there are still fantastic oyster beds off the Essex coast near Mersea Island, their high price and scarcity have made them a luxury food.

One exciting feature of February is the arrival of purple sprouting broccoli, which sees us through to the middle of April, nearly connecting with the bounty that late spring eventually provides. There are white and purple versions of sprouting broccoli, and a dish with the two together is very attractive. It's often called 'the poor man's asparagus' and can be served in many of the same ways. It's particularly good steamed and served with a poached egg and hollandaise – add a piece of toast or muffin and it's a seasonal variation of eggs Florentine. I like it with a dressing of lightly toasted and crushed almonds, chopped egg, tarragon, white wine vinegar, crushed garlic, mustard, salt, pepper and olive oil. Like Calabrese, it also loves preserved fish and chilli flavours; it's lovely tossed in a dressing of fresh chilli, soya sauce, sesame oil, lime and fish sauce, then sprinkled with lightly roasted black and white sesame seeds.

I once created a meal at Leila's Shop in Shoreditch for Paul Godfrey, the writer behind 'Spitalfields Life', one of the most extraordinary blogs on the internet. The meal was for the launch of a book he was publishing by the photographer Colin O'Brien, and the ingredients came from Leila's grocery next door. Leila's commitment to seasonal food and attention to the quality of produce she sells are impeccable. Her philosophy is similar to mine in that she focuses on regional ingredients in season, but she's also excited by seasonal produce from other parts of the world, especially Europe. Because of this the meal included blood oranges in a salad with fennel and radicchio, but the reason I bring up the occasion was for the sprouting broccoli dish I cooked as the starter. The season was drawing to a close, but Leila still had lots of both purple and white sprouting broccoli in very good condition. I served it with anchovy sauce, chopped chilli and large, crispy breadcrumbs – simple but very delicious.

Sprouting broccoli with anchovy sauce

Serves 4 as a starter

16 stems sprouting broccoli – preferably a mix of purple and white

1 medium onion

1 tsp fresh thyme leaves

1 sprig rosemary

1 bay leaf

2 garlic cloves

4 anchovy fillets

1 glass white wine

Olive oil

2 sprigs parsley

In a medium saucepan, heat a couple of tablespoons of olive oil. Finely dice the onion and add it to the pan. Strip the rosemary and chop with the thyme leaves. Add these to the pan with the bay leaf. Cook gently until the onions are soft and translucent. Peel and finely chop the garlic and add to the pan. When the garlic is thoroughly cooked through, remove the pan from the heat for a minute and add the anchovies – allow them to melt into the hot oil, stirring gently and mashing them a bit where needed. Add the white wine and return to the heat, cooking off the alcohol and reducing until it starts to thicken a little. This can be made ahead to this point and warmed through to serve.

Pick through the broccoli, removing any very large or yellow leaves and trimming any tough bits. They may be very different sizes so either cut the biggest ones in half lengthwise or cut into the stems, as with Brussels sprouts. Plunge into boiling water and cook until tender – I like it when the heads are a little soft, but many prefer them firmer. Drain well, drizzle with a little extra virgin olive oil, and arrange on plates with the sauce spooned on top. Scatter some roughly chopped parsley and serve.

February doesn't have many food-related events to shout about, but it does have Shrove Tuesday. The exact date changes and every four or five years it comes at the beginning of March. It takes place 47 days before Easter and was originally a pagan ritual. The Slavs believed that Jarilo, the god of springtime, needed help in the struggle against winter and so they ate pancakes for a whole week. The round pancake represented the sun, and at the end of the week some were burned as a sacrifice to the gods. Christianity co-opted the festival and it became a feast to usher in the beginning of Lent, a period of fasting and circumspection.

I remember making pancake batter at a very young age and took the matter of eliminating lumps very seriously. It was then that I learned about the technique of slowly stirring the liquid ingredients to gently incorporate the flour so that no lumps would occur. For some reason I had it in my head that a whisk was cheating and so only a wooden spoon was allowed. While I still adopt this gradual approach I've subsequently found there is nothing detrimental to the quality of the batter should a whisk be used, although it may mean a little more resting is required.

Everyone has their favourite pancake filling, from lemon and sugar, via jam of any sort, to Nutella and banana. A friend's son likes them with jam, honey or maple syrup spread all over and rolled up so they can be cut into pieces he can manage with his hands – he calls them 'rock and roll pancakes', and I doubt I'll ever be able to call them anything else. The French go mad for a good pancake, or crêpe, especially in the north, where they're often made with buckwheat flour and called galettes. I once visited Mont Saint-Michel, the small commune built on a rock in the Channel near the border between Brittany and Normandy. You can walk across the sand at low tide, but it's cut off from the mainland when the tide comes in. It's packed with shops and cafés selling galettes served in every possible way you can imagine. I made my way through several different varieties before waddling back to my car and continuing my journey.

I've got two pancake recipes here. One is a simple batter for a crêpe-style pancake and the other is one we used to make in the café – these puff up in the American style and use a fair whack of baking powder. I could eat them all day with bacon and maple syrup, but they're good with compote, jam, honey, lemon and sugar, chocolate spread, whatever takes your fancy.

Classic pancake batter

There are a million and one recipes for pancake batter and they're all very similar – flour, milk and eggs are the basic ingredients but no two flours are the same and eggs vary in size so you may need to modify the quantity of milk in order to get the right consistency. You can make this in a blender or food processor but I like doing it by hand. Serve each pancake as you make the next – they're best fresh from the pan.

110g plain flour
2 eggs
330ml milk
1 tbsp melted butter or vegetable oil

Sieve the flour into a large bowl and make a well in the middle. Lightly beat the eggs and pour them into the well. Add 50ml of milk and the butter, and with a whisk or wooden spoon stir the mixture, slowly incorporating the flour. Add a dash more milk if needed. This should form a thick, smooth paste. Once this has been achieved, and you're happy that there are no lumps, steadily pour in the rest of the milk, whisking with a moderate amount of vigour until the batter is only just the thickness of cream.

Heat a heavy-bottomed frying pan until it's pretty hot, and then wipe a paper towel dipped in vegetable oil around the pan, or swirl a knob of butter around, tipping out any excess. Pour in a small ladleful of the batter and tilt the pan in circles to cover the bottom evenly – tip any extra back into the bowl as you want the pancake to be thin. When the sides start to curl and the bottom has started to go golden brown, flip it and cook it on the other side for a minute or so. Tip it onto a plate and move on to the next one.

Re-grease the pan after each pancake and adjust the heat as you go – every batter is different so a little tweaking is necessary.

Puffed-up pancakes

I always make this in a food processor, but you can use a hand-held blender or an electric whisk.

> 250g plain flour
> 1 tbsp baking powder
> 3 whole eggs
> 50g butter, plus more for frying
> 250ml milk

Melt the butter and then set aside to cool a bit. Put all the ingredients in the bowl of the processor and blitz until smooth, but no longer. This one prefers to rest in the fridge for half an hour or more, if possible, but you can use it straight away.

Heat the pan and grease it – getting the right amount of butter or oil in the pan takes a little practice, but aim for just over the minimum you need to cover the bottom of the pan. I like using butter for the frying but vegetable oil will do just fine. Dollop spoonfuls the size of a drop scone into the pan and carefully flip them when bubbles form. Remove from the pan when risen and coloured on both sides.

Stocks are peculiar things and chefs will go on about them for as long as you can keep your eyes open. They play an important role in culinary tradition, forming the basis of many sauces, and great care is taken to preserve the purity of the flavour and the clarity of the liquid.

Big, meaty stocks are a cornerstone of classical French cuisine, a discipline my career has only touched upon. Making chicken stock is more up my street, perhaps because of my, rather distant, Jewish heritage. Producing a good one is an art in itself, and very satisfying. You can roast the bones, which gives it a richer, rounder flavour and more colour. The roasting process also renders off some of the fat and solidifies some of the toxins, making the stock slightly easier to manage. That said, I like the less obtrusive flavour you get from making a stock with raw bones. Whether roasted or not, simply chuck them in a pan with cold water to cover generously and slowly bring to a boil. As the stock gets close to boiling, grease and foamy scum will rise to the top. Carefully skim it off so it doesn't get boiled back into the liquid – the stock will be clearer and have a cleaner taste. You can boil the stock to reduce it later, but at this stage simmer and don't let it come to a rolling boil.

You'll notice I haven't suggested putting any herbs, spices or vegetables in yet, and there is a good reason for this. I add them after the first time it's come to the boil because I don't want to skim them out of the stock, so I wait until the main skimming is done. Once skimmed I add onions, carrots, celery, spices and robust herbs such as bay, rosemary and thyme, but anything green or more delicate, like leek or parsley, I only put in for the last half an hour or so. I rarely cook a vegetable stock for longer as this is the best way to extract only the most aromatic flavours from the vegetables – any longer than this and the flavour starts to become bitter. If this is the case with vegetable stock, why should it be any different when you put vegetables into a meat stock? Fish stock is similar in that 25 minutes at a gentle simmer is all that's needed to bring the best flavours out of the bones; any longer and it will start to take on an unpleasant and bitter taste.

The spices depend on the final use of the stock and the region of the dish. Solid standbys for me are whole peppercorns, fennel and juniper seeds, a clove or two and a few coriander seeds for a delicate orangey hint. Escoffier always said that the pepper should only go in for the last nine minutes as it can lend bitterness to the final flavour. I almost always add a bay leaf or two, fresh thyme and a sprig of rosemary. Later on the veg will follow and the standards for this are garlic, onion, carrot, leek, celery and parsley stalks. Other veg or fresh herbs will go nicely in there, such as tomatoes (which change the colour a great deal), coriander stalks and basil stalks; the Italians sometimes put a Parmesan rind in for a bit of savoury amino oomph.

Keep skimming the stock throughout, and when the veg have been in for about half an hour gently strain it through a colander. If it's still a bit murky and you're using it for a broth you can clarify it by letting it cool to a manageable temperature and then briefly whisking in a few egg whites and crushed eggshells – the number depends on the amount of stock, but I would suggest one egg white for every half litre of stock. Reheat over a medium flame and bring to a simmer for a couple of minutes. The eggs and shells will form a scummy layer. Strain it through a damp, clean tea towel or muslin and you will end up with a lovely clear stock. It can then be reduced to bring out the intensity of flavours before finally seasoning with salt if necessary. Heston Blumenthal suggests freezing stock in ice-cube trays in its cloudy state, then letting it melt through a coffee filter paper when it's required.

These last stages are only necessary if you want to show off a bit. It's actually really easy to make a simple and very tasty stock with a few leftover chicken bones and whatever else comes to hand. Stay away from salad leaves, cabbages and the majority of root veg (carrots are good, but not much else), skim it thoroughly and you can't go wrong. A nice bit of chicken stock in the fridge or freezer is a wonderful resource, and if you haven't put it into ice-cube trays you can still break it up into pieces, or if it's really gelatinous, such as stocks made from ham hocks, you can cut them up before you freeze them.

Other than Shrove Tuesday, there aren't many events to break up the interminable dreariness, which is one of the reasons that Valentine's Day stands out. It was first named Valentine's Day in 496 by Pope Galasius and honours many different Christian martyrs about whom little is known. The first reference to its romantic connotation comes in Chaucer's 'Parlement of Foules', written in 1382:

> For this was on seynt Volantynys day
> Whan euery bryd comyth there to chese his make.

A great deal of the culinary significance of Valentine's Day lies in the domain of the chocolatiers, but not everything is in their hands. It's at this time of year that foods with aphrodisiac properties reach the peak of their popularity. Of these, oysters are perhaps my favourite, and happily are in season. Whether they or any other food are genuinely aphrodisiac is not for me to say, but they undoubtedly contain a complex cocktail of minerals and other goodies, and the taste and texture can set the imagination racing.

Truffles score high on the aphrodisiac scale due to their musky, evocative aroma. The first time I tasted them was at the house of my chef mentors at Moro, Sam and Sam. They served an outrageously simple dish of freshly made pasta with shaved white truffle, very good olive oil, salt and just a touch of pepper. I'll always remember the smell of them – sweet, nutty and earthy. The scent of fresh truffles is olfactory nirvana. Like all the best things in life, it's not immediately obvious what all the fuss is about, or even if you actually like it, but it grows on you, becomes part of you.

The truffles in season at this time of year are mostly black – still frighteningly expensive but around half the price of white truffles – and whilst delicious raw, cooking brings out their full flavour and aroma. White truffles are almost always served raw, shaved over eggs, risotto or pasta.

I enjoy designing the menu for Valentine's night. Beetroot produces dishes with a pink colour, so it always features on the menu. It makes a vivid and delicious soup, but one of my favourite ways to serve beetroot on Valentine's night is as the stuffing for pierogi, a Polish pasta dumpling. They're often rather stodgy so I roll the pasta a little thinner than usual and shape it like a tortellini instead of the traditional half-moon. I was originally taught how to make this shape by Sonya Dyakova, a member of the graphics design team who I worked with when I was opening the café. Just after it opened Sonya organised a Russian night, and together we made hundreds of pelmeni, small beef-filled parcels you find all over Russia and some parts of Eastern Europe. I fry the pierogi in a little butter after boiling, a bit like gyoza, and then serve them with sour cream, brown butter and breadcrumbs. For Valentine's night service I add the juice from the beetroot in the dough so it really packs a pink punch.

Basic pierogi recipe

Any number of ingredients can be used to fill pierogi. The classics are potato, onion, quark (curd cheese), spinach, mushrooms, cabbage or meat. I provide a recipe for a beetroot and goat's cheese filling (page 150), and a nettle and goat's cheese filling on page 159, but you can let your imagination run wild. Traditionalists will say you should add mashed potato to the dough, but I never do and have always been very happy with the result.

Makes 35 pieces, enough for 6
265g plain flour
200g double cream
1 egg
2 or 3 slices of sourdough bread
1 tbsp olive oil
75g butter
Butter and oil for frying
Sour cream
Salt and pepper

Bring the flour, double cream and egg together in a bowl with a wooden spoon, then tip out onto a floured surface and knead for 12 minutes, or until the dough is smooth and elastic. You can add chopped dill or other herbs, and a pinch of ground caraway is nice too. These are by no means traditional additions, but they add layers of flavour to the final dish.

Wrap the dough in cling film and set aside to rest in the fridge while you make the filling.

When you've made the filling and the dough is well rested you can assemble the pierogi. Roll the dough out as thinly as you can, to around 1mm, on a well-floured surface. (If the dough has gone hard in the fridge you may need to let it relax a little first.) Cut out circles 8–10cm in diameter using a cutter if you have one, or a cup or glass if you don't. The scraps can be rerolled several times to make more pierogi.

Put a teaspoon or so of filling on each circle, slightly below the centre. Dip your finger in water and moisten the bottom edge of the circle, then fold the top over and seal with your fingers to make a half-moon shape. You can leave them like this, or pick up each one, fold the curved edge back on itself to make more of a sausage shape, and then curl the pierogi around your finger (with the seam on the outside), bringing the two pointed ends to meet and sealing them with a little more water. You should be left with something looking a little like tortellini. At this stage you can put the pierogi on an oiled tray in the fridge, covered with cling film, and they will keep quite happily for a couple of days.

Make some coarse crispy breadcrumbs for scattering on top by roughly tearing up slices of bread and tossing them in the olive oil. Spread out on a baking tray, sprinkle with a little salt and toast at 170°C until dried out and golden brown. Put on a plate to cool and then store in an airtight container. These will keep for days.

To make the browned butter, melt 75g of butter in a small saucepan and continue to heat over a medium heat until the solids have lightly caramelised. They will continue to darken once removed from the heat, so be careful not to overdo it. Tip out into a small container to cool.

To cook the pierogi, bring a large pan of salted water to the boil, and have ready an oiled plate. Add as many pierogi to the pan as will comfortably fit in a single layer and cook them for a couple of minutes or until they float to the top. Fish them out with a slotted spoon, give them a gentle shake and put them on the oiled plate.

Melt a pat of butter with a drop of oil in a heavy-based frying pan. When the butter foams, fry the pierogi (again, don't overcrowd them) on two sides until golden. Serve them hot, with sour cream, the browned butter and the breadcrumbs sprinkled over.

Beetroot and goat's cheese pierogi filling

4 medium beetroot (around 350g)
125g butter
200g soft goat's cheese
A good pinch of ground allspice
Salt and pepper

Peel and grate the beetroot. Melt the butter in a heavy-based frying pan over a medium heat and sauté the beetroot for around 15 minutes until soft. Allow the beetroot to cool, then add the goat's cheese while they're still a little warm. Season the mixture well with salt, pepper and a generous pinch of ground allspice. Don't hold back on the seasoning as the filling must provide the flavour for the dough too.

Valentine's night is generally less stressful for the kitchen than for the front-of-house. Tables for two are easy for chefs to catch up on, so even though it's a busy service the kitchen doesn't mind so much. The waiting staff, on the other hand, have to run further the more tables there are. To make it more interesting, the clientele are under as much pressure to deliver as we are, so keeping everyone happy can be harder than usual. Nonetheless, it's always a fun night to work, full of conjecture about how the dates are going on the different tables.

February is bleak, but it has its moments. It brings love and pancakes, which is never a bad combination. Its close also marks the end of winter, and from here on we start the steady trek towards summer. The hard times aren't yet over for the seasonal cook, but at least we can start looking forward to gentler times ahead.

MARCH

—

Nettles

Wild wood sorrel

Wild garlic

Rhubarb

Japanese knotweed

Alexanders

Angelica

Spinach

In like a lion, out like a lamb.

Proverb

The transition from autumn to winter is one of bowing to the inevitable, but by the time we reach the end of March, it begins to feel like we're coming out the other side.

March marks the beginning of spring, and as we leave February behind we make a foray into new seasonal territory. The chill and rain might linger but our spirits begin to lift and it's easy to feel optimistic. In the Mediterranean spring starts more predictably with an earlier flourish of spring crops. In the UK, however, we're still eating much the same produce as we were in the middle of winter, and some of these are becoming difficult to find.

There are a few new things to alleviate the seasonal drought, but not many. One is a plant that some are only just coming to appreciate as a food source – most of the time it's associated with stings and dock leaves. I remember making nettle soup with my sister in our garden in Sussex when we were small. We made it in an old billycan over a wood fire and it didn't taste very nice. This might have been because my tender taste buds weren't ready for such a vegetal flavour, but these days I eat it with enthusiasm. Nettles, like many wild plants, are high in vitamins A and C, iron, potassium, manganese and calcium. It's also thought to be good for hay fever, some non-cancerous prostate conditions, and as a diuretic to flush the system or, as some people like to say, cleanse the blood. It stands to reason that foraged herbs and vegetables are packed with nutrients as they only grow in places that sufficiently suit them and they won't have been crossbred for incidental factors like appearance and flavour. It's said that Milarepa, the canonised Buddhist monk, lived to the ripe old age of 83, and that during his many years in the Tibetan wilderness he survived on nettles alone. His hair and skin turned green and his meagre diet left him weak and emaciated, but it was enough to keep him going and lead him to impart such wise words as these:

> If you do not acquire contentment in yourselves,
> Heaped-up accumulations will only enrich others.

> If you do not obtain the light of Inner Peace,
> Mere external ease and pleasure will become a source of pain.

> If you do not suppress the Demon of Ambition,
> Desire for fame will lead to ruin and to lawsuits.

My early nettle memories include an episode I'm sure many will relate to – I fell off my bike one summer and landed right in the middle of a big nettle patch. It was quite a trauma as every area of skin left bare by shorts and T-shirt was covered in nettle stings. It was an experience that took me years to forget, but with time I came to understand that the fear of nettle stings is generally worse than the sting itself. These days I handle them boldly, finding the old adage to be true:

> Tender-handed, stroke a nettle,
> And it stings you for your pains.
> Grasp it like a man of mettle,
> And it soft as silk remains.

> *Aaron Hill (1750)*

The stinging is caused when our skin brushes against the tiny silica trichomes, or glassy hairs, that grow all over the leaves. The tops break off and they turn into tiny hypodermic syringes which inject a minute amount of a chemical cocktail that includes histamine, acetylcholine and, strangely enough, serotonin, the chemical we produce to make us feel happy. Soaking nettle leaves in water helps draw out this stinging compound, and cooking destroys the stings themselves.

The debate about whether dock leaves actually help with nettle stings, other than as a placebo, seems endless, but the connection runs deep and many swear by it. Sadly, dock hasn't any culinary uses, even though it's from the same family as sorrel. The lemony flavour in sorrel comes from oxalic acid, which is named after the unrelated wood sorrel – *Oxalis acetosella* – from which the substance was first isolated. I've cooked with wood sorrel on several occasions, but it's small, spindly and difficult to find in any real quantity so it rarely constitutes much more than a garnish or lemony highlights in a salad.

Oxalic acid has a very low toxicity rating, but eating plants that contain it in significant quantities can be fatal. Oxalic acid is also present in rhubarb; there is only a small amount in the stems but the leaves contain much higher levels. In the Second World War there were many cases of poisoning from rhubarb leaves after the government ill advisedly recommended them during rationing. Most of the tart flavour in rhubarb comes from malic acid, which was isolated from apples by a German-Swedish pharmacologist in 1785 and was named two years later. The root of the word malic comes from the Latin word for apple, *malum*, and it is this substance which makes green apples and grapes taste sour.

You need a fair amount of nettles to make a good soup. The taste and texture are best when you use only the light green tender leaves from the tip of the plant. There's a delicate hint of anchovies in the aroma and flavour if you make it really well, and it's lovely if combined with another spring arrival, wild garlic.

Nettles tend to darken and go grey when cooked, so combining them with wild garlic not only adds flavour but also adds colour. If you want to make the following recipe with nettles alone adjust the quantities accordingly. Spinach can do the job of making it greener if you don't have wild garlic or want to simplify the flavours. In this recipe I blitz it until it's smooth, but you can leave it chunky if you like. I remember making this soup in Wales a while back and mixing in some sea aster instead of wild garlic. I left it unblitzed, roughly chopping all the leaves before putting them into the soup to cook. It was wonderful – sea aster is an unusual foraged herb to cook with, but it lent a hint of ozone and medicinal freshness to the soup.

Nettle and wild garlic soup

Serves 4
2 large onions
2 celery sticks
2 bay leaves
Plenty of good olive oil
1 litre or so of vegetable or chicken stock
1 large potato
About 750g nettle tips
250g wild garlic
Salt and black pepper
4 tbsp crème fraîche

Heat a few tablespoons of the oil in a saucepan, enough to cover the bottom and then an extra glug. Dice and add the onions and celery. Cook until translucent and light golden brown. Add the bay leaves. Peel the potato and cut it into 1-inch pieces. Add to the pan and cook with the onions for a minute or so, then add the stock. Cook until the potatoes can be easily crushed on the side of pan with the back of a spoon.

In the meantime, pick through and wash the nettles and wild garlic – a pair of clean washing-up or latex gloves are useful for the nettles, but I find I rarely get stung as long as I handle them gingerly and grip the leaves firmly when necessary.

When the potatoes are nearly done add the nettles, and when they're cooked add the wild garlic. Simmer for another minute or two until the garlic is well wilted.

Remove from the heat and blend until really smooth. You may need extra stock or water, or milk or cream to get the consistency you need, and you can pass it through a sieve with the back of a ladle if feeling pernickety. Season well with salt and pepper. I love a dollop of crème fraîche and a drizzle of olive oil on top.

Soup isn't the only thing you can make with nettles – they're a good substitute for spinach in lots of recipes. I've eaten fabulous nettle ravioli several times, and made very successful nettle and goat's cheese pierogi on many occasions.

Nettle and goat's cheese pierogi filling

This recipe works just as well for ravioli fillings. I aim for an end weight ratio of 1:1 nettle to goat's cheese, but this depends on how hard you squeeze the nettles, so be prepared to adjust a little. You can also add some blue cheese or Parmesan into the mix.

Serves 4
220g nettle tips
125g creamy goat's cheese
Zest of ½ a lemon
A good pinch of freshly grated nutmeg
Salt and freshly ground black pepper

Pick through the nettles, discarding any that are old, damaged or woody. Again, clean washing-up or latex gloves are useful for this. Wash the nettles well in cold water and then drain in a colander. Bring a big saucepan of water to the boil and blanch the nettles until well wilted – this will take about a minute from when the water boils again. Cooking the leaves destroys the tiny needles which deliver their sting. Drain and refresh in cold water and then drain and squeeze out as much of the water as you can.

Chop the cooked nettles finely and combine with the rest of the ingredients. If it doesn't seem unctuous add a tablespoon or so of cream, crème fraîche or cream cheese. Season highly, as the pasta will draw flavour from the filling. To make pierogi, see page 148.

At Konstam we used to make a cocktail with nettles. We called it the Konstam Sting. It was very refreshing and the nettles gave it a gentle, green, elderflower undertone. I recommend using the grape variety Bacchus, which has a nettle note and a hint of elderflower. Grown extensively in Germany, it thrives in colder climates and many vineyards in the UK use it for winemaking.

The Konstam Sting

1 shot of vodka
1 shot of nettle syrup (see below)
½ glass dry white wine, preferably Bacchus or ortega
Soda water
Lemon zest
Ice cubes

Fill a large wine glass with ice cubes, pour over the vodka and syrup. Add the wine and top up with soda water. Taste and add more syrup if needed. Garnish with the lemon zest.

Nettle syrup

When foraging for nettles try to pick only the bright green tips, as these are the freshest and most aromatic. The large, darker leaves tend to taste grassy.

750g caster sugar
500ml water
500g nettle tips
½ tsp citric acid
Lemon zest – 2 strips

Pick through the nettles and give them a good wash in plenty of cold water. Bring a saucepan of water to the boil. Drain the nettles and blanch a handful for a minute or so in the boiling water until wilted. Drain and refresh in cold water. Drain again and gently squeeze. Chop finely, put in a small bowl, cover and refrigerate. Put the rest of the nettles in a large stainless steel or glass bowl with the lemon zest.

In a saucepan heat 500ml of water with the sugar until it dissolves, bring to a boil and immediately pour over the nettles and lemon zest. Stir in the citric acid and leave to stand until cool.

Strain and combine with the chopped nettles. Pour into bottles or jam jars and keep in the fridge.

Wild garlic is a very special ingredient. Not only is it beautiful to look at, with sweeping spear-shaped leaves and white flowers like clusters of tiny stars, but the flavour is amazing too. It's sweeter and more subtle than bulb garlic, but with a little punch of its own. It generally comes to the fore in early to mid-March, or late February if you're lucky. It likes shade and grows mainly in woodland. I remember seeing swathes of it on trips to the countryside when I was young, but found the slightly cloying and overpowering smell a bit sickly. When I was working at Moro we went on a foraging mission in Dorset and brought back eight or nine black bin bags of the stuff. After that I didn't look back. It cooks very quickly, like spinach, and is really versatile. You can put it in frittata, spätzle, pasta stuffings, and a simple wild garlic and potato soup is a joy to behold. I like it sautéed with butter, a splash of vermouth and a dash of seasoning and then served on crunchy sourdough toast with a poached egg. Like purple sprouting broccoli, it's something you can make a feature of and it really brightens up the season. It also goes well as a side dish or with almost any fish or meat. My friend Sanchia Lovell folds it into her mayonnaise to make a wild garlic aioli. Below is her recipe, in her own words.

Wild garlic aioli

This recipe arose from a surfeit of wild garlic. It's good with almost anything but particularly on a salad of soft-boiled duck eggs, frisée and lardons, or with grilled chicken or spring lamb chops.

You can make the aioli with a hand whisk, an electric whisk, or in a food processor. I prefer the first two for the lightness they bring.

2 egg yolks
225ml rapeseed or other light vegetable oil (but not cold-pressed oils, which impart too much earthiness)
50ml extra virgin olive oil, a smooth, mild variety such as Arbequina is best
2 handfuls of wild garlic leaves, or to taste
Sea salt
Juice of half a lemon

Put the egg yolks into a large bowl and give them a good beat on their own with a pinch of salt. Start to add the lighter oil drop by drop to form a smooth emulsion, whisking constantly – you can start to add it in a steady stream about halfway through. When you've added all this oil, continue with the extra virgin olive oil. Add the lemon juice.

Finely chop the wild garlic leaves – I like to really go for this to release as much of their greenness as I can. Fold them into the mixture. Taste the aioli, adding more salt or lemon if needed.

꧁꧂

The strikingly handsome forced rhubarb of January has tailed off by the time we get to March. Now, the garden rhubarb, deep green and dark pink, is being picked, and provides us with a much-needed resource through the next couple of difficult months.

Interestingly, rhubarb, *Rheum rhabarbarum,* is from the same family, Polygonaceae, as *Fallopia japonica*, or Japanese knotweed, which can be cooked in almost all the same ways as rhubarb. In the past I've made some pretty nice jams and compotes with it. The flavour is less delicate and the texture isn't as refined, but whereas rhubarb is a welcome addition to any garden Japanese knotweed is so difficult to get rid of and so pervasive that it's illegal to dispose of it in normal garden waste. It's also flagged up on house surveys and has a negative impact on property value – so the more of it we eat, the better. Buckwheat, *Fagopyrum esculentum*, the seeds of which are an important food crop in many parts of the world, and which is increasingly popular in the UK, is also a member of this family.

Stewed rhubarb goes well with countless things, like meringue, or spooned on top of porridge, and it's delicious on its own with a generous dash of double cream. I've served it with pork, skate cheeks, scallops and mackerel. With pork it welcomes a spot of horseradish, and for skate a few leaves of tarragon sprinkled on top. With mackerel it does the same job as gooseberry, and for this I like it quite sweet.

I make rhubarb compote in two ways. The first is to make a syrup, bring it to the boil and drop in diced rhubarb, then let it cook in the heat of the syrup – this way is suited to more finely diced rhubarb. The other method is to use only a little liquid and cook the rhubarb with it. Either way, it can be difficult to get the timing right. The trick is to stop cooking it before it really breaks up but has just started to go soft. This is much harder than it seems as it keeps on cooking after you take it off the heat. As is often the case, the window of opportunity is small and it's easy to get it wrong.

Rhubarb compote

This is a recipe for the second type of compote.

  375g rhubarb
  115g sugar
  75ml rosé wine
  1 fresh bay leaf and/or 1 scraped vanilla pod

Wash and trim the rhubarb. If some stalks are much thicker than others, split them lengthways into two or even three, so they're roughly equal to the skinnier ones. Cut all the stalks into 1-inch lengths.

Put the rosé in a saucepan big enough to hold all the rhubarb in one layer, bring to a boil, then add the rhubarb, bay and vanilla pod with its seeds, and the sugar, stir together briskly and cover with a tight-fitting lid. Be careful in case the rosé catches fire.

Keep the heat high and stir once or twice while the rhubarb is still firm. When it just starts to soften – this will only take about 5 minutes – remove from the heat. Leave to cool, with or without the lid on (depending on how close to being cooked you think the rhubarb is), then remove from the pan and refrigerate. If you're worried that it's gone too far, take it out of the pan while it's still hot so it cools a little quicker. The timings for this are very variable and depend on the size of the rhubarb and the pan and the power of the cooker. The rhubarb is nicest, in my opinion, when it's really tender but still whole, so don't stir it around too much. It will keep in the fridge for a week or so.

Rhubarb compote is great to have in the fridge as it can be made into many things, such as fool or trifle. If you do get it wrong and overcook it a little, add an extra 260g of sugar and some orange zest, bring it back up to heat and put it in a sterilised jar as jam. It has next to no pectin, so if you're making proper rhubarb jam it's a good idea to either add pectin or mix it with something else – strawberries, for example – or use a small muslin bag of apple cores and seeds while you cook it. That said, I have made successful, if less jammy, batches without any additional setting assistance. Rhubarb jam tends to develop mould quite quickly, but I'm of the scrape-it-off-and-eat-it-anyway mindset.

If you want to make rhubarb sorbet, blitz the compote in a food
processor or blender, add a dash of rose water or orange blossom
water, and churn it. This is very easy to do if you have an ice cream
machine, and pretty easy if you don't. Just put it in a bowl in the
freezer and keep coming back to it every half an hour or so to give it
a good stir or whisk until it's frozen. Make sure you cover it once it's
made. It may get quite hard after a day or so, but let it thaw for a
few minutes before serving and it should be fine.

I've known about *Smyrnium olusatrum*, or Alexanders, mainly from
dipping into Richard Mabey's *Food for Free* when I was younger.
But no recipe I've ever read made it sound particularly appetising,
so I've never foraged for it or taken it when it was offered by other
foragers – until recently, when Anton, a Russian forager I used
when I was working in Clapton, caught me unawares and managed
to sell me a few kilos. This led to great success on two counts; the
first was vodka infused with Alexanders leaf. This one is easy – get
a bottle of vodka and stuff the washed young leaves into the top
and replace the lid. Leave it for a week or two and you'll find you've
made yourself an excellent aquavit or schnapps-type drink. The
second is roughly chopping a few of the stems and cooking them
with rhubarb to make crumble. This was truly delicious. When
I told Anton about it he was very excited as he'd never heard of
it. Nor had I, and I'm amazed it isn't a classic combination; the
aromatic Alexanders and the sharp rhubarb marry beautifully when
mellowed by cooking and sugar, bringing a new dimension to a
classic pudding. Make the compote as above, but substitute about a
quarter of the rhubarb for Alexanders stems, chopped into quarter-
inch pieces. There are many recipes for crumble topping, but here's
one I think works best.

Crumble topping

Crumble is not only adaptable, it's easy and cheap to make. You can use just about any fruit – I even had a passable strawberry crumble once.

75g plain flour or spelt flour

50g ground almonds

25g rolled oats

125g chilled butter

75g sugar – use golden caster for summery fruits, and light muscovado for autumnal fruits

A generous pinch of sea salt

Optional:

A handful of flaked almonds to top

Put the ground almonds and flour into a bowl and roughly grate the butter onto them. Rub the butter in lightly and quickly until you have large crumbs (not fine crumbs). You can do this in a food processor by using the pulse setting – a few short bursts will do.

Stir in the sugar, salt and oats, and refrigerate the crumble until you're ready to top your fruit. This will encourage crumbliness rather than clagginess.

When you put the crumble on top of the fruit, sprinkle it on loosely and don't pat it down. Sprinkle flaked almonds on the top. Bake at 200°C for about 25 minutes or until the top is golden and the fruit's juices are oozing around the edges.

In 2015 I was asked by the excellent men's health charity Movember to write a menu for the opening meal of Eroica Britannia, a vintage bike-riding festival they support in Derbyshire. It was a great evening, set in stunning Hassop Station on the Monsal Trail, and we served some fabulous local produce, ranging from trout and sirloin to asparagus and strawberries. It was much later in the year than

March, but I mention this meal for the rhubarb and angelica pickle we made to go with the Hartington's stilton we served at the end. I'd intended to make it with Alexanders, but it was unavailable so I asked the chef, Graham Mitchell, to order in some candied angelica instead. Garden angelica comes from the same family as Alexanders, and they both have a pleasantly medicinal flavour. The Apiaceae family of plants is huge – the sixteenth largest – and also includes anise, asafoetida, caraway, carrot, celery, chervil, cicely, coriander, cumin, dill, fennel, hemlock, lovage, parsley and parsnip.

Rhubarb and angelica pickle

This should be made at least a day or two in advance to let the flavours mingle. The rhubarb is used raw, so it won't keep as long as other pickles but will still last a week or so in the fridge.

Makes about 750ml

250g rhubarb
90g candied angelica root
1 onion
½ cup vinegar
¼ cup water
½ cup sugar
1 bay leaf
1 tsp white mustard seed
A pinch of fennel seed

Finely dice the rhubarb and the angelica, aiming for about quarter-inch pieces. Combine in a very clean mixing bowl.

Dice the onion the same size as the rhubarb and put it in a saucepan with the vinegar, water, sugar, bay and spices and bring to the boil, then immediately pour over the rhubarb and angelica. This will slightly cook the rhubarb but should let it keep a little bit of crunch. Transfer to sterilised jam jars and refrigerate once cool.

It was because of its early harvest that spinach was adopted in England in the 14th century, and reached us via Spain, Italy and North Africa from Persia. It's high in vitamin A, beta-carotene, folate and manganese, and incredibly high in vitamin K. It's a prevalent ingredient, always good as a side dish or soup and as a basis for any number of pasta stuffings. It also works well in soufflés, tarts, frittatas, gnocchi, dumplings, sag aloo – my mind goes into a spin in an effort to write them all down, and a book of spinach recipes would be no hard task. One of the great things about spinach is that it keeps its colour well during cooking, so any time a boost of green is needed, a touch of spinach is just the ticket.

Twice-baked soufflé is one of my favourite spinach dishes. It's dinner party heaven – not only does it taste amazing but it can be made well ahead and finished at the last minute.

Twice-baked soufflés

Serves 4
200g spinach
20g butter, plus extra for brushing ramekins
15g flour
80ml milk
Salt and pepper
A pinch of ground mace or nutmeg
2 large eggs
100ml double cream
20g grated Parmesan or other hard cheese, plus extra for ramekins

Preheat the oven to 180°C. Blanch the spinach in salted boiling water until wilted, about 1 minute, then drain, refresh in cold water and drain again. Squeeze firmly to dry and then chop finely.

Brush ramekins with melted butter, and sprinkle a little grated cheese into each one.

Melt the butter and stir in the flour. Cook gently for 3 minutes, stirring occasionally. Stir in the milk and continue to stir occasionally for another 5 minutes or so. Add seasoning and a pinch of ground mace or nutmeg. Remove from the heat and allow to cool a little.

Separate the eggs and beat the yolks into the white sauce. Stir in the chopped spinach and tip into a large mixing bowl. Whisk the egg whites to stiff peaks and gently fold into the spinach mix. Spoon the mixture into ramekins until filled level.

Set the ramekins in a deep baking tray and fill it 1 inch with boiling water. Bake for 20 minutes or until well risen. Remove from the tray and leave to cool for 10 minutes. Carefully remove the soufflés from the ramekins and place, right side up, on a buttered ovenproof dish.

The soufflés may be made ahead to this point and kept in the fridge. The rest takes 10 minutes or so and should be done just before you serve them.

Preheat the oven to 200°C. Pour the cream over the soufflés, sprinkle with the cheese and bake until the cream bubbles. Check seasoning before serving. The cream left in the bottom of the dish is delicious, so try and give a bit to everyone.

This chapter began with a quote about the weather at this time of year. The transition from the wildness of winter to the calmness of spring takes place over the course of March – but in like a lion, out like a lamb makes the end of the month sound harmless. We're using up our food funds, polishing off the last dribs and drabs of our carefully harvested stash, but as the sun starts to show its face we're lulled into a false sense of security. And just as we think it's all going to start getting better, April arrives.

APRIL

—

Spring onions

Radish

Spring greens

Bees

Honey

Crab

Watercress

Steak

Crème fraîche

Rocket

Sorrel

Pigeon

Eggs

April is the cruellest month, breeding
Lilacs out of the dead land, mixing
Memory and desire, stirring
Dull roots with spring rain.
Winter kept us warm, covering
Earth in forgetful snow, feeding
A little life with dried tubers.

T. S. Eliot, *The Waste Land* (1922)

 few years ago, during the first year after Konstam opened, I wrote:

> The sun has started to win its own private battle for some time now, ever since the last week or so of March, but all through early April I've had my head hunkered down between my shoulders, begrudgingly shedding my overcoat only when the sweat began to trickle down my face, secretly insisting that it was still winter. My idea of seasonal change is now determined by the food calendar and I won't confess to spring until the new veg start to appear at my door.

It captures the lag during spring between the change in the weather and the change in the seasons. You have to be fully immersed in the process of seasonal food to feel it, but it's there and April is when it happens.

I have on many occasions felt a similar sense of seasonal displacement while writing this book. I become immersed in the food available in a particular month as I write about it, then go to the market and find a completely different range of produce to the one I expect, sometimes confused which month I'm in.

My memories of how hard April can be have their roots in my time spent working within the extreme set of restrictions I'd set myself, and which I'm no longer bound by in quite the same way. However, I feel it was from undergoing that process and trying to see it through to its inevitable conclusions that I learned so much about what it really signifies. The lack of variety at this time of year in particular meant that the highlights became accentuated and I appreciated them in a way I hadn't expected.

For most people the truly seasonal year has become a distant memory, but what we tried to achieve at the restaurant made it clear to us what a lifestyle dominated by the seasons really means – without harkening back or romanticising, we started to understand how people coped in earlier times with different resources. On an extreme level you only have to go back 170 years to the Great Potato Famine in Ireland to see how an entire population could be completely dependent on a single crop.

The reason April is so difficult to navigate from the perspective of seasonal food is that the supply of almost everything from the winter has dried to a trickle, and yet very little of the produce we typically associate with spring is ready to harvest, so you're caught in an exasperating no-man's-land. Fortunately, this period doesn't last long and how bad it is depends on how strict you are with your geographical limits and whether you have access to farms growing a full range of early spring produce. By the end of the month things are looking a bit better, but there are a few really tricky weeks before you get there.

April was the month we opened Konstam at the Prince Albert. Getting there was exhausting and stressful. We'd been filming *The Urban Chef* for five or six months leading up to it, and the series captured something of the situation during that period. The filming was a massive commitment in its own right and, on top of my workload with the café and setting up the restaurant, it contributed in no small way to my stress and fatigue levels.

One advantage to the filming was that I absolutely had to visit a lot more farmers and growers than I would have done otherwise. The idea of sourcing from within the limit of the Tube network was to put the produce within the reach of Londoners, making it easier for them to connect with it and the narrative behind it.

Although the producers were all within travelling distance, if I hadn't had to visually represent the process I would probably have made most of the arrangements concerning produce by phone, and spent more time working in the café and looking after things on-site at the restaurant. So, despite the additional pressure the filming brought, I'm glad it pushed me to visit all those farms, gardens, allotments and growing projects and meet the people running them – it brought the process home to me in a way it never would have otherwise. We didn't use all the producers I met while filming, but I went on to forge long working relationships with several of them. I doubt these connections would have been so strong if it hadn't been for those early visits.

As well as all this, making the programme was a lot of fun – running around London with a film crew behind me, sitting on the Tube with boxes of veg and a camera in my face. I also enjoyed watching it on television when it came out – always getting my own jokes more than anyone else I was watching it with. I remember the morning after the first episode came out, I was sitting in front of the café with a couple of my staff, having a cigarette, when a man walked by, looked at me and said, 'You're that bloke off the telly, aren't you?' It was perfect, exactly what people are supposed to say when you've just been on TV – and nobody's ever said it since.

There were many trials and tribulations before the restaurant was ready, to do with money, banks, design, sourcing produce, staffing, equipment and the daily demands of running the café, but eventually the big day arrived. We had invited as many people as we could for the opening party, but as it got closer it became more and more apparent that the restaurant itself might not be ready to open.

I was in close liaison with the contractors and they assured me that although it would be tight, we'd get there. But they still weren't done two days before, or for that matter the day before. I was lucky enough to have enlisted Jacob Kenedy and Victor Hugo – who were at that time putting together plans for their own restaurant, Bocca di Lupo – to help me get the restaurant up and running. And so the job of prepping for the opening night canapés fell to Jacob, who had to make everything in the café, down the road, as the kitchen wasn't installed in time. To Victor fell the task of keeping the trickle of early guests happy on the pavement outside with glasses of sparkling Chapel Down while we discreetly lugged the last bits of equipment out the back door, swept the floor and brought tables up from the basement. Then we finally let in the small crowd of people who were standing outside in the early evening sunshine, and I was able to turn my attention to the food.

It transpired that the brand-new hob hadn't come with the correct gas hose, so we had to steal the one from the grill in the café to finish off the canapés. It was all down-to-the-wire stuff, but by that time, after all the filming and making arrangements and running the café and finding investors and general mayhem, I can genuinely say that even though it seemed like we were only seconds from disaster, I felt very calm, as if everything had a rhythm – a pretty quick rhythm to be sure, but one that I could hear and co-ordinate things to. If you're lucky it can get like that when you're running the pass on a busy service – everything flowing to a beat only you can hear. It's not always like that, sometimes it's chaos, but on this special evening it was just right, and I felt like I could see how everything was going to fit into place. And it did, in the end.

The evening was a success, the canapés were great, nearly everyone was there that we'd hoped would come. No one seemed upset by the odd glitch and I even remembered to make a speech – I forgot to say thanks to Sam and Sam from Moro, but apart from that, it was all good. And at the end, when my long-suffering girlfriend at the time, Julie, had fallen asleep on the pass and I was sitting there finishing off a bottle of champagne with Adam (the friend who'd made the TV series), I remember looking around at it all – the open kitchen, the bar, the incredible chandeliers – and laughing because only days before it had been covered in dust and full of builders and their tools, and feeling that we had finally got there – it was Konstam at last.

One of the most successful canapés we made that night was baby doughnuts, inspired by a recipe from Jacob's grandma Agnes. This is how you make them.

Agnes's doughnuts

Makes 12
300ml milk
280g flour
4 egg yolks
1 tsp dried yeast
25g caster sugar
½ tbsp dark rum
Zest of ¼ lemon
A pinch of salt
100g butter
Vegetable oil for deep-frying

Warm a third of the milk to blood heat and dissolve the yeast with a little flour and sugar. Put the butter aside, then mix everything else together in a big basin.

Slowly add in the butter, mixing as you go to form a soft dough. Cover with a tea towel and leave in a warm place to rise to twice its size.

Knock back the dough and roll out to half a centimetre. Cut into rounds and leave to rise again.

Heat the oil in a medium saucepan to 180°C and fry the doughnuts a couple at a time, turning occasionally to colour evenly. Lift from the oil and leave them to drain and cool on kitchen paper for a few minutes. Roll them in caster sugar and eat them when they're cool enough.

———

So the restaurant opened and we were left with the problem of trying to source enough food. Having spent six months meeting farmers and producers, the main problem wasn't that there was a lack of food growing in and around London but that most of the farms and projects I was working with were too small to distribute their produce to me on a regular basis. Some produce came from inner-city growing projects that were close enough to deliver, and some came from larger operators such as Stanhill Farm in Dartford and S.J. Frederick in Roydon, who make regular deliveries into town, but there were a lot of producers who just didn't have the wherewithal to drive all the way to King's Cross more than once a week, if at all.

In the end I found a group of farms quite near each other in the north-west, around Amersham and Chesham – we arranged for them to deliver to each other and then two of them would make the trip to Konstam. Duncan Mitchell from Mitchells Dairy would come on Mondays, and Keith Bennett from Stockings Farm (where we got our pork and lamb) on Wednesdays. This meant we could get deliveries twice a week.

In most London restaurants it's easy as anything to get deliveries every day, sometimes twice a day from most suppliers: each night the chef works out the orders, and in they come the following day. We, on the other hand, had to calculate our orders for the whole week and then figure out how to keep them fresh. Problematic at times, but it was exciting too – not only had we set up a restaurant but we'd developed a distribution system that allowed us to buy produce from the farms it was growing or reared on and have it delivered to us in the middle of London. Many of the farmers hadn't known each other before we met them, but they soon

used these networks to make other deliveries too. We'd made a
new community.

Focusing on the wait for asparagus, peas or broad beans later in
the spring makes it easy to forget about the more unobtrusive
or commonplace vegetables that come out just before them. I
remember breathing a sigh of relief during our first full spring at
Konstam when Peter Clarke, one of our key farmers, mentioned that
he had spring onions. I was desperate for good fresh produce at that
point but was so focused on the big boys that I'd forgotten about
the imminent arrival of the humble scallion. It threw him when
I ordered them in kilos instead of bunches – he hadn't thought of
a price for them in that quantity. In they came in a plastic crate,
slightly muddy but long and slender. We trimmed and washed
them immediately, then gently steamed them with butter in a
pan with a tight lid until they were just tender. When I saw them
served with grilled brill, boiled Barnet potatoes and beurre blanc, I
realised that behind my back the season had changed.

Buttered spring onions

Trim the spring onions (leaving as much of the green on as possible)
and slice off the roots – if they're more than 7 or 8 millimetres
across, cut them in half lengthways part of the way down. Give
them a really good wash, soaking them for a bit, and then let them
drain for a few minutes. Melt a large knob of butter in a wide,
heavy-bottomed pan. Arrange the onions in one layer in the pan
and salt. Stir to cover with the butter and salt and raise the heat,
stir again, add a couple of tablespoons of water, cover with a close-
fitting lid until the onions are just tender and then remove them
from the pan. Be careful not to overcook them as they will lose
their colour and some freshness of flavour. Serve with white fish or
chicken, and Jersey Royals if you're are lucky enough to find them.

If you don't have a big pan, or want to play it safe, blanch them in boiling water and then toss them in butter and salt.

The next year I realised they would make a great substitute for grilled baby leeks, blanched and then chucked on top of really hot charcoal or on a griddle for a few seconds. Done like this they go beautifully with almost anything – steak, lamb, chicken and especially fish. The slightly smoky flavour goes really well with hollandaise or béarnaise sauce too. When grilling leeks you can put them raw on the grill and peel away the burned outer layers, leaving the tender, cooked flesh inside. With spring onions there isn't really enough to them to do this so you have to adopt a more roundabout method. Calçot (a big, Spanish type of spring onion) has enough layers for this, but not the spindly domestic variety.

Another commonplace vegetable that rears its lovely little round head at this time of year is the radish. I rather like radishes but I know not everyone appreciates them. Dipped in good salt and served with a knob of butter, as the French do, makes them into a wonderful hors d'oeuvre or picnic classic. You can also serve them with anchovy butter.

Radishes with anchovy butter

When buying radishes, pick a bunch with nice fresh leaves if possible.

Serves 4
125g unsalted butter
4 anchovy fillets
1 shallot
1 tbsp chopped chives
Zest of ½ a lemon
Salt

Cut the butter into dice and place in a bowl – leave to soften. Chop and mash the anchovy fillets in a pestle and mortar or with the flat of a knife on a chopping board. With a fork, mash them into the softened butter until evenly distributed. Finely dice the shallot and fold it into the butter with the lemon zest and chives. Try the butter with a radish to check for seasoning – I don't use pepper in this recipe as the radishes have a pepperiness of their own.

Trim the radishes as desired. I like to keep the leaves on if they're in good nick, but I usually trim the little hairy tails off the bottoms. If they're really big you can cut them in half lengthwise, leaving a bit of leaf on each half – they're good for scooping up the butter. Soak them in cold water – iced if possible – for 15 minutes, then drain. Be careful not to damage the leaves – trim off any that are still wilted, damaged or brown.

Arrange the radishes on a plate and serve with the butter in a small bowl. If you made the butter ahead and kept it in the fridge, remember to leave it out to soften before serving.

Radish and tarragon go well together too; the slightly soapy flavours mesh and the anise of the tarragon and the white pepper of the radish match perfectly. Dressed with a sharp and light mustardy dressing, you can serve them with all sorts of fish, especially poached. At this point it would be remiss not to mention the radish dish that Jacob Kenedy does at Bocca di Lupo. I worked in the kitchen there for a little while, and every time the person on the cold section made a radish salad the waft of white balsamic and truffle oil dressing would drift over and really turn my head. I'm generally a bit snooty about white balsamic but in this salad it's perfection, partly because they use a very good vinegar but also because the mild sweetness and low acidity work so well with all the other flavours on the plate, acting like mirin and rice wine vinegar might in a Japanese dish.

Some of the best radishes I've ever had come from Chegworth Valley's farm in Kent. They were crisp as a spring shower, with bags of flavour and just the right amount of peppery sweetness. I was bowled over by how good they were. It's always a revelation when something you thought would be uninspiring turns out to be exceptional.

It would be negligent to go through spring without mention of spring greens. These are the first cabbages of the year and are loose-leaved. They're extremely good for you, with masses of vitamin C, folic acid and fibre, and lend themselves to very simple cooking.

Spring greens with crème fraîche and garlic

Serves 4 as a side dish

2 or 3 heads of spring greens
25g butter
2 garlic cloves
2 tbsp crème fraîche
2 tbsp chopped chives or chervil
Salt and pepper

Bring a large pan of salted water to the boil. Pick through the greens, discarding any discoloured leaves. Put the greens into the boiling water and cook for 2 minutes. The stems should give way between your fingers after an initial resistance. Drain and refresh in cold water. Drain and shake dry.

Peel and slice the garlic. Heat the butter in a pan until it stops foaming and add the garlic over a medium heat. When the garlic starts smelling creamy and is just starting to turn brown, throw in the greens. Toss and add the crème fraîche. Season, toss again until everything is heated through, add the chives (or chervil) and serve.

When the going gets tough in the seasonal food calendar the bees get going. April is when the hives start buzzing. Although there isn't much in the way of fruit and vegetables for us to forage, the preponderance of spring flowers means it's time for the bees to get busy. They'll keep on going through the late spring, summer and early autumn, until it gets too cold for them and they pack up for the winter around November. Only the queen lasts the whole season, and will live for several years. The worker bees born in April only live a few weeks. Later in the year they spend more time in the hive and can live up to a couple of months.

Hives are often placed in areas where one type of flower predominates, and this lends different flavours to the honey. There are more and more beekeepers in London these days, and the city provides a varied and rich ground from which bees can forage. All the gardens and their many different species of flower make it impossible to get honey of one type, but there are times of the year when specific plants, such as ivy, are in flower and are predominant enough to impart a particular flavour.

Bees get their pollen from an area within an eight-mile circumference, and I like to think of all the amazing gardens this would cover in London – gardens we don't often get to see but which the bees can visit at will, each one contributing something to the honey they make. The honey thus becomes the fruit not only of their labour but also of an army of gardening Londoners – selecting, transporting, digging, planting, sowing, tending, watching and pruning; all that work going into a pot of honey. And that's before you take into account the estimated 10 million foraging journeys the bees will have to make for every pot.

However, over the last decade or so bee populations have been ravaged. Colony collapse disorder (CCD) – when whole colonies go into sudden and steep decline, dying or disappearing for days at a time – has struck hundreds of thousands of hives across northern

Europe, much of North America and parts of Asia. Bees are vitally important to our food systems, and not just because they make honey but because they pollinate around 80 per cent of the plants we rely on for food.

Current research into the problem suggests that a variety of factors contribute to the phenomena. Although a great deal of evidence points to systemic pesticides such as neonicotinoids and the invasive varroa mite, it may be that changes in habitat and diet and new ways of industrially managing bees could be contributory and exacerbating factors.

It isn't necessarily the case that systemic pesticides are directly responsible for the deaths of bees, but it is possible that they cause sufficient damage to their nervous, digestive and immune systems and that this makes them more susceptible to previously less serious threats. In many cases the bees simply disappear from seemingly healthy and well-stocked hives, leaving no trace. This has led beekeepers to suggest that the damage to the bees' nervous systems – disrupting their finely honed ability to navigate – means they can't find their way home.

In France and Italy action has been taken to suspend usage of some of the pesticides thought to have a particularly damaging effect, but the UK and US governments are both dragging their feet. Ironically, the data on which the original decision to allow the use of these chemicals comes from the companies that manufacture them, and which therefore stand to gain the most from their use.

Despite these pesticides seeming to be a significant factor and common to many cases of CCD, no one can pinpoint with certainty the cause of this worrying syndrome. Michael Pollan – author of *In Defence of Food*, talking in the documentary *Vanishing of the Bees* – says that intensive agriculture is the common factor, and that decades of farming in this way is finally taking its toll. Many people feel that the bees are like the 'canary in the coalmine', and their complex biosystems are fragile enough to be an early indicator of the damage being caused by unsustainable food-growing practices.

Bees and the way they live continue to fascinate us – and we never tire of honey, their magnificent, labour-intensive gift to the planet. The very idea of looking for local honey in London shops would have seemed eccentric just a few years ago, but the rise in beekeeping means it's now stocked in delicatessens and health food shops throughout the capital. There is a nice theory that people who suffer from bad hay fever should eat honey that comes from the area they most frequent. Supposedly, ingesting the pollen of the plants that cause the problem builds up a level of tolerance. I can't testify to the effectiveness of the principle as I don't suffer from hay fever but some people swear by it.

I know a beekeeper called Steve Benbow who used to keep hives on the roof of his apartment building in Bermondsey, and who still looks after the hives on the roof of Fortnum & Mason. He used to provide us with honey and honeycomb at Konstam, and we loved serving it with Norbury Blue, a locally produced blue cheese from just south of London.

Honeycomb ice cream

You can make honeycomb ice cream with cinder toffee, for which there's a recipe on page 42, but this one calls for real honeycomb. It's good to find a local beekeeper and get it from them. Otherwise you should be able to find it in a good deli. The flavour is amazing, though you might get a few bits of wax stuck in your teeth when you eat it.

Makes around ¾ litre of ice cream
285ml whole milk
285ml double cream
1 vanilla pod

50g caster sugar
5 egg yolks
140g honeycomb

Whisk the egg yolks and sugar together in a big mixing bowl until the sugar is dissolved.

Bring the milk and cream to the boil with the scraped vanilla pod and its seeds in a saucepan and remove from the heat. Stir one ladle of the hot milk mixture into the eggs, then another, and then stir in the lot.

Return to the pan and cook over a low heat, stirring continuously with a wooden spoon until it coats the back of the spoon. Run a finger across the back of the spoon to leave a stripe – if the stripe holds then it's thickened enough.

Remove from the heat and immediately pour into a jug. Allow to cool, remove the vanilla pod and churn according to your ice cream machine's instructions.

Break up the honeycomb and fold it into the ice cream before putting in the freezer – this is sticky work so hold the honeycomb over the ice cream as you do it so as not to waste any of the honey. Don't worry about incorporating it fully – streaks of honey will be an added bonus when you come to eat it. Reserve a couple of pieces of honeycomb to serve with the ice cream.

To make without an ice cream machine, chill the base over an ice bath until cool, then freeze. When it starts to freeze around the edges, whisk to churn it – an electric whisk is ideal for this. Put it back in the freezer and repeat every half an hour until it freezes. This will take about 3 hours depending on your freezer. On the last churn, layer it with the broken honeycomb, fold and let it freeze. It will be a little icier than the machine-made ice cream, but still delicious.

Serve with a piece of honeycomb on the side or on top for each person.

The hay fever theory aside, although to me it makes sense intuitively, it's hard to say whether there are any measurable health advantages to eating local food. One point that has been made by nutritionists who support the cause is that because the food has less distance to travel the nutrients have less time to break down than in food that has been transported from further away, and less processing of the produce is required to maintain its freshness.

As I touched on in the February chapter, I believe wholeheartedly that eating local food is better for us, not only because I think the food is healthier but because it increases our awareness of the produce, gives it meaning, enhances our personal dialogue with food, and enables us to make better judgments regarding what we eat.

April is definitely a dry spell in the food calendar, but at this time of year our coastal waters are full of crab, and those from the east and south-east are particularly good. Crabs are fiddly to prepare, and although it's more convenient to buy ready-picked crabmeat it usually tastes a bit tired. Besides, you get a real sense of achievement when you buy whole crabs to cook and pick yourself.

Cooking crabs means killing them; the raw flesh in a dead crab degrades so quickly you should always buy them when they're alive. Much of the time this means they get plunged directly into boiling water, which we all agree isn't a very nice way to go; so it's more humane to kill them just before cooking them. This can be tricky: you need to drive the tip of a knife or skewer through two points on the underside as they have two main nerve areas. The same procedure applies to lobsters, but at least they have only one set of nerves running all the way down the middle of their bodies, so a big sharp knife through the brain and midline of the body should do it. You can chill lobster and crab in the freezer first, which will render them insensible, but if they freeze too quickly this might be just as inhumane as the hot-water method. I tend to go for the knife in the back of the head technique with lobsters, as I know I wouldn't like to be dropped alive into a boiling vat of water myself. Crabs I'm usually guilty of boiling.

Cooking crab is pretty simple, but picking them once they're cooked is a pain. I have an early cheffing memory of making one of Moro's signature dishes, crab brik. I think this is almost certainly the nicest crab recipe I've ever come across, though it involves a lot of work. I was enjoying the experience – seeing six huge crabs from the east coast come out of the boiling water, all pink and amazing was exactly why I was loving my new job – but then it was explained to me that I had to pick the crabmeat out of the shells. I was handed a funny-looking double-wedge-shaped mallet type thing and a wooden skewer. After about 20 minutes of scraping, picking, cracking and breaking and only having made the slightest impact on the first of the crabs, I started to panic.

The job is split into two and the person making the warka (a fiddly and time-consuming pastry made from a particularly wet dough) was going great guns, but the mountain of a task that lay ahead of me was starting to seem insurmountable – picking the crab and checking for shell, washing and chopping all the herbs and chilli for the filling, grinding the cumin, then seasoning and mixing everything together before service and in time for the briks to be rolled. Sam, who was running the kitchen that day, saw I was behind and asked how I was getting on, pointing out that the warka was nearly made and I still hadn't washed the herbs. By this time it was nearly 5.30, service started in an hour and I was only on my second crab. So I put my head down and worked like crazy. The time ticked by rapidly and the pressure increased. In the end, the crab briks were late for service, and before we were even halfway through the evening I was rolling them to order, which is a faff during a busy shift. It wasn't my best night.

This might not sound serious in retrospect, but there is so little room for error that small things out of place can have a significant impact. At Moro, as with every restaurant kitchen, we were always up against it – we had to get things done in a short space of time, and to a very high standard – but I learned so much, in such a passionate environment, from chefs with food and cooking in their bones, that even though it was a trial by fire, a job that always pushed me, I count myself lucky to have had that experience.

The crab brik recipe is reproduced below, and though it pains me to say it, you can use filo pastry instead of the laborious warka pastry they use at Moro. Samuel and Samantha have been kind enough to allow me to include the brik recipe here. If you want to try making warka, remember that the dough needs to be just loose enough to dab, but not so loose that it falls off your fingers, and the metal plate needs to be very well seasoned and just the right temperature over a pan of simmering water. Too hot and the pastry cooks too fast, too cool and it sticks like a sticky thing. If you want, you can use a non-stick frying pan that fits snugly into the top of a large saucepan. This works well, but with really new pans the surface can be too non-stick, meaning the pastry doesn't actually catch at all.

Crab brik

Once you've mastered warka, try making our version of the Tunisian brik – made with crispy warka, moist crabmeat lightly seasoned with cumin, chilli and herbs, it's a real treat. At Moro we cook and pick fresh live crabs, and although this is quite a laborious process, if you can get hold of fresh crab, we think it's worth it. However, crabmeat from a fishmonger is a good alternative.

Serves 4

- 1 crab, about 1kg in weight, boiled for around 10 minutes, cooked and picked thoroughly, keeping the white meat separate from the brown, or 400–500g crabmeat, ¾ white ¼ brown
- 1 medium fresh red chilli, halved, seeded and finely chopped

1 large bunch fresh coriander, roughly chopped

1 small bunch each of fresh mint and flat-leaf parsley, roughly chopped

½ garlic clove, crushed to a paste with salt

2 dsp lemon juice

½ tsp freshly ground cumin

To finish, cook and serve:

8 warka sheets

750ml sunflower oil for deep-frying

Harissa

1 lemon, quartered

If you do a quick job of picking out the meat, or you use two smaller crabs instead, 1.25–1.5kg of crab will be necessary. If you pick the crab quickly you won't get so much meat, and if the crabs are smaller there is a higher proportion of shell to meat than in one large crab. Mix the white meat of the crab with the brown meat and add to the rest of the ingredients. Taste for seasoning.

Lay two sheets of warka on top of each other and put a quarter of the crab mixture into the centre. Lightly moisten the edges with some water and fold them into the centre in a pleating fashion so the crab mixture is sealed inside. Now turn the brik pleat-side down onto a floured surface. Repeat this three more times with your other remaining six pieces of warka.

Put the oil in a large saucepan (never more than half full) and place over a medium heat. Carefully lower one brik at a time into the oil. Cook for a couple of minutes until a beautiful golden brown. When ready, take out with a slotted spoon and pat dry with kitchen paper before serving. Serve with some harissa, the lemon and a little salad if you like.

The full recipes for warka and harissa can be found in the first *Moro* cookbook (Ebury Press, 2001).

I went to university in Winchester. King Alfred's College, now the University of Winchester, is situated near the top of a steep hill overlooking the south side of the town. Below it are the famous boys' school and the water meadows on the banks of the River Itchen. Watercress has been cultivated there for nearly two hundred years, and although the future of these watercress beds is uncertain, Hampshire remains one of the country's most significant areas of production. It is a leaf less well known now than in the days of Pepys when it was sold in bunches on the streets of London to be eaten on the hoof, but the punch of its peppery flavour, its elegant curled stems and dark green leaves are still appreciated the country over. It thrives in slightly alkaline waterways with chalk beds, and it floats due to its hollow stems. It must be eaten fresh as it doesn't last long after picking, but good watercress will keep in the fridge if you remove the dead stems and immerse it in water. I rarely buy it except from a wholesaler, as it tends to be limp and unappealing once it's sat in a supermarket for more than a few hours. The quality can be very inconsistent and there's no point buying it out of season as the further it travels the lower the quality.

The peppery flavour of watercress goes perfectly with beef in any form, and with almost any kind of fish. The piquancy also complements pork, and it will transform a sandwich or a green salad. The dark green of watercress soup, served hot or chilled, is the ideal starter for any spring or summer meal.

Watercress soup

You need plenty of watercress to make this soup – it should be deep green and unctuous.

Serves 4

3–4 bunches of watercress (around 450g)
2 small onions
1 celery stick
1 small fennel bulb (optional)

50g butter
1 bay leaf
1 sprig thyme
1 small potato
1 litre chicken or vegetable stock
Salt and pepper
A little olive oil
Crème fraîche or sour cream

Dice the onion and celery. Trim and dice the fennel, if using. Heat the butter in a large saucepan and add the diced vegetables. Cook over a low to medium heat until softened and sweet. In the meantime, dice the potato and add this to the pan with the bay leaf and the thyme. After a minute or two on a low heat, cover with chicken or vegetable stock. Bring to a gentle simmer and cook until the potato is easily crushed against the side of the pan, about 15 minutes. Remove from the heat.

While the potato is cooking, bring a separate pan of water to the boil. Pick through the watercress. Wash and discard only the woodiest stalks, then roughly chop the rest. Plunge into the boiling water for 30 seconds to a minute, drain and refresh in cold water. Add to the hot soup, removing the bay leaf and the thyme stalks first, and blitz until very smooth. You may want to add some more liquid here – I often use milk, or you can use cream instead. Check for seasoning and heat very carefully before serving – don't let it boil – stir and remove from the heat when it bubbles just a couple of times.

Serve with a swirl of sour cream or crème fraîche, a drizzle of olive oil, crusty toast and lots of butter.

I worked for some time at a pub called the Windsor Castle in Clapton a few years ago, and we served stunning skirt steak from Nicola Bulgin at Beatbush Farm in Essex – some of the best I've ever tasted. They only slaughter a few animals each week, so I had to make sure I got my order in well ahead of time. Skirt steak, known as *onglet* in France and hanger in the US, is cut from the diaphragm and there are only a few portions on each animal. It's probably my favourite cut of beef, high in flavour and with a firmer texture than some of the more celebrated cuts. When I ran Konstam we bought exceedingly high quality skirt steak from Natural Farms in Kent. It was practically the only cut we served during the four or so years the restaurant was open. We marinated it with bay, thyme, garlic and juniper, and grilled it over Kentish charcoal.

At the Windsor Castle I would often serve the steak with a watercress and home-made crème fraîche relish, run through with chopped shallot and fresh horseradish.

Watercress relish

This goes really well with beef, particularly rare skirt steak.

Enough for 6 roast dinners
1 bunch or half a packet of watercress
4 tbsp crème fraîche
1 or 2 shallots, depending on size
1 tsp wholegrain mustard
1 tsp extra virgin olive oil
1 tbsp red wine vinegar
½-inch piece of fresh horseradish
Salt and freshly ground black pepper

Pick through the watercress, discarding any brown or wilted leaves. Only discard the very thickest stalks – the rest will go into the relish. Chop to medium fine with a sharp knife and combine with the crème fraîche in a mixing bowl. Finely dice the shallots and grate the horseradish on the fine side of a box grater, or on a microplane, and add these to the watercress with the rest of the ingredients. Check for acidity and punch, adding vinegar and mustard if needed. Season well with salt and freshly ground black pepper.

Making your own crème fraîche, like making yoghurt, is surprisingly simple and very rewarding. You can make yoghurt from any other live yoghurt by creating the right sort of home for the bacteria and then setting them free to multiply and grow. Bring a pint of milk, or half milk and half cream, up to 80°C then let it cool. When it gets to blood heat – meaning you can keep your finger in it for a count of ten – add a couple of tablespoons of live yoghurt, cover with a clean tea towel and leave in a warm place overnight – an airing cupboard (if you have one) or the warmest part of the kitchen.

Crème fraîche is even easier. Simply put a tablespoon of buttermilk or yoghurt into a pint of double cream, cover with a clean tea towel and leave to stand at room temperature for 24 hours. Refrigerate after this and it will keep for a week or so. It will continue to thicken a little, even at fridge temperature. The milk and cream ferment as the bacteria convert lactose to lactic acid. This creates an environment hostile to other bacteria, and so once they've taken hold it will keep for some time.

Watercress isn't the only leaf available in April. Rocket and sorrel are cropped from now on and will carry on through the summer and into the autumn, with rocket outlasting sorrel by a month or two. You can now get rocket everywhere and it's sold all year round in most supermarkets. Italian wild rocket is the most easily available in the shops, but it's very easy to grow yourself and keeps coming back after cutting.

When I started the café I had a herb bed in my grandmother's beautiful garden in Hampstead. On Mondays, the day we were closed for the first year or so, I would do the banking then get the bus to Parliament Hill Fields and walk across the Heath to her house so I could tend to the herbs and bring some back to use in the café kitchen. We grew parsley, chervil, fennel, mint, chives, thyme, sage, rosemary, lemon balm and rocket. She had a golden marjoram plant next to the herb bed, which I would frequently raid for salads. Cropping the rocket was a bit fiddly at first, but I loved the fierce pepperiness you only get when it's fresh. I noticed that the hotter and drier the weather the more intense the peppery notes would be.

Rocket leaves have an elegant curling shape and bring life to any salad. It's so ever-present on restaurant plates now that people can be quite snooty about it, but I still love the fresh tang it brings and stubbornly persist with it on my plates. As a key ingredient it has such a strong flavour so it doesn't feature in many recipes, but you can make great pesto with it. It's important not to use too strong or fresh an olive oil with it as together they can be overpowering. I also like it paired with walnuts instead of pine kernels.

Sorrel is less easily bought, but you can grow it yourself. It feels old-fashioned, like something my grandparents would have eaten, but its vibrant lemony flavour always brings me to my senses. I mentioned sorrel in March when we were talking about oxalic acid, the substance that makes it so zingy, but April is when it comes into season. Sorrel sauce goes really well with fish, and I like it shredded it into an omelette with chives, dill, parsley and goat's cheese. I make soup with it using the watercress soup recipe above, swapping the watercress for sorrel and adding a dash of double cream. Sorrel has the annoying habit of going limp and dark grey-green as soon as you cook it, but the flavour stays sharp so don't worry about that. If you're making soup it's perfectly acceptable to borrow colour from a big handful of spinach or wild garlic.

There is no official season for hunting woodpigeon as it's largely seen as an agricultural pest, and along with the collared dove it can be shot all year round. It's the most common of the pigeon species, even more so than the domestic pigeon. This is the one we see all over our cities and which is descended from the rock dove. The two are hard to tell apart, but the latter is protected and it's illegal to shoot them at any time of the year. You can shoot domestic pigeons at will, but they will feed on practically anything so I wouldn't recommend eating them. Despite our cultural connections with various species within the pigeon family, there is no hard taxonomical distinction between the terms pigeon and dove, both being used to refer to different species within the pigeon family.

Although there is no set season for woodpigeon, there are times of the year when it's at its best; it's scrawniest in winter, when it's rummaging around for food. It will still taste good, but when the ground has thawed and food supplies become more plentiful the quality rises. From April onwards the breasts get plumper and increase significantly in size.

You can roast pigeon whole and many recipes find a use for the legs, but I've always found the breast the only part worth the time and effort. Keith Bennett, the wonderful man who rears sheep and pigs in Amersham, brought it to my attention that they shoot pigeon on his farm all year round, so he always had pigeon breast in his fridge. In the early days at Konstam a constant supply of almost anything was a blessing, so I told him to bring them on down with the delivery of lamb and pork, even though I wasn't too sure what I was going to do with them. I can't remember how we first served it but they were delicious. In the months and years that followed we cooked them in any number of ways, but soon learned that the trick is to marinate them well and cook them very quickly.

One of the things I love about pigeon breast is that it goes really well with both savoury and sweet, dark fruit flavours. Its dense meat tastes great with sour cream or crème fraîche, as well as with vinegary dressings and stock-based sauces. I've served it with leeks, beetroot, onions, Jerusalem artichokes, celeriac, carrot, broad beans and just about anything. The two most common pairings were with beetroot and crème fraîche, and with barley and red cabbage salad.

Seared pigeon breast with roast baby beetroot, elderberry dressing and seasoned crème fraîche

I generally only cook this dish over charcoal, the smoky taste adding something I feel is quite crucial to the dish, but I realise this isn't always possible. If you do use charcoal, however, make sure it's absolutely piping hot when you put the pigeon over it. The recipe says seared and it means seared – the inside should be rare and the outside coloured.

Serves 4 as a starter

4 plump pigeon breasts
2 garlic cloves
5 juniper berries
½ tsp fennel seeds
8 white peppercorns
½ tsp wholegrain mustard
6 baby beetroot and their leaves
Extra virgin olive oil
Maldon salt and black pepper
4 tbsp crème fraîche
1½ tbsp Cabernet Sauvignon vinegar
½ teaspoon Dijon mustard
A pinch of nigella seeds
2 tbsp elderberry syrup – see page 336.
    If you don't have elderberry syrup, the juice from crushed bilberries,
    blackberries or blackcurrants make a good stand-in.

Crush the garlic in a pestle and mortar and set half of it aside. Add the juniper, fennel seeds, white pepper and wholegrain mustard to the mortar and crush to a fine paste. Add a teaspoon or two of olive oil to the mix and then rub it into the pigeon breasts, removing the skin and the mini fillets first. Put in a closely covered bowl in the fridge with a little extra oil drizzled on top and leave to marinate for up to two days.

Preheat the oven to 180°C and put a medium-sized pan of salted water on to boil. Separate the beetroot leaves from the roots and reserve the leaves. Peel the beetroots and cut in half. Toss in a bowl with a little oil, salt and pepper. Place on parchment on a baking tray and roast in the oven, turning occasionally, until tender and caramelised (about 25 minutes). Remove from the oven and leave to cool.

Plunge the beetroot leaves into the boiling water and return to the boil, cooking for about 30 seconds, or until the stems give way when pinched. Lift out of the pan and refresh in cold water.

Mix half the remaining crushed garlic with the crème fraîche and a drizzle of oil. Season with salt and black pepper.

Make a dressing with the Cabernet Sauvignon vinegar and 4 tablespoons of olive oil. Season it well and split it in half. Add the rest of the crushed garlic, the Dijon mustard and the elderberry syrup to one half. Leave the other half as it is.

Get your coals, griddle or frying pan piping hot. Drizzle a little oil on the pigeon and season it. Add oil to the frying pan (if you're using this) and sear the pigeon. When it's coloured on one side (about a minute), turn it and repeat. It should still have a pleasant amount of give when prodded. Remove immediately to a gently warm plate and leave to rest for a minute or two.

Toss the beetroot – leaves and tuber – in the remaining Cabernet Sauvignon dressing and arrange on the plate. Slice the pigeon breast at an extreme angle into 3 or 4 slices and set it, with the slices still almost together, onto the beetroot. Put a dollop of the crème fraîche on the side and a good drizzle of the elderberry dressing over it. Sprinkle a few nigella seeds and a touch of salt and pepper over the lot.

I could probably write a whole chapter on eggs. Breakfast was one of my first cooking explorations as a fast-growing teenager, and I would cook huge plates of eggs and bacon for myself and my friends.

Although we're used to getting eggs all year round, many breeds
of chicken only really start to lay when the days get longer,
hence their mention in April. However, my friend Anna Koska,
an amazing artist who keeps chickens, says her brown chickens,
Warren Hybrids, are good workers and lay an egg a day regular as
clockwork, even through the winter.

There are thousands of recipes for eggs, and many spring to mind
to include here, but since it is the simple things I enjoy, I'm still
fascinated by the challenge of poaching the perfect egg. In the end
it comes down to one key factor: the freshness of the egg. You can
see why by cracking a fresh egg and comparing it to one a few days
older – the white will hold together better than the white in the
senior egg, in which the proteins have become watery and thin.
The older egg won't kill you, but when you break it into boiling
water it will disperse before it has time to form. Most of us probably
aren't lucky enough to have eggs as fresh as Anna's regular supply,
so although you probably shouldn't bother with eggs that are close
to their use-by date, there are a few things you can do to help your
egg along.

Some chefs put salt in the water, and although this doesn't seem
to affect things one way or another, I can't get my head away
from the theory of adding a pinch of salt to egg whites before
whipping them in order to break down the albumen a little bit. I
find that a generous glug of white wine vinegar helps keep the egg
together. The other key factor, after the freshness of the eggs, is the
temperature of the water. My technique is to bring it to the point
where small bubbles are just rising up from the bottom, give it a
gentle stir, tip the egg into the water from an eggcup touching the
surface, then bring the temperature up until the water is gently
buffeting the egg. It's this buffeting that lifts the egg off the bottom
of the pan and helps create a spherical shape: boil too hard and
it can pull the egg out of shape, too low and the egg stays at the
bottom and comes out flat. Once it's started to firm up, turn down

the heat and let it finish cooking gently – the proteins in eggs tighten up so much that the emulsions break down and the texture suffers once they reach about 70°C.

How well done you like your eggs is up to you, but I like mine with the white just set and the yolk really runny, so when you cut it the yolk bursts out and runs all over the toast, or mingles with the hollandaise, or lathers the smoked haddock. However you like it, prod it and if it responds in the right way, lift it out and either serve it straight away, or, if you need to finish off other elements of the breakfast you can dip it for a few seconds in cold water to stop it cooking and then put it into a bowl of slightly hotter than blood heat water until you need it. This is also a good moment to discard any bits of errant or over-cooked white. Sometimes a spot of egg vanity pays off, especially if you're cooking breakfast to impress.

While we're on the subject of eggs, I thought I'd include another favourite of mine. A very simple recipe, and one I've used as a canapé or a bar snack.

Quail's eggs with mace salt

I love the taste and smell of ground mace, and I make the salt for this in my coffee grinder (cleaning it carefully afterwards). If using ground mace, or you don't have a grinder, use a pestle and mortar or the back of a metal spoon on a board.

Serves 4 (3 eggs per person)
12 quail's eggs at room temperature
10g Maldon salt
4 blades of mace, or 1 tsp ground

Put a pinch of salt and mace in the bowl of the grinder and blitz to a fine powder. If the oil in the mace makes it clump, push it away from the sides, add a touch more salt and blitz again. Combine with the rest of the salt and toss to mix evenly.

Bring a saucepan of water to the boil. Fill a bowl with cold water and set it to one side of the stove. Drop the quail's eggs into the boiling water. Cook them for 2½ minutes if you want them runny or 3 minutes if you want them just set. I like them runny, but they can be more difficult to peel. Lift them out and drop them into the cold water. Leave for 10 minutes or so to cool thoroughly.

Serve peeled or unpeeled with the salt in a little dish on the side for dipping.

In Spain scrambled eggs are called huevos revueltos, the word *revueltos* having the same two meanings in Spanish as in English – to scramble an egg and to scramble for the line. I like that words translate in more than one way across languages; in French the word *mortier* has the same four meanings as the word mortar in English. In my experience, revueltos are cooked quickly in olive oil, instead of slowly in butter, and often include ingredients like mushrooms, chorizo, asparagus or prawns. When I was developing the café menu I remembered having revueltos a few years earlier on a trip to Spain with my old friend Jack Pickering, and I decided to put them on the breakfast menu. They quickly became a favourite of my morning regulars and never left the menu. The five main ways we served them were with chorizo, morcilla, mushrooms, smoked salmon – sliced and beaten through at the last second – or just plain with herbs. The herb mix was always the same, a combination of chopped flat-leaf parsley, chives and diced spring onion. I always loved it when someone would order them 'lightly scrambled', a phrase you rarely hear, and it's the way I like mine cooked too.

Revueltos

A recipe for scrambled eggs might seem a waste of time as everyone likes them differently and there are a million and one ways to make them, but the Spanish don't only eat them for breakfast – revueltos can often be found as a light lunch or a starter for dinner. They combine the eggs with a huge range of ingredients, from wild asparagus, mushrooms and prawns through to blood sausage, squid and sheep's brains.

I never feel that two eggs are quite enough. When I cook for myself it always ends up as three, but I think five is good for two people as a light lunch and four for an evening starter.

Serves 2 for lunch
5 fresh medium organic eggs
1 tbsp olive oil
1 handful chopped flat-leaf parsley
Salt and pepper

Break the eggs into a bowl or jug and season them – be careful as eggs don't need much salt or pepper. Lightly beat them to mix.

Heat the oil in a pan and quickly fry whatever you're scrambling your eggs with. If you're using chorizo try and find the small, lightly cured cooking chorizo the Spanish use, instead of the large sliced ones we mostly get here. Dice it small and fry it quickly. Sobrasada is also nice, but barely needs any time in the pan. Morcilla is Spanish black pudding, softer and more crumbly than ours. Prawns and squid only take a second, and asparagus is best blanched for 30 seconds or so then cut into chunks. Mushrooms need a minute or so to let some of their water content extract and evaporate. Whatever you mix in with the eggs, make sure the heat is pretty high at the end of their cooking time.

Tip the eggs into the pan and stir them quite quickly, removing the pan from the heat if you need to. The eggs will cook fast and it's important not to overcook them, so be ready to share them out onto the plates as soon as you think they're done. Again, people like their eggs done different ways. They will continue to cook even when out of the pan, so err on the side of caution.

The final egg recipe in this chapter is for another dish I used to love serving in the café. I loved it so much I called it Eggs Konstam. It wasn't a complicated dish, and it had a naughty un-local, a-seasonal ingredient in it too, but it worked so well it went on the menu. Eggs Konstam is poached eggs on rye bread with grilled morcilla and avocado. I sometimes added a dollop of mayonnaise on the side, but the juiciness of the morcilla was enough really. The bread was Troels Bendix's delicious rye and the morcilla with onion was from Brindisa. The sourness of the rye adds just the edge the dish needs to cope with all the other rich flavours. You could mash the avocado with lemon or lime if you want sharper flavours, but I felt the balance was good as it was and we simply sliced half an avocado onto the toast before plonking the eggs on top.

All this egg talk paints a certain gloss over things, but April really is a tricky month in the seasonal food calendar and it hurts each time it comes around. As it draws to a close there is a tendency to raise one's hopes in the belief that things will start to look up soon, but seasonal change doesn't happen from day to day; it's a gradual process and the good times, though near, haven't yet arrived.
So we head into May with very little yet to show and the waiting just gets harder.

MAY

—

Asparagus

Elderflower

Jersey Royals

Lamb

Carrots

Lovage

Lemons

Broad beans

Now the bright morning-star, Day's harbinger,
Comes dancing from the East, and leads with her
The flowery May, who from her green lap throws
The yellow cowslip and the pale primrose.
Hail, bounteous May, that dost inspire
Mirth, and youth, and warm desire!
Woods and groves are of thy dressing;
Hill and dale doth boast thy blessing.
Thus we salute thee with our early song,
And welcome thee, and wish thee long.

John Milton, 'Song on a May Morning' (1660)

We know May as the last month of spring, but historically it's often been seen as the beginning of summer. In Irish tradition the celebration of Beltane comes at the beginning of the month, heralding the start of summer, and in Roman times the Festival of Flora was celebrated for the same reason. May Day, the first Monday in May, is supposed to be the first day of summer, but few of us see it that way. In our mind's eye May is mild-mannered, a genuine spring month. The lambs are jumping around like crazy and nobody has a care in the world. Even a delicate shower of warm rain isn't enough to dampen the May spirit as we know sunnier days are soon to come.

I don't think that's the whole story though. I see May as an in-between month; like April, it's a lull between seasons. In folklore it's associated with a sense of unease – for instance, it's supposed to be very bad luck to be born or to marry in May, and for some reason washing blankets is frowned upon. April's themes relate to daffodils, swallows and nature making its entrance, while May's are much more geared up to anticipating a good or bad harvest. I'm not entirely sure if there is a direct connection between this seasonal anticipation and the fateful atmosphere, but I can imagine farming communities being on tenterhooks at this time of the year, waiting to see if the early crops were going to bear fruit, and that uneasy feeling finding its way into our traditions.

As in April, the produce that appears in the midst of this seasonal food vacuum becomes all the more noticeable, but there is one particular ingredient that provides a welcome glint in the darkness, and for me it's become a symbol of seasonal produce.

Anyone who goes out for a meal with me and orders asparagus at any time other than May or June knows how I feel about the issue. In the UK we grow pretty much the best asparagus in the world, with production centring on the east and south-east, so we should embrace it wholeheartedly when it arrives and concentrate on other vegetables when it's gone. The asparagus season expresses many of the things I would like to change about the way we relate to food. We have six to eight weeks during which we can eat asparagus until we're fit to burst and our pee smells to high heaven, and yet we feel the need to have it all year round, which ultimately undermines the singular relationship we have with it. I can remember when asparagus was served only on special occasions, but this is no longer the case as it's imported from Spain, Peru and Chile all year long in pencil-thin, uniform bundles lacking in taste and substance. It pains me to think of future generations not knowing what all the fuss is about.

The British asparagus season typically starts at the beginning of May, but if the weather is right it can come earlier. The first spring after we opened the restaurant was very warm and everything came up early. I rang Toby Williams at Stanhill Farm in mid-April to order some rhubarb, but he had a surprise for me and told me that the asparagus had taken it upon itself to poke its head up early. Within seconds I'd ordered a couple of boxes of beautifully firm, splendidly irregular and incredibly tasty south-east London asparagus. We served it as simply as we could – melted butter, a sprinkle of Maldon salt, a pinch of lovely golden sourdough breadcrumbs and a wedge of lemon. I love it with a poached egg and hollandaise oozing all over the plate, but we figured there would be plenty of places serving it like that and wanted to make it a bit different, so instead of elaborating we went bare ... almost naked, in fact.

Part of my enjoyment of serving asparagus at Konstam was that while I was looking into the history of food in the capital I found out that asparagus was a traditional London crop that thrived on the banks of the Thames near Battersea a few hundred years ago, when the area was still agricultural. I got great satisfaction from knowing that we were serving a true London dish.

The flavour of asparagus is verdant but never overbearing and its versatility makes writing recipes for it almost an irrelevance as you can use it in almost anything – salads, soups, risottos, in an omelette, frittata, stir-fries – I could keep going but I do have to pick a couple, so here's one of my favourite asparagus dishes, a simple tart with crème fraîche, chives and cheese.

Asparagus tart

This tart is brilliant for early picnics. Bake the shell without the filling first – this is called baking blind and is the way to ensure you get lovely crisp pastry however rich and creamy the filling. I rarely add water to the pastry as it is slightly lighter without, but this pastry is very crumbly and a tablespoon of water will make it a little easier to roll and handle.

Makes about 10 slices
Pastry:
450g plain flour
250g unsalted butter
2 large eggs, or 2 whole and 1 yolk if medium
1 scant tbsp cold water, if using
A pinch of salt

In a food processor blend the butter, salt and flour until you achieve the texture of fine breadcrumbs, then add the eggs and water and blend until the pastry just comes together in a ball – don't mix it anymore than you have to. Tip it out of the blender, pat it into a log. This makes enough for 2 tarts, so cut it in half, put half in the freezer and half in the fridge. Leave to rest for at least 30 minutes.

Remove from the fridge and leave out for 15 minutes. Roll out to about 3mm and line a 25–30cm loose-bottomed fluted tart tin. Fold the sides back on themselves, tucking the edge down inside the tin to form a double layer and gently pressing the pastry into the fluted edge. This makes the edges a little higher and the pastry a bit flakier. Return to the fridge to rest again for another 20 minutes.

Preheat the oven to 225°C, and when it's hot prick the base of the tart with a fork, line it with parchment and fill it with baking beans to keep it flat while baking. Reduce the oven to 180°C and bake for about 10 minutes or until the edges start to turn golden brown. Remove the beans and parchment and continue to bake until the whole tart shell is golden and crispy. Lightly beat an egg with a small dash of milk and glaze the inside of the tart shell, taking care to fill any fork holes or cracks, and return to the oven for a further 2 minutes. Remove from the oven and allow to cool completely.

Filling:
100ml milk
200ml cream
½ cup crème fraîche
4 whole eggs

½ bunch of chives, thinly sliced
1 tbsp roughly chopped parsley
Salt and pepper
2 bunches of asparagus
150g cheddar cheese

Set the oven to 165°C. Arrange the asparagus in a wheel in the completely cooled tart shell. Mix together the rest of the ingredients (except for the cheese), season, then pour around the asparagus. If you want you can chop the asparagus into chunks, add to the filling and pour it all in together. Sprinkle the cheese on top. Place in the middle of the oven, and when slightly puffed, only just set and golden brown on top, remove from the oven and allow to cool to just above room temperature before serving.

Fortunately the asparagus season coincides with the change in the weather, so you can start dusting off the barbecue. One of the best ways to cook asparagus is to grill it. You can do this on a griddle indoors, but do it over charcoal and it becomes something else entirely. Grill it quickly over hot coals to get a touch of colour on it – it doesn't take long and cooks a little in its own heat after you've removed it, so don't overcook it. It needs nothing more than olive oil and salt.

This next asparagus recipe was an accident, but a happy one, and was inspired by a tweet that Jackson Boxer from Brunswick House posted about raw asparagus dipped in salad dressing. I was writing late at night and needed a snack, so I had a look in the fridge and saw a bunch of big, chunky asparagus I'd bought that day and a little jar saying 'vinaigrette'. Out they came and I started dipping the raw asparagus in the jar, loving the crisp texture and the greenness of the flavour. The vinaigrette, made with Cabernet Sauvignon vinegar, was really good but I felt it needed something more, so I had a quick rummage in my kitchen cupboard, grabbed

the pomegranate molasses and poured a slug of it in the jar.
It was exactly what was needed, and I worked my way through
the whole bunch.

Pomegranate dressing

Makes enough for 1 bunch of asparagus
1 garlic clove
1 tbsp pomegranate molasses
1 tbsp Cabernet Sauvignon vinegar
4 tbsp good extra virgin olive oil
Maldon salt and black pepper

Crush the garlic and mix with the vinegar and molasses. Season
with salt and pepper to get a good balance and then mix with
the olive oil.

At this time of year there are a few fleeting highlights that really
stand out. In the last few months, wild garlic, purple sprouting
broccoli, nettles, rhubarb and spring onions have saved the day. This
month's big hitter is asparagus, but another ingredient that comes
into season around now is elderflower, exerting a subtle influence
on not only our palates but our olfactory systems. This is one of the
truly lovely foods that May has to offer. As soon as there's a little
warm weather the green buds the elder has been unobtrusively
developing burst into intensely fragrant umbrellas of small cream-
coloured flowers. The smell they give off has more than a hint of
cat's pee, especially later in the season when the flowers are past
their best, and only give a bare indication of the delicate citrus and
vanilla notes that can be gleaned from them.

The taste of elderflower captures the mood of early summer, and
there's nothing better than a jug of iced water laced with home-
made elderflower cordial and a couple of slices of lemon. However, it
took me a while to work out which direction to come at it from, so

when I occasionally meet people who don't like it I can understand why, though I feel it's my mission to convert them, knowing the pleasure it will give them in the long run.

The elder is a large and unassuming tree that grows all over the country and is happy in most soil types; this makes it great for foraging. It's common to most woodlands and hedgerows, and when I need some I usually pop down to the Regent's Canal near my house in Camden. The flowers are charming if not particularly striking, and its ritual and medicinal uses are mythologically revered. It is perhaps this that has led the Christian Church to demonise it, claiming the cross used to crucify Christ was made of elder, and that Judas Iscariot hanged himself from an elder branch. Both tales are unlikely to be true as the elder is not native to Palestine. It was also claimed that burning it will summon the devil, and allowing it into your house would bring bad luck, suggesting an attempt by the Church to undermine the power it held for pagan worship. The word has a nice etymology, probably coming from the Anglo-Saxon word *aeld*, meaning fire, as the hollow stems were used to blow air into fires. The Latin name is *Sambucus nigra*, thought to have given its name to sambuca, which contains elderflower and was originally a Greek drink made from elderberries.

Although both the flowers and berries of the elder are mildly poisonous before cooking, especially when unripe in the case of the berries, the elder tree gives us several medicinal treatments. A tea made from the flowers, either fresh or dried, is supposed to be good for flu, colds, excessive mucous, sinusitis and other problems relating to the respiratory tract. The fruit helps with rheumatism, and the bark and roots ease constipation and arthritis.

Ground elder, *Aegopodium podagraria*, is much more closely related to the carrot than to the common elder. Its season comes to an end about now so it's best in February, when it's most tender and the flavour is aromatic and less grassy. It flowers in May and June, at which time it has a laxative property when eaten. Ground elder grows everywhere in the wild – but it's a terrible weed, so whatever you do don't encourage it in your garden as it will take over and is hard to get rid of.

The Romans brought it here to provide themselves with an early spring supply of greens and, like the Scandinavians in modern times, apparently used it like spinach. Ground elder cordial has a nice aromatic and slightly medicinal flavour and I recommend giving it a go. Its best-known medicinal use is to treat gout, hence one of its common names – goutweed. To make the cordial, use a similar recipe to the one for elderflower cordial given below, using about half a shopping bag full of tender young leaves instead of elderflowers.

I've read many recipes for elderflower cordial and they all have lemon in them. Some recipes call for oranges too, but it adds a warmness to the flavour which detracts from the clean, refreshing finish. I've often toyed with the addition of lime but I usually serve them together anyway so have always omitted it from the recipe.

The addition of a little powdered citric acid helps to preserve it and also lifts the flavour, sharpening it and giving it clarity. If you're foraging in areas where dogs are walked it's advisable to avoid low-hanging elderflowers – the pollen supplies most of the flavour so you mustn't wash them before use. Carefully pick through your elderflowers looking out for insects – though they won't survive the entirety of the process and it's strained at the end. I've found that fastidiously picking off as much stem as possible will help the flavour, and it's best to make cordial early in the season when the flowers have a fresher, less dusty flavour.

Elderflower cordial

Makes 1½ litres
20–30 heads of elderflower
1kg sugar
1.2 litres water
3 unwaxed lemons
75g citric acid

Gently shake the elderflowers to remove dust or insects, then pick through carefully and put them in a large, clean metal bowl.

Bring the water and sugar to a boil in a large saucepan, stirring until the sugar has completely dissolved.

Zest the lemons with a peeler or paring knife in wide strips and put them in the bowl with the elderflowers. Slice the lemons (discarding the ends) and add them to the bowl. When the sugar has dissolved in the water, pour it, still boiling, over the flowers and lemons, then stir in the citric acid. Cover the bowl with a cloth and leave at room temperature for 24 hours.

When the mixture has steeped for long enough, strain it through muslin or a new, rinsed J-cloth and pour into sterilised glass bottles with air-tight lids. It's best when left to settle in the bottle for a few days, but essentially it's ready to go.

Although the lack of variety and dearth of basics continue well into May, it's around now that Jersey Royals get going in earnest. Other new potatoes appear now and in the coming months, but Jersey Royals are traditionally the earliest and easily the tastiest. They were originally called Jersey Royal Flukes and came about when a Jersey farmer called Hugh de la Haye bought a couple of giant potatoes in a shop. He was so impressed by these potatoes that he showed them to his friends at a dinner that evening. One of the potatoes had 15 eyes, and this caused so much excitement that they cut the potatoes into 16 pieces and planted them. The next year they found that one of the plants had produced a crop of kidney-shaped potatoes with paper-thin skin and an excellent flavour. Thus was born the Jersey Royal.

During the potato harvest Jersey now exports around 1,500 tonnes a day to mainland Britain, providing the island with an industry worth about £35 million. This is their biggest crop export by far, and the potatoes can only be found in Britain and on Jersey itself. Jersey Royals are protected by the European Union in the same way as champagne and the apple brandy of Somerset, and can't be called Jersey Royals if grown anywhere else. This meant that when I was running Konstam at the Prince Albert I was unable to use them, but I was lucky enough to have an enterprising grower with an allotment who grew some of the same variety for me. There wasn't a great deal of them, and we had to call them Barnet Royals on the menu, but each year we had a brief flurry of new potatoes in May.

Jersey Royals taste so good that you barely have to do much more than boil them with a sprig of mint, drain them and slather them with melted butter and a decent pinch of salt – done like this, there's a reasonable chance they'll be the best thing on the plate. They are extremely good for potato salad too, and recipes for this break down into two main types: dressed with a vinaigrette, which can be served hot or cold, or with mayonnaise, sour cream or crème fraîche. Dressed new potatoes make a simple and delicious salad, but are best if tossed with the dressing while still a bit warm and then left to rest so they absorb the flavours. Chop some parsley and add it just before serving so it keeps its flavour and doesn't go grey.

When I worked at Rose Bakery in Paris in early 2003, we served a *salade tiède* of new potatoes, bacon and chicory. We would fry the bacon, warm the diced boiled potatoes and toss this mix with a red wine vinaigrette, sliced chicory and flat-leaf parsley while the bacon and potatoes were still hot. The salty bacon counters the sharpness of the slightly wilted but still crisp chicory and the waxy potatoes provide a perfect textural backdrop. You can throw in a few lightly roasted walnuts and a couple of chunks of blue cheese, but I do like the simplicity of the original. It's great on its own as a quick lunch or as an accompaniment to chicken or pollock.

A potato salad made with home-made mayonnaise is a joy. I like lots of herbs in mine and sprinkle chopped chives and parsley with abandon. A good potato salad always needs one or two ingredients that are sharp, salty and preferably crunchy. The list that makes a potato salad special is endless: spring onions, shallots, cornichons, gherkins, capers, mustard, horseradish, cayenne, anchovies, pickled walnuts, un-pickled walnuts, raisins … it goes on and on. And that's before you've combined it with other vegetables. Potato, beetroot and herring salad is a central and northern European classic my aunt Ellen (who is originally from Germany) makes at Christmas and other big family events. This is the recipe as she told it to me:

Ellen's potato, beetroot and herring salad

All the ingredients are approximate, so you'll need to experiment until you've got the balance right for your own taste buds, but basically think central European-Jewish. Also, the matjes herrings are only to be found where the Jewish-Polish-Russian population goes shopping. I go to the deli in Belsize Village – a lovely shop.

It would be worth talking to them about those herrings – they're different from the better-known pickled variety – steeped in oil and very tender.

Mix together:
8–10 matjes herrings, cut up
6 medium-sized cooked beetroots, roughly diced
2–3 large or 5 smaller Bramley apples, diced
6 sweet-sour pickled cucumbers (careful there, it might be too many)
Salad potatoes (i.e. ones that don't crumble)
Onion (chopped very fine)
Capers (a small jar, drained and rinsed)
Oil, vinegar (usually not much is needed), pepper, salt to taste
Chopped, hard-boiled egg to put on top

On reflection, this is a huge amount as it's for Christmas and we eat it over several days, or else invite lots of people over.

Another of my favourite potato salads is when you toss thoroughly cooked (a salad is no place for an underdone potato), halved and lightly crushed potatoes with chunks of hard-boiled egg, wholegrain mustard, mayonnaise, chopped anchovy, cracked black pepper, finely sliced spring onion or chives, and diced pickled walnuts. The flavours are amazing and the texture of the pickled walnut makes the whole thing work. I find that the dark, sweet-yet-vinegary brine in the jars of pickled walnuts is lovely in a whole host of dressings and meat sauces – a good drizzle in a dish of devilled kidneys is fabulous.

The emphasis of this book is firmly on fruit and vegetables since their range over the course of the year easily outweighs the variety of meat and fish. However, there are times when meat and fish come to the fore, and May is one of them. Some would say the lamb reared in the Black Mountains of Wales is the best in the land, others might say Dartmoor. In fact, they thrive across the British Isles and high-quality lamb is found all over the country. Keith and Liz at Stockings Farm near Amersham, just north-west of London, provided us with all the lamb we used at Konstam and it was always of incredibly high quality.

Sheep start giving birth around Easter time, so it's not until late April that the first of the new season lamb is available. Lambs born this early are generally forced through with a high-protein diet, and it's in May that the grass-fed lamb season really starts. Lambs continue to be born throughout the year, but most are born in the spring. New season lamb is the most tender and highly sought after, but as the year goes by their flavour develops, so although summer and autumn lamb is perhaps more delicious, the early lambs are very, very tender.

Lamb is called lamb until it's a year old, at which point it becomes hogget. When it is two years old it becomes mutton. As the sheep gets older its flavour develops, as does its texture. Some equate this to tougher meat, but I think this is the wrong term. Mutton is slightly denser but as long as it's of good quality it shouldn't be chewy or stringy.

A 2007 study by Lincoln University in Wellington, New Zealand, claimed that due to the scale on which lamb is produced there and the warmer climate leading to lower heating demands, lamb shipped by sea to the UK contributed less greenhouse gases than domestically reared lamb. It's a claim worthy of consideration, but when I read the report I saw that the data was incomplete and presented in ways that produced a skewed picture. Taking into account that it was effectively funded by the New Zealand government, there is enough to suggest it was published as a response to their lamb industry's fears of a backlash against global agriculture.

This report still crops up in the media and in general conversation, and it clearly strikes a chord with many. While it's important to take an objective approach to the issues of local and seasonal food and weigh up the pros and cons, especially when it comes to efficiency, I feel this kind of approach is in danger of missing the point. Sourcing food from all over the world without regard to locality or seasonality dislocates us from it and makes us see it as a commodity. My argument is that in order to make the right decisions about food and how it intersects with society and the economy we need to be as connected to it as we possibly can. As I mentioned earlier, the industrialised global food infrastructure might be more efficient than smaller, more localised food networks, but the amount of time, effort, money and political will that has been invested in this infrastructure over the past centuries is mind-boggling. Until we invest considerable resources into making seasonal and local food a priority it may well be that the rewards we stand to reap remain unattainable.

I'm pretty good at butchery, it's a side of my job I rather enjoy – I find it quite calming. Like baking bread, there's something fundamental about it. Although butchery has been a feature of my work for the past 20 years, some experiences stand out. At Brandt and Levie, some outstanding sausage-makers I know in Amsterdam, I spent a day working with them and a wonderful man who had been a butcher for 40 years. I was astounded by his sensitivity to even the smallest sinews and muscles deep within the meat – it was like he could see with the tip of his knife. And when I was doing my internship at Chez Panisse in California I spent a lot of time working in their beautiful kitchen on whole lamb, half pigs, quail, duck and chickens. I found these butchery sessions very grounding, in a way you don't often feel when you're abroad.

Lamb is incredibly versatile and goes with a huge range of flavours. The most classic pairing in this country is with garlic and rosemary, but it takes strong spices very well. Younger lamb, such as is available in May, needs less seasoning as the flavour is milder, but older lamb, hogget and mutton are all perfectly happy to take whatever you can throw at them.

I like matching mature lamb and cuts with more flavour, such as shoulder, with anchovy, a classic and often underused combination that works beautifully. The following recipe came about by necessity. It was late and I needed the lamb in the morning, so I put it in a very low oven overnight and hoped for the best. I knew it would be fine in theory, but turning off the lights and going to bed with something cooking in the oven felt rather unsettling. I woke up, still slightly anxious, and went to see how it was. It was perfect – moist and falling off the bone. Now I find the thought of it cooking away as I sleep a comforting one.

Despite the strong flavours in the rub they don't overpower as they mingle gently in the long, low heat of the oven. If serving the lamb in the evening, start cooking it in the morning; if it's for lunch, start the afternoon before. There isn't a massive amount of preparation time, but an hour or two marinating before going in the oven won't hurt.

Slow-cooked lamb shoulder with anchovies and celery

Serves 5–6

1 shoulder of lamb, skin on, bone in (about 2–2.5kg)

6 garlic cloves

6 anchovy fillets

1½ heaped tbsp capers

1 tbsp wholegrain or Dijon mustard

3 sprigs of fresh rosemary

1 head of celery

3 carrots

1 onion

2 bay leaves

1 sprig of thyme

1½ glasses white wine

Salt and freshly ground black pepper

Remove the lamb from the fridge and trim any excessively fatty bits, but don't be too severe as the fat keeps the meat moist and full of flavour. A lot of the fat melts during the cooking and is easily skimmed off the resulting juices.

Crush the garlic to a fine purée in a pestle and mortar with a teaspoon of salt. Strip and chop the rosemary and add it to the mortar with the anchovy and capers, and crush them all in too. Add the Dijon mustard and a good pinch of black pepper, and combine. This mixture is quite intense and should provide enough seasoning for the dish, but it all depends on the size of the lamb shoulder, so if you feel it might need a little more salt then add it now.

Rub the mixture over the lamb shoulder, making sure to massage it into the skin and any nooks and crannies. Cover and leave in the fridge for an hour or two.

Preheat the oven to 90°C. Trim and clean the celery, cut it into 3–4-inch lengths. Peel, trim and cut the carrots in half lengthwise and then into thirds. Peel and cut the onion into chunky wedges. Put the lamb into a generous baking tray and arrange the vegetables, bay leaves and thyme around it. Pour the wine in over the vegetables – don't let it wash the rub off the lamb. Scrunch up a piece of baking parchment large enough to cover the tray and run it under the tap. Gently squeeze it a few times and unfurl it, then put it over the lamb and the vegetables and tuck it in around the edges. Cover very tightly with tin foil.

Put the lamb in the oven and go to bed, or to work, or for a long walk. It's almost impossible to overcook the lamb at this temperature, so don't be scared to leave it for a long, long time – 8, 9 or even 10 hours will be fine.

Remove the lamb from the oven an hour and a half before you want to serve it. Check it's done and leave it to rest with the tin foil on for 30 minutes. Remove the vegetables but do not discard, then strain the liquid into a jug. Set this aside and leave to settle before skimming off the fat.

You can cook it to this stage well in advance – even a couple of days ahead. If you do, remove from the fridge for at least an hour to come up to room temperature before moving on to the next step. Leaving the juices – strained but unskimmed and unreduced – in the fridge overnight makes it very easy to remove the solidified fat that will rise to the surface.

Half an hour before you want to serve the lamb, preheat the oven to 220°C and cook for about 10 minutes or until the skin is golden brown. Heat the vegetables in the oven too.

Reduce the juices to thicken a little but keep an eye on the seasoning – it can easily become too salty.

Remove the lamb from the oven and pull the bones from the joint. They should come out very easily and it will pretty much fall apart at this point. Discard the bones and pull the meat into nice big chunks, discarding any large and unpleasant fat deposits. Transfer to a warm platter, cover with tin foil and leave to rest. Put the vegetables on the platter next to the lamb and drizzle some of the seasoned juices over the top of both. Serve the rest in a warm jug.

Be careful to serve everything nice and hot as cold lamb can be unappetising. Delicious with mashed potato and a fresh green salad.

Approached with sensitivity, the flavours of lamb and fish go well together in a variety of ways. In the past I've matched home-salted sprat (see February), shallot and parsley relish with leg of lamb. I've served all sorts of cuts with anchoïade, from shoulder to mutton chops, and I've paired braised shoulder with oyster, pea and baby onion sauce.

I haven't given carrots as much of my cooking love as I could have over the years. They do end up being taken for granted, but carrots are essential in stocks, stews, soups, sauces, salads, casseroles and all manner of dishes, though they rarely get the lead role and struggle to make their culinary mark. Despite this, I do have a couple of recipes up my sleeve and feel that roast carrots should get a mention. May is the time for baby carrots in sweet crunchy bunches. Roasted whole with just salt and oil and they really are good. When they get a bit bigger my favourite way of cooking them is to steam them with lots of butter and some sugar and salt until they're covered with a sweet, sticky glaze. Done like that they're called Vichy carrots and are traditionally cooked in the soft-water of Vichy, which is supposed to tenderise them.

Vichy carrots

This is one of those simple recipes that takes a little experience to get right. How they cook depends on a few factors that don't remain the same – freshness, size and age of the carrots, the size of the pan, the heat underneath it, the efficiency of the cartouche – not rocket science, but it always needs a spot of last-minute adjustment. I used to caramelise the butter and sugar more than I do now, preferring a sweeter result, but it can be nice to get a little bit more complexity from the sugar and butter if you like.

Serves 4
500g carrots
50g butter
1 tbsp sugar
Salt
1 sprig of parsley

Peel and cut the carrots into chunks. I do this by cutting them at an angle and rolling them about a third of a turn each time, so they end up a bit irregular and with several flat edges. You can cut them into thick slices but this makes the cooking time more precarious.

Put the carrots in a pan large enough to hold them in one layer, add the butter and the sugar and a good pinch of salt. Turn the heat up high and add enough water to come about halfway up the carrots. Crumple some baking parchment and run it under a tap, squeeze it a few times and then carefully unfold it. When the water is boiling, place the paper (known as a cartouche) over the carrots, tear a small hole in the middle and tuck it into the edges a little.

Wash and chop the parsley. Cook the carrots for about 10 minutes, until they're just starting to become tender, remove the cartouche and evaporate any remaining water over a high heat. As the water disappears, lower the heat and gently toss the carrots in the glaze left by the butter and sugar; this will take another 6–8 minutes. When the glaze has thickened and is covering the carrots nicely, toss in the parsley and serve.

—

I once ran a pop-up restaurant on Jersey with a friend of mine, India
Hamilton, during a film festival called Branchage. One of the dishes
on the menu was a scallop carpaccio with lemon, gin and thyme,
but we had vegetarian options for each course, and for this dish, to
replace the scallops, I decided to smoke some carrots and thinly slice
them. I was very pleased with how they turned out, slithery and
tender, with a delicate wisp of applewood smoke curling around the
sweetness of the carrot.

I had to come up with all sorts of salad recipes when I was running
the café. We had five different salads each day, and although there
were regular favourites we still needed variety and thinking of new
ideas wasn't always easy. One day I was feeling very unadventurous
and just grated some carrots, squeezed a whole load of lemon juice,
slopped in some olive oil, tossed it with salt and ground fennel seed
and put it out on the counter. Simple and easy but it turned out to
be very good.

Lovage is an underused herb and can be difficult to approach at
first, due to its strong and complex flavour. It's tender in May but
gets a little tougher and even more pungent as the season draws
on, so this is a great time to use it, especially if you're not used
to it. I distinctly remember the first time I tasted it, the unusual
combination of flavours – parsley, celery, aniseed and something
medicinal, almost like eucalyptus – completely turned my head.
I was instantly intrigued and wondered for some time how to use
it. It wasn't until a few years later – when I made a connection
with a growing project around the corner from the restaurant
and started raiding their patch – that I managed to incorporate
it into my cooking.

I'd been making persillade sauce – chopped parsley and garlic with olive oil – for some time and decided to switch the parsley with lovage, adding a little lemon zest for balance. I remembered that squid could take the force of chopped fresh chilli and wondered if cuttlefish would deal with lovage. We grilled it on the fantastic charcoal grill we had in the restaurant and found it worked perfectly.

Grilled cuttlefish with lemon and lovage dressing

It isn't always practical to cook over live coals, but the extra flavour really makes this dish. The punch of the garlic, the brightness of the lemon and the complex aromatics of the lovage all work perfectly with the richness of the smoky cuttlefish.

Ask your fishmonger to clean the cuttlefish for you, separating the tentacles from the body; it's a messy job and not one you're likely to want to do at home.

Serves 4
4 medium cuttlefish
20 lovage leaves
3 garlic cloves
Zest of ½ a lemon
8 tbsp olive oil
Salt and pepper
A couple of handfuls of rocket or frisée

If you're feeling adventurous, to prepare the cuttlefish at home, pull the cuttlefish heads from the bodies, scraping out any innards that remain, being careful not to break the little ink sac inside. Cut the tentacles from the head just below the eyes. Open the cuttlefish bodies down the seam. Pull off the wings and scrape the membrane from both sides. Score the inside surface of the body in a crosshatch pattern with the knife at an angle; this will allow the body to curl on the grill, keeping it moist as it cooks. Leave the tentacles whole, pulling off the outer membrane as much as possible.

Finely chop the lovage and garlic and zest the lemon. Combine with 4 tablespoons of olive oil and season.

Season the lemon juice with salt and add the other 4 tablespoons of oil to make a simple lemon dressing.

When your charcoal, or griddle, is hot, season the cuttlefish with salt and just a little pepper and grill until it turns opaque – a couple of minutes on each side but no longer. If you overcook it the flesh will become tough.

Remove from the grill and serve with the lovage dressing spooned over the top and the rocket with lemon dressing on the side.

Cuttlefish was something of a feature on my restaurant menu. I love squid almost as much as octopus, but until we opened the restaurant I hadn't really eaten cuttlefish. I knew about them from finding their smooth, white, oblong skeletons on the beach as a child, but I didn't know you could eat them. Due to the arrangement we had with Ben's Fish on Mersea Island we occasionally ended up working with fish that were less well known at the time, such as cuttlefish, skate, dab and grey mullet. Again, it was a sourcing policy that presented us with some headaches but which also led to many happy accidents.

While there is a clear and distinct season for oranges grown in any one spot – the trees flower and fruit just once a year – this isn't quite the case for lemons. Lemon trees flower and ripen concurrently, so you'll often see blooms and fruit on the tree at the same time. They are quite happy in the cooler parts of the year too, which means they have an extended season. When this is depends on where you are, and in Europe the best lemons are found on the

Amalfi Coast in southern Italy. The season there runs for most of the year, ebbing and flowing from March or earlier through to November. It's said that the best part of the season is from May to September, hence their arrival at this point in the book.

Lemons don't need a great deal of heat to ripen. They can be grown in the UK, but our climate isn't ideal so the flavour will be lacking in comparison to lemons grown in sunnier countries. This being the case, they don't warrant much of a place in the British seasonal calendar, despite our love for them and their immense contribution to our culinary adventures. The main reason I'm weaving them into the story is to include two of my favourite recipes. One is a classic British dessert, lemon posset. Starting out as a variant of a syllabub, posset is probably the easiest recipe you'll ever come across. It goes very well with shortbread, and I think it's nicest with a couple of stewed gooseberries plonked on top.

Lemon posset

Lemon posset is the most elegant of desserts, and one of the quickest to make – excellent for low-stress late spring and early summer dinner parties. The tartness of the lemon is underpinned by the richness of the just set cream and the end result is surprisingly light. How tart you want it is up to you – too sweet and it can become cloying, but an extra spoon of sugar works when serving it with another tart fruit, such as bottled gooseberries or rhubarb compote.

Serves 6–8
300ml double cream
75g caster sugar
2 lemons

Remove the zest from one of the lemons, then juice both. Place the zest and juice in a saucepan along with the sugar and cream. Heat gently, stirring occasionally, until gently boiling. Simmer for 3 minutes then pour into serving glasses and chill until set.

The other recipe I want to mention definitely needs to be in this book, and the only place it fits is in this section. My grandmother, Nancy Farquharson, née Konstam, was a formidable character who could be strict and dismissive, inclusive and charming in equal measure. She had one of the best memories I've ever come across and loved to tell me about her past. Unfortunately my memory isn't as good, so I've forgotten most of the stories she told me, but I haven't forgotten that her favourite dessert was castle puddings. These are little sponge cakes made in dariole moulds and served, while still warm from the oven, with a lemon zest and golden syrup sauce. They first appear in the *Radiation 'New World' Cookery Book*, a thick, hardback tome that came with a particular model of cooker manufactured in the 1920s and 1930s. My copy of the book, which I inherited from my grandmother, was published in 1937 and was the 18th edition. I used to serve these little puddings as Castle Cakes in my café, and have used this sponge recipe in numerous guises since.

When my grandmother passed away in 2007 I was asked to read at her funeral. This was a great honour as she had a huge circle of friends and a lot of relatives. She was buried on her 100th birthday and left behind 21 great-grandchildren. I cast around me for what to read and quickly settled on this recipe. When I mentioned the book it had come from and then asked how many people still had a copy, three people put up their hands – 70 or so years after the book was published.

Nan didn't only give me this recipe, of course; she gave me many things, tangible and intangible, but perhaps the most significant was her name, or rather her maiden name. It was her brother who changed it from Kohnstamm to the simpler and more manageable Konstam in the 1950s, but it was through her that I came to it and it was the name I used for my café and my restaurant. I did this partly because I liked the Jewish deli names you get in New York and I wanted something that resonated with this, but mainly because I wanted a name that was steeped in the idea of family, that represented my belief in food being at the heart of community; and I wanted to make a place that felt like home to as many people as possible. Konstam fitted the bill perfectly and so that's why I used my grandmother's name, and that was why I read the recipe at her funeral.

This is how the recipe was first published (it serves 6):

Castle Puddings

2 ozs. butter
3 ozs. flour
2 ozs. sugar
1 egg
½ teaspoonful baking powder
Little milk

Cream the butter and sugar together, beat in the egg, add flour and
baking powder, and lastly a little milk. Pour into greased dariol
moulds which may be decorated with pieces of cherry and angelica
according to taste.

All I can add to this is to make sure you really cream the butter and
sugar, sieve the flour with the baking powder and learn to gauge the
milk by eye as it never seems to be quite the same amount – 35ml
is a good starting point – the mixture should be stiff but still have
a little give. Grease your moulds well and preheat the oven to
220°C, turning it down to 180°C as soon as you put the puddings
in. They'll need about 20 minutes.

My grandmother's housekeeper, Lore, who I talk about in the
December chapter, always used to serve it with golden syrup
warmed through with lemon zest. I use the zest of half a lemon
with 150 millilitres of golden syrup, heated until thin and quite
hot, but not boiling, then left, preferably in a warm place for half
an hour or so. Make this before you make the puddings and then
reheat before serving.

May trundles on. It starts off slowly but soon gathers momentum
until, usually quite late in the month, the broad beans arrive. When
they arrive you really know that the wait is over. From now until
late winter there's a new crop of fruit or vegetables every week or so.

Broad beans are immensely versatile and one of the oldest-known
cultivated plants, originating in the Fertile Crescent and the eastern
Mediterranean. They are pretty easy to grow and survive well in
harsh landscapes. They can be found in culinary use across most of
Europe, much of the Middle East, North Africa, China, Pakistan,
Latin America and North America. To many they are dried and
known as fava beans, the main ingredient in Egypt's national dish,
ful medames. Falafels are generally made from fava beans, although
they're often made from chickpeas too. In cooler, wetter climates,
when drying beans on the vine isn't an option, broad beans are eaten

fresh, preferably when they're young and tender. Much of the time they are blanched and then popped out of the somewhat bitter outer pod. Once they reach a certain age they're almost inedible fresh, becoming crumbly and tannic. It's at this point they are only good for drying, but there isn't often enough sunshine in the UK to do this reliably.

I love broad beans, especially the little ones. Heralding, as they do, the start of the summer produce there is an excitement about eating the first ones each year, and a certain reverence in the cooking that you don't get from many foods. When they're super-fresh, just off the vines and very young, they can be eaten raw, sprinkled on or run through a salad, stirred into a risotto to cook in its heat, or put in the bottom of a bowl before pouring broth. Broad bean and ham soup is delicious, and broad bean purée goes with all sorts of things – it's great as a substitute for mushy peas with battered fish.

Broad beans are also good tossed with loads of herbs, hazelnuts and cooked barley, or stirred into spätzle with cream and sorrel or dill. Spätzle is an uneven noodle that comes from Germany and Alsace, and we used to cook it a great deal at Konstam; I liked it as it fitted into our northern European culinary remit. I'd chosen this area as I didn't want to be chasing after the produce to make Mediterranean dishes, pulling my local sourcing policy all out of shape. Therefore we took the geographical area that relied on the same produce as we grow near London – this meant the UK, Ireland, northern France, Germany, Austria, Switzerland, the Czech Republic, Hungary, Slovakia, Poland, the Low Countries and Scandinavia. We didn't quite get round to mastering the cuisines of all these countries, but it was an interesting mix and one with a certain gastronomic communality. These areas don't have that many light carbohydrate options. Rice is off limits, as are most types of pasta. Dumplings are found all over the region but tend to be very heavy. Pierogi from Poland were a godsend, and the Alsace provided us with some options too – not only flammekueche, a sort of pizza bianca, but also spätzle, which I was over the moon to discover.

Spätzle, or spaetzle, are a type of noodle native to a swathe of central Europe starting in the Alsace and moving east through Swabia, Switzerland, Austria and Hungary. They come in varying shapes and sizes, depending on the technique or equipment used to make them. The traditional way is to flick pieces of wet pasta dough from a board into boiling water, but this is tricky to master so most households will have a special press for pushing the dough through. I use a piping bag – disposable ones are perfect. Or you can use the top section of a steamer, pushing the dough through the holes with a spatula, but it can be difficult to get them the right length. A potato ricer with a wide plate setting is also an option. Spätzle are made in batches that take very little time to cook, and if making enough for several people each batch is refreshed in cold water and then the whole lot is reheated in one go. Once made they can be combined with any number of other ingredients to make a main dish, or simply served with melted butter to accompany schnitzel, beef, chicken, fish or pork. They're also great served with stew to soak up the juices.

Spätzle with broad beans and lovage

Serves 4 as a side, or 2–3 as a main with green salad

200g plain flour

A pinch of ground fennel seed or nutmeg

¼ tsp salt

2 whole eggs

40–50ml cold whole milk – the amount depends on the water content of the flour and the size of the eggs

1 small onion

75g butter

100g cooked and double-podded broad beans

3 tbsp crème fraîche

10–15 lovage leaves

We used to make this in big batches by hand and developed a vigorous paddling, kneading action that was very tiring but gave a good result, folding air in as we went. You can make it in the bowl of a mixer with a dough hook – the result is just as good and much more efficient for smaller quantities.

Put the flour, spice and salt into the mixer and crack the eggs into a well in the centre. Add half the milk and set the mixer on its lowest speed. Add more milk after a while as necessary. The texture of the dough should be loose and glossily wet, more than sticky, almost like a very slow-moving liquid. You should be able to see the glutinous strands being stretched as the mixer works. The dough is ready when you start to see bubbles as the mixer pulls at the dough; this will take 10–15 minutes. Be careful not to over-knead it.

Put the dough into a piping bag with a plain, unfluted 3mm nozzle if you're using a classic piping bag; trim later if using disposable. Tie the end and leave to rest in the fridge for at least 20 minutes. If using a spätzle press or other such paraphernalia, set to rest in the fridge in a covered bowl. The dough can be made ahead to this point and cooked later, but the cooked result keeps well in the fridge for a day or two, so I would recommend reaching this stage before leaving them.

Take the dough from the fridge and leave it to come back to room temperature for 10 minutes.

Put a pan of water on – the biggest you have is a good bet, two-thirds full – salt it well and bring to a vigorous boil. Set a big bowl of cold water next to the cooker and get your spider or slotted spoon ready.

Cleanly cut off just the very end of the piping bag, leaving a 3mm hole, and hold the bag over the water, about a foot from the surface, and start to squeeze the dough from the bag. Be careful not to cut too much off the nozzle of the bag or they will be fat and undercooked. If the hole is too small and the dough doesn't come out, cut another slither of plastic from the tip of the bag and try again. The dough will relax a little as you hold it over the pan – the heat from below and from your hands will warm it quite quickly, meaning it will get looser as you go. You want a fairly steady stream of dough to come out of the bag, snapping just at the point it hits the water. If you hold it too low you'll end up with long spätzle worms, which aren't right at all, and if you hold it too high the dough will snap and spring back and end up too short and stubby. Experiment with different heights before going for a whole batch.

If using a spätzle press it will be a lot easier, but a little experimentation might still be needed to get the height required.

Cook until they rise to the top and then a couple of seconds more; this takes about 2–3 minutes. Scoop out with a spider, slotted spoon or small sieve, then immediately put them in the bowl of cold water.

Make the noodles in 3 or 4 batches, depending on the size of your pan and the speed of your technique. Drain the spätzle, toss in a bowl with a little oil and place in the fridge.

Dice the onion. Heat half the butter in a small saucepan and sauté the onion with a pinch of salt until soft and golden brown. In a large frying pan, heat the rest of the butter over a medium heat until it stops frothing, put the spätzle in and fry until the noodles take on some golden brown bits, then toss in the onion, broad beans and add the crème fraîche. Toss and cook a little more until the crème fraîche starts to thicken and coat the noodles, then add the chopped lovage. If it looks a little dry, add another tablespoon of crème fraîche. Season, stir to mix and serve.

You can make a good early summer bruschetta by podding some blanched broad beans, mashing half of them with a fork, then adding the rest with plenty of olive oil, lemon zest, seasoning and mint. Dollop this onto freshly toasted Pugliese-style sourdough, crumble on a bit of goat's cheese, tear a few mint leaves over them and add a drizzle of the best olive oil you can lay your hands on. A small amount of really good oil can make or break dishes like this and it's worth investing in.

Broad beans, the first of the spring-sown deluge, signal the change of season, ushering out the spring and calling hail to the summer. Their arrival is the start of the flurry and from here on out there's abundance. It also means the beginning of the jamming, pickling and preserving that makes the bareness of winter and the solitude of spring a little more bearable. We started the month in austerity, but the food recession has drawn to a close and the wealth of June is upon us at last.

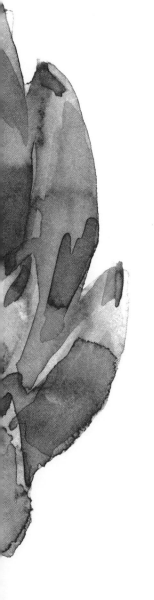

JUNE

—

Onions

Peas

Pea shoots

Bean sprouts

Lettuce

Courgette flowers

Artichokes

Beetroot

Strawberries

Cherries

Gooseberries

Mackerel

I realised

*June had never been
just a month*

*music . . .
never just a tremble
on my lips*

*warmth was never
merely a blanket.*

Sanober Khan

June is a happy time in the seasonal food calendar – there is a steady flow of new produce cropping up between now and the end of October. We can heave a sigh of relief and start thinking about what we want to cook, instead of fretting over whether we have anything to cook with. While there are a great deal of fresh vegetables and lots of fruit, one of the wonders of the season is the array of alliums, the family onions, garlic and leeks belong to. If you're lucky, and know the right people, you can find four or five different types of onion around now. There are the usual white onions (the UK ones tending to be a little stronger than the big ones from Spain), red onions, shallots and spring onions. We also have Welsh onions, which are like spring onions but bigger; in France they call them *grelot*, and in Spain they're similar to calçots – a vegetable so revered the Spanish hold festivals to celebrate its season. In all their forms, onions are one of the lynchpins of the kitchen and deserve a good mention in this book.

—

When I was a teenager, long before I had any notion of becoming a chef, I struggled with the best way to chop an onion. I remember an advert for Marks and Sparks that showed some perfectly chopped onion and I would watch it transfixed. My knife skills at this point were extremely limited, but I was keen to learn. At the age of 16 I remember asking a friend who was working in a kitchen how to cut up an onion. He seemed surprised that I was interested, but for me it was fascinating. I had an inquisitive mind in general, but looking back I realise I probably thought more about food than most boys my age. My cooking escapades weren't that frequent or grandiose, but they were a tangible part of my youth, and it seems onions were a part of my burgeoning chef brain.

Cooking onions is one of the great arts of the kitchen, and I've only met a handful of cooks and chefs who are really skilled at it. It must also be understood that there is no 'wrong' way to cook onions, since all their many different flavours and textures have a place, but used without care and consideration these flavours can easily be out of place or inappropriate. The potential of the onion flavour in a dish is often ignored or its importance underestimated, which means that the cook can either miss out on an important element or inadvertently incorporate a flavour.

Most good soups begin with a base of carefully cooked onions – they provide the round, savoury sweetness that all the other flavours rest on. There's no point in just throwing onions and other ingredients into a pot with some water, leaving them to boil and then blending them. With enough seasoning and cream you might get something edible, but the taste of an onion develops very little by boiling; soup made like this will just taste half-cooked. Not every soup needs deep flavours and powerfully caramelised onions, you just need to take care to get the onions to the right point before you add any liquid.

Onions are high in sugar, of which the majority is glucose, one of the key sugars we absorb in our diet. Boiling onions softens their flavour but it doesn't caramelise the glucose, which intensifies the sweetness and gives depth. This roundness is what skilfully caramelised onions bring to a dish and it is this that makes them so special. Simply adding sugar would add sweetness but is no substitute for the complexity of caramelised glucose. If you're cooking lots of onions use a wide enough pan that they form a layer no more than an inch or so deep, and make sure the oil is very hot before placing the onions in the pan – the water the onions release will start to evaporate immediately and they won't stew. The steam this produces will also help get the cooking off to a quick start. If you're using butter you have to be very temperature conscious and cook them at a more gentle heat.

I learned a great deal about cooking onions from making tortillas. Tortilla is a very simple recipe, but to make a really good one you need to make sure that each of the three major ingredients is just right. The onions must be really well cooked, very soft and well caramelised but without being jammy, and they need to be sliced quite thin so that they almost disappear into the mix.

Although I often bang on about slicing onions across the grain to increase their tenderness, in Chinese and other Asian cooking styles onions are frequently sliced from top to bottom so they retain their shape. This is ideal for rapid cooking and perfect for stir-fry – it also gives a range of flavours and textures as the thicker bits cook differently to the thinner bits at the end of the slice. And I'm very happy for a salad to have raw onion in it, I just don't want that taste in my soups.

The more you cook onions the more intense the caramel flavour. Some of my favourite soups come later in the year when celeriac, parsnips and squashes come to the fore, and then you can really dig into the onions, cooking them until they're really sweet. In June the soup ingredients are more delicate, such as peas or broad beans, so you need to be a little more careful with your alliums, bringing out a more delicate sweetness and allowing subtle traces of their piquancy to remain.

Pea and bacon soup

Serves 4

700g fresh peas

3 garlic cloves

1 celery stick

1 carrot

3 onions

1 bay leaf

50g butter

6 rashers of streaky bacon

2 sprigs mint

1 little gem lettuce

Crème fraîche or sour cream to serve

Salt and pepper

Pod the peas and place the pods in a saucepan with the garlic, roughly chopped celery, peeled and chopped carrot, 1 onion, peeled and roughly chopped, and the bay leaf. Cover with cold water. Bring to the boil, simmer for 15 minutes and leave to stand.

Meanwhile, chop the other 2 onions and melt the butter in a medium saucepan. Add the onions and cook, stirring frequently, over a medium flame until translucent and light golden brown – don't let them caramelise too much. Matchstick the bacon and then add two-thirds to the pan. Continue cooking for another 5 minutes until the bacon is cooked through and tender.

Add the peas, and enough pea stock to cover, and bring to a boil. Immediately reduce the heat and simmer until the peas are tender but still nice and green – this depends on how fresh the peas are and may take up to 10 minutes.

When they're cooked, blitz until smooth. You can pass it through a sieve if you want it really smooth. Season with salt and pepper. Add more reserved pea stock or a dash of milk to thin if required. Return to pan and reheat, but don't boil. This can be cooked up to a day or two in advance to this point.

So serve, fry the rest of the bacon with a little oil until the fat has rendered and it's crispy. Lift from the pan with a slotted spoon and leave to cool on a piece of kitchen paper.

Pick, wash and roughly chop the mint.

Wash, dry and shred the lettuce. Share this between the bowls you're serving the soup in then pour in the hot soup.

Put a dollop of crème fraîche or sour cream in the middle and scatter the mint and crispy bacon.

As this recipe indicates, June is when the peas get going. Peas are lovely, and fresh peas are even lovelier, but before we come to them I want to say something about the lettuce in the last recipe. Braised peas with shredded lettuce stirred through towards the end of cooking is straight out of the classics. Simply braise the peas with lardons, a dash of Noilly Prat, and wilt some shredded romaine or little gem into them for a quick and delicious dish or accompaniment. Many cooks would use a softer, round lettuce, but I like the wilty crunch the romaine or little gem bring to it. I love using lettuce this way as it adds an indefinable something to the dish and brings it alive. If you really want to push the boat out, a dollop of crème fraîche on top, a sprinkle of chunky breadcrumbs and some chopped chervil will finish it off nicely.

Peas are every child's favourite green vegetable. They're unthreatening because they're small and round, and there is a poem, often attributed to Ogden Nash, about them sticking to his knife with honey, which is a bit irreverent and therefore appealing to children. I think peer group conversation may have something to do with so many children losing an early acquired taste for varied food, but somehow the pea seems to stay in fashion as we grow up. Peas are easy to grow and freeze very well, making them a convenient year-round source of greenery, and although it can be time-consuming there's something quite fun about podding them.

With peas come pea shoots – and I don't mean bean sprouts, I mean pea shoots (the tips of young snow pea plants). These have, to my knowledge, only recently been grown in the UK, although I wouldn't be surprised if they've been doing so forever in China and other parts of Asia. Pea shoots look great and you can pop them into salads for a lovely texture and a subtle pea-flavoured hint. When they get a little bigger you can sauté them with butter and vermouth – excellent on toast with poached eggs.

While we're on the subject of shoots, it's worth mentioning that the majority of bean sprouts used in London are grown in London, in a warehouse in Park Royal. I've seen huge pallets of them at the Chinese trader stalls in New Spitalfields Market. Apparently, the man who founded this bean-sprout factory, Joseph Pao, is something of a germination genius and has dedicated his life to industrial scale bean-sprout production. Bean sprouts of all descriptions were a bit of a health food fad in the 1970s, and with good reason: sprouted beans are extremely nutritious considering their high water content, with a very high protein level – over 35 per cent – making them a useful alternative to meat or dairy. They also provide calcium, phosphorous, B vitamins, vitamin C and iron, and we're able to absorb the minerals in them more easily than from many other plants because of an enzyme reaction they undergo during germination. The sprout fad has definitely returned in recent years and we now have quite a range. I particularly like radish sprouts; they look amazing – all purple and curly – and have the same peppery flavour they get when they've grown into radishes.

The end of May and the start of June both shout 'salad', as this is when we start harvesting not just fresh young vegetables like peas, broad beans and salad onions but when we start cutting lettuces too. Nothing tells us that spring has arrived like a good salad. I once saw Alice Waters, head chef at Chez Panisse, and her daughter, Fanny, give a cookery demonstration in San Francisco about how to make a green salad. They took a good 40 minutes explaining how to wash and dry the salad and make a basic vinaigrette. Despite the sparse subject matter their talk was enthralling and it really brought home the idea that it's the simple things in cooking that are the most important — if you pay attention to these, the rest will follow naturally.

Lettuce is supposed to have a slightly soporific effect. It contains two chemicals — lactucarium and hyoscyamine — in very small quantities, both of which can cause mild drowsiness. This effect isn't noticeable in a salad, but a whole head of lettuce before bed is said to be sleep-inducing. It's also said that bathing babies in water with lettuce leaves helps them sleep. I first read about this in Laura Esquivel's novel *Like Water for Chocolate* but haven't really come across it again, except for some quite amusing posts on Mumsnet.

On the whole, lettuces grow very well in the cooler climate of the UK, but they're very susceptible to drought, and slugs and snails love them, so they need a lot of care. It's great how ready to eat they are once they're grown — just step outside with a small knife, lop them off at the root, give them a wash and they're ready. Washing lettuces really needs a gentle hand and lots of water. I pick the leaves off, place them in a sink or big basin of very cold water, give them a gentle shake, then leave them for a few minutes to crisp up before lifting them out and placing them in a colander to drain.

Once you've washed and dried your lettuce, you can make a vinaigrette. I like it with a little garlic, well crushed with a generous pinch of salt in a pestle and mortar, some Dijon mustard, red wine or cider vinegar, more salt if required, pepper and some good quality olive oil. You can make dressings with rapeseed oil — it works very well with dishes such as cabbage salads — but I think olive oil has a better all-round flavour. It's very important not to make the dressing too weak. Season the mixture before you add the oil to get the balance of flavours just right, and then add just enough oil so that you still get a punchy acidity coming through and you can taste the rest of the flavours. Many people put a touch of sugar in too. Alice and her daughter said between 3 and 5 parts oil to other ingredients – and that's certainly a punchy dressing. You'll find the ratio varies when making lemon dressing, so start at 3:1 and work your way up. Again, season the lemon juice with salt before adding the oil.

When I was little I couldn't stand the sharpness of salad dressing and the bitterness of lettuce, so I wasn't really a salad lover. Now I have a particularly sour tooth and am a fiend for pickles, chutneys and the like, so a good sharp dressing appeals to me.

Recipes that involve cooking lettuce are unusual and I'm attracted to their rarity. Of course, you can simply braise whole heads of lettuce; little gem or the hearts of romaine are perfect for this as they hold their shape just enough to prevent a mushy and inedible mess. I once came across an Escoffier dish, in one of my favourite recipe books, *A Taste of France* by the photographer Robert Freson, which is filled with amazing and elaborate still lifes of food and ingredients, where sea bass fillets are wrapped in blanched lettuce leaves before poaching. I was immediately intrigued by it and served it for a while at Maquis in Hammersmith, where I was head chef for a year. It took a while to get the seasoning and the wrapping of the leaves right, but once we did it was delicious, the slightly slimy lettuce adding wonderful texture to each mouthful of fish. A few new potatoes to go with it and some of the poaching liquid and you have a very elegant summer dish.

Courgettes come a little later in the year, but they produce flowers in June. The Italians love them, and although we're using them more and more over here it's taken us a while to cotton on, especially considering how well the plants grow in the UK. In Italy the flowers are traditionally stuffed with ricotta, tomatoes and herbs before being lightly battered and deep-fried. At Konstam we used a local blue cheese called Norbury Blue, which was a little heavy on taste for the delicate flowers but it oozed out on the plate in a very satisfying fashion. Since then I've used goat's curd and home-made soft cheese, as well as more classic ricotta fillings. At Salt Yard in Goodge Street they use a Spanish goat's cheese called Monte Enebro and drizzle the courgette flowers with mountain honey just before serving.

The courgette plant produces a male and a female flower, and although both can be used it's the female ones that are most sought after. The best time to crop these is when the petals are still firm and a baby courgette has formed at the base. This little bit of courgette not only tastes great but makes them easier to handle when stuffing and frying. Male flowers can be cooked but the petals tend to be a mite tougher. I think they're good unstuffed, simply battered and deep-fried using the same tempura for the stuffed female flowers. Great as an antipasto or tapa, they also go very well with fish. This is the batter I use.

Batter for courgette flowers

100g plain flour
50g cornflour
12g baking powder
Ice cubes
Soda water

Chill the soda water in the fridge. Mix the flours and baking powder with a whisk – don't sieve them. This mixture lasts forever, so you don't need to use it all in one go.

Pour the soda water over a few ice cubes, then immediately pour it into the flour leaving the ice cubes behind, while very gently whisking. You want it to have a coating consistency but not too runny and not stodgy, a little like thick double cream. Don't worry if it isn't smooth – in fact, this is desirable as the lumps explode in the hot oil and this action is one of the things that gives a crisp finish to the end result. Let the batter rest in the fridge for 10–20 minutes, then use while still cold.

~✒︎✒︎~

Although it has very little place in traditional British cooking, largely because it doesn't grow as well here as in warmer climes, we have very much taken the artichoke to heart. This is mainly down to the popularity of Mediterranean food in the last couple of decades – both for its simple use of fresh ingredients, making it accessible to the home cook, and because of its perceived health benefits in comparison with heavy northern European cuisines. The Italians and French hold the artichoke in particularly high esteem, but it's also prized in North Africa, on the other side of the Mediterranean. Just as the food from all these cultures has had a significant impact on our own, both recently and historically, so the artichoke is fast becoming a more regular feature of our kitchens and our gardens.

The few childhood memories I have of artichokes are of eating them boiled whole, peeling the leaves off one by one and dipping them in as much melted butter as possible. I loved scraping the frugal flesh from the leaves but found the heart a bit much to take, partly because of the hairy choke which was too much of a challenge for my little fingers, but also because I wasn't so sure about the texture – soft, smooth but also stringy in places. I can't help but think there was also something about the disappointing easiness of it after all the struggle for scrapings among the thorny leaves. Occasionally you'd get a few slices of grilled, preserved artichoke heart from a jar on a pizza, but on the whole they were seen as relatively exotic. Nowadays, however, they feel very familiar and we know so much more about how to cook them.

I remember cooking them with Jacob Kenedy, of Bocca di Lupo, and his family in Sperlonga, Italy. We trimmed them, then filled the scraped-out hearts with a mixture of crushed garlic and chopped parsley, seasoned them well, turned them upside-down, placed them in a saucepan with an inch of white wine and a couple of millimetres of olive oil and placed a parchment cartouche over the top. We simmered them until the wine boiled away and the rims of the hearts went crispy in the olive oil. When cooked like this the Italians call them *carciofi alla giudia*, or Jewish artichokes, a speciality of Roman-Jewish cuisine, although I think they're usually more deeply fried than the ones we made. Nonetheless they were superb and were received with great compliments from Jacob's family.

Artichokes, *Cynara scolymus*, are a type of cardoon and part of the thistle family. Each artichoke is an unopened flower bud – the leaves we peel off and strip with our teeth aren't petals but bracts, a specialised type of leaf that usually forms beneath, or cups, the flower. The petals, tucked deep inside at the point when we eat them, are thin and purple like those of the thistle, and when it's in flower you can see how closely related they are. The heads of cardoons, though spinier and less fleshy, can be eaten in the same way.

Due to our cool climate artichokes aren't grown extensively in this country and it can be difficult to get good results, but I hear that Guy Watson at Riverford Organics tends personally to the small crop they have there, and I know from experience that they produce very good ones. My sister and several of my friends grow them, so clearly it can be done. Even if they don't bear good fruit, they look fantastic. Owing to their sunnier climes the Spanish, French and Italian seasons are earlier than ours, and the Turkish season is earlier still, so good ones are available to buy from spring but the harvest peaks in summer.

Most recipes for artichokes require only the heart, but there's no getting away from the fact that they're a pain to prepare. There are lots of different ways to go about this. The edible part forms a sort of cup shape in the middle of the globe and you need to find a way of trimming away the rest of it – painstaking and fiddly. Making a dish of artichokes at home need not take hours, but when you have to prepare enough for restaurant use this may mean several boxes, so learning how to prepare them quickly becomes a necessity. Seeing as the flesh is so important, it's vital not to trim them too hard, but if you don't trim them enough you end up with tough, stringy bits.

Almost every chef I know has a slightly different approach, but my method is as follows: first break the outer leaves off at the base, until you start to see the shape of the cup. If the stalks are very woody snap them off, otherwise cut them off two or three inches from the base of the heart. Then I get a small, very sharp knife or a peeler and peel the strings from the sides of the stalk, and finally I trim back the hard, stringy green flesh from around the bowl of the artichoke heart. I use a teaspoon to scoop out the hairy choke in the middle of the heart. Have a large bowl of water ready with lemons squeezed into it to keep the prepared hearts in while tackling the next ones. This prevents them from discolouring. It doesn't hurt to wear latex gloves while doing this job as it will discolour your skin and leave a bitter and hard to remove taste on your fingers.

This is the first stage to a multitude of artichoke recipes. Grilled and marinated in oil they make a classic antipasto, and they're great lightly braised with garlic and tossed in a salad, or stirred into paellas, pilafs and risottos. You can make them into an extravagant soup, and they're divine stuffed or cooked as in the recipe on pages 250–1. You can also shave them raw to add a crunch to a summer salad.

June is thoroughly spoiled, and not only by some of the food year's seasonal fly-bys – it's also when many of the root vegetables start to come into season. Beetroot is among them, and you'll notice it crop up throughout the book. Partly because its growing season is long and it can be eaten at any point along the way – from micro herb, through its baby stage to mature plant – but also because it stores so well once harvested. This means you can cook with it all year round, but for flavour and freshness you can't really beat the small bunches of bright purple beetroot with hard flesh that start hitting the farmer's markets around now.

As well as many healthy vitamins and minerals, beetroot is high in a compound called geosmin. This is the chemical that gives beetroot its earthy taste and aroma, and is the same substance that gives earth its distinctive smell. It also finds its way into river fish and sometimes wine. We are incredibly sensitive to it, detecting it in concentrations as low as 5 to 10 parts in a trillion. It appears that we developed this sensitivity because it is present around water, and it's thought that camels have an even higher sensitivity to it than we do, allowing them to detect water from up to 50 miles away. Geosmin breaks down in acidic conditions, and this is the reason why the earthy taste often caused by the presence of the compound in some freshwater fish is countered by wiping or rinsing with vinegar. It may also be why we like beetroot cooked or served with vinegar; it mellows the geosmin and brings out the other flavours.

Because of its year-round availability beetroot has been a mainstay of my kitchen for several years, finding its way into scores of dishes from salads, soups, canapés and starters to main courses and even a few desserts. I couldn't really pick my favourite, but I do love it and find it to be one of the most versatile vegetables around. There is a beetroot and orange recipe in the February chapter, and it comes up in a couple of other chapters, but this is its seasonal starting point. One way I've served it in June is tossed through a warm salad with lightly roasted red onion and thyme.

Beetroot and red onion go so well together, both flavour-wise and visually. This is a roast version of a salad I've made a million times over the years. Thyme works well in this recipe, but I also love beetroot with marjoram – cook some beetroot as described on page 34 and let them cool in the cooking water, then peel and chop them into chunks, slice or dice some red onion into them, dress with red wine or cider vinegar, olive oil, salt, pepper and some freshly picked marjoram and you have a fantastic summer salad.

This salad is great as part of a summer lunch or served warm with almost any meat or fish at any time of the year. It stipulates Cabernet Sauvignon vinegar (the sweet variety), which will make any salad sing; standard red wine vinegar will be fine, but add a teaspoon of honey to the recipe.

Beetroot and red onion salade tiède

Serves 4
4 or 5 medium beetroot – about 600g raw
2 or 3 red onions – about 600g unpeeled
100–150ml olive oil
1½ tbsp Cabernet Sauvignon vinegar
2 sprigs thyme
2 garlic cloves
1 tsp Dijon mustard
Salt and pepper

Preheat the oven to 220°C. Put the onions, unpeeled, into a baking dish and roast whole for about 15–20 minutes, until softened but not collapsed – the idea is that they have some sweetness but also some crunch. Remove from the oven and leave to cool – they'll continue to cook a little. When cool enough to handle, but still warm, pull off the peel and cut into 1-cm wedges lengthwise.

While the onions are cooking and cooling, make a dressing with the vinegar, 4½ tablespoons of olive oil, salt and pepper and the mustard. Strip off the thyme leaves and add them. If serving immediately, while still warm, crush and add the garlic. Otherwise, leave until later. Toss the warm onions with the dressing and set aside.

Peel the beetroot and cut it into large bite-size chunks or wedges. Toss in a bowl with a couple of tablespoons of olive oil and some

salt. Spread out on parchment on a baking tray and roast for 20
minutes or so, agitating occasionally and turning the tray. They
should be nicely caramelised and tender. Remove from the oven and
leave to cool for a second, then lift out of the tray and toss with the
onions. If using warm at this point, let the flavours mingle a bit,
toss again and serve. Otherwise, set aside to cool and then toss in
the crushed garlic.

Although it's only now that many of the vegetables we associate
with spring are being harvested, the fruits that start to come
through in June belong to summer. Think of strawberries and you
think of summer. They always make me think of Wimbledon,
even though I'm a transient tennis fan and most years only watch
a few significant matches. Nonetheless, tennis and strawberries
are a classic combination etched on our social almanac by years
of tradition.

I've always preferred raspberries to strawberries, but the strawberries
come earlier and are more ubiquitous over the course of the summer.
The boundaries of the strawberry season have become somewhat
blurred over the last decade or so – although the British season is
relatively short and runs from late May to the end of July, they are
now available all year round, and you can buy strawberries from the
UK for a large part of it too. This is a massive bone of contention
for me since it's only possible because of growers using heated
polytunnels or greenhouses to extend the season beyond its natural
limits. We've used greenhouses for a long, long time and they're not
what I have a beef about: it's the heating them that's the problem.
Not only is it a huge waste of energy and an unnecessary drain of
our carbon resources, but the result barely warrants the time it takes
to eat them.

Like tomatoes, out of season strawberries are nearly always tasteless
and sharp, which undermines their cultural and culinary value –

we'll always be aware of fluctuations in quality, but if something
is available all the time we get less excited by it than we would if
it were only around for a fraction of the year. This also means that
farmers won't be prepared to invest in growing them properly as the
general level of mass production will undermine their market value
too. However, when June arrives and you finally taste strawberries
that are grown properly, you realise once again the poor quality of
the ones you've been eating throughout the year.

After apples, garden strawberries are our second biggest fruit crop,
and were first cultivated in the 18th century. Wild strawberries are
native to many parts of the world but larger, sweeter varieties were
brought over from Chile and North America in the 1750s, and the
strawberry we now eat was bred from them. The name comes from
the layer of straw traditionally spread underneath the plants to stop
the fruit from touching the earth and spoiling before ripening.
Strawberries don't ripen after picking, so if you're growing them
yourself, which is easily done, always make sure you leave them
on the plant until they're really ready to pick, and when buying
them select shiny, red and, most importantly, fragrant ones. The
smell degrades quickly after picking so this is a good indicator
of freshness.

Apparently the crowds at Wimbledon go through 27,000 kilos of
strawberries and 7,000 litres of cream in the course of the two-week
tournament, a combination credited to the household of Cardinal
Wolsey in 1509. It's hard to know with simple food combinations
like this whether such a story is true, but this was the first time it
was served to the court. These would have been much more similar
to the strawberries we find wild in hedgerows – smaller, less sweet
but with a more floral flavour. I always think they have a hint of
Parma Violets, and are a welcome treasure on a long walk.

Other than in jam, strawberries aren't that good once they're cooked
as the texture becomes mushy and can be off-putting, so they're
usually used fresh, either served on their own, in fruit salads, in ice

cream or as a garnish for just about any fresh summer dessert you care to mention; strawberry pavlova is one of the best puddings the summer has to offer and is a personal favourite. I love strawberry tarts but have rarely found them to be quite as nice to eat as they are to look at. Strawberries go very well with elderflower – you can macerate them with cordial before serving, but you can also make the elderflower cordial into a semi-gel before tossing them with it. This may sound strange but it really works. Simply set some elderflower cordial with agar agar, using more than the manufacturer recommends so it sets quite hard, blitz it with a hand blender to loosen it up and then use a few spoonfuls to coat the hulled and halved or quartered strawberries.

Cherries also ripen around this time and are ready to harvest. They grow very well here, and although the vast majority of the global crop is grown in Turkey, the US, Iran and Italy, you can – and should – buy British ones in season. The British cherry harvest has fallen by 90 per cent in the last 50 years and we now import 95 per cent of the cherries we consume. There have been campaigns in the last few years to help promote home-grown cherries, but it's an uphill battle. Good cherries can easily be grown in most gardens, especially in the south, and Kent, where the growing conditions are ideal, is renowned for its orchards. We're not always aware just how many cherry trees grow on the streets of London, and although the birds get most of the fruit the blossom they produce in the spring is spectacular, unexpectedly transforming the city and collecting in drifts on the pavement.

Working with fire and very sharp objects, as one does in the kitchen, means that risk of serious injury is never far away. Nicks, cuts, bruises and light stabbings are par for the course, and although really serious accidents are rare, there will always be near-misses, one of which springs to mind when I think of cherries. This happened in 2001, when I was at Maquis. I was poaching about 5 kilos of cherries and had put a massive pan on the stove to heat up while I picked and washed the fruit. By the time I'd finished the pan was exceedingly hot. I tipped the cherries in and by the sound they were making I quickly realised how super-heated the pan was and I was worried they were going to burn. The liquid I was poaching them in was Pernod and as the bottle was immediately to hand I thought I'd better pour it in to stop them from catching on the bottom. The pan was about two feet across and I was standing right over it, looking in, curious about the wild bubbling and sizzling. Out of the corner of my eye I suddenly saw flames forming around the entire edge of the pan, which was directly beneath my face. As I jerked my head backwards a column of fire the width of the pan shot up, missing my face by a matter of millimetres but taking off a good portion of my fringe. The whole of the extraction canopy above the stove was filled with fire as I took a step backwards, staggering slightly and somewhat dazed. Eventually I found the wherewithal to slam the lid on, not only to extinguish the flames but because I didn't want the cherries at the top to burn in the intense heat. The cherries were great – in fact, they tasted amazing, but they nearly took my face off.

Cherries poached in Pernod

Select a pan that will comfortably fit the cherries in a layer 3 or 4 inches deep, and put it on a medium heat for a minute, so it's piping but not red-hot.

Tip the cherries in and add about 1 cm of Pernod – be careful as this may flame, so make sure your face isn't over the saucepan and that there isn't anything flammable above the pan. If you're worried you can get rid of the alcohol by warming the Pernod for a few minutes in a smaller pan first. It may still ignite, so attend it at all times. If it does, remove it from the heat and put a damp tea towel over it until it's cooled down.

Once the danger of the Pernod igniting is over add some sugar – how much will depend on the tartness of the cherries. Add a handful or two and come back to it later when they're cold. You can add more then if needed.

Let the cherries simmer with a lid on for a minute or two and then remove from the heat and allow them to cool in the pan. Transfer to Tupperware and refrigerate. You can add a vanilla pod or star anise while they cook if you like, but the anise has a lot of aromatic botanicals in the flavour so I prefer to let the liquor, the cherries and the cherry stones do their thing and develop their own flavour. This works well with all sorts of liquors such as brandy, kirsch, gin, vodka, schnapps and calvados, but experiment and see what you come up with.

Back in the days when I owned the café I stumbled upon a recipe for mackerel with gooseberries; just reading about it sent me into a complete spin – the juxtaposition of oily fish and sharp fruit was unlike any recipe I'd seen before. It's hard to remember where I first came across it, but I have since seen it – or references to it – in recipe books from both sides of the Channel, and it seems it's a bit of an Anglo-French classic.

The word gooseberry in French is *groseille à maquereau*, which translates into English as 'mackerel currant'. For a long time I thought the name derived from the stripes on the skin, but apparently it's because of this culinary association. I like to serve it with the gooseberries left quite coarse and with a lot of sugar to balance the sourness, otherwise the gooseberry overpowers the fish. Perfect for a barbecue, just give the mackerel a good clean and put it in the fridge until you're ready. Top and tail the gooseberries and cook them with a splash of water and a few tablespoons of golden caster sugar until they just burst. Grill the mackerel on your barbecue and serve with the gooseberries. You can add dill, mint, coriander, tarragon, horseradish, orange zest, bay, sour cream or mustard, but make sure you let the gooseberry flavour sing over the top of any additions.

I've swapped the gooseberries in this sauce with rhubarb a few times and thought it worked very well, leading me to try it with other fish. Rhubarb compote with pan-fried cod or skate cheeks and sprinkled with tarragon is superb. Or you can deep-fry the cheeks, using the batter on page 249 , and serve them with either of the two fruit compotes and a spoonful of mayonnaise.

Gooseberry compote can be folded into whipped cream to make a fool – whip double cream to very soft peaks and fold in a few spoonfuls of the compote (sieved first if you want it smooth), then fill small glasses with the mixture. Leave these in the fridge for half an hour or so before serving and they make a lovely and very easy dessert. You can layer cream and compote in the glasses to get a nice striped effect. Again, this works well with rhubarb and raspberries. Garden rhubarb is still around, so take your pick.

In the south-east mackerel are just coming into season. It's one of my favourite foods now, although this wasn't always so, and two unforgettable events helped change my mind. Strangely, they both took place in Scotland. When I was quite young I was given a rod and a fishing licence for a river near where we used to go on holiday in Sussex. I sat by that river for hours, having read all sorts of books about the best place to fish, the thickness of the line, the types of fish to be found in different parts of the river, and exactly what tackle to use. It was very nice sitting in the sun by the mill pond on the river, but I eventually gave up because I didn't catch so much as a minnow, despite all my research.

Soon after I'd given up my angling aspirations we went on a family holiday to Skipness on the Mull of Kintyre. One day three of us went out fishing in a boat, my sister, my cousin and I all clutching little rolls of orange nylon string with hooks knotted into it. When we were out deep enough we let out our fishing lines and settled down to wait. Unlike my unsuccessful earlier fishing ventures, it wasn't long before the fish began biting. I remember the feeling as the line started to run away and then the tug as I started pulling back. Fish are pretty powerful when they're trying to get away from you with a hook in their mouth, and it was a real fight to get them into the boat. After quite a battle, and all of a sudden, I had one in the boat and in my hands. It was slippery and hard and thrashing around. Eventually we got the hook out of its mouth, and just as I was wondering what the hell to do with it I remembered someone had once told me that to kill a fish you hit its head on the side of the boat. It took a few goes before it gave up the ghost, but several whacks later it was laying in the bottom of the boat, a smear of its blood on the gunwale. It nearly flipped itself out of the boat in one last dying spasm, then finally rested, staring blankly up at the sky. It was the first time I'd killed anything bigger than an insect and I remember the moment very clearly. When it had just come out of the water I could feel how alive it was, and now it was dead. It was an unsettling and morbid moment but also an exciting one – in my memory it seems like we landed hundreds, but it was probably more like five.

While we were out fishing my mum found some wild gooseberries and that's what she served them with. This was all lost on me as I still didn't like mackerel at that point, or gooseberries for that matter. The real turning point for me with mackerel was on another trip about ten years later, this time to the island of Mull. I was there with my sister and a few friends for a very rainy week of walking. We decided we should take advantage of our coastal location and buy some fish, but we were in the middle of nowhere and couldn't find a fishmonger. We had just given up when we spied some fishermen coming up the beach from their boat. When we asked if they'd caught anything we could buy they said they'd had no luck. They were just about to walk away when one of them turned back and said, 'I don't suppose you'll be wanting these mackerel, will you?' We practically took his hand off and were amazed when he wouldn't take any money for them. For him they were just bait but for us they were an exotic treasure – fresher than almost any fish we'd ever come across before.

We found a spot at the end of the beach to cook our precious haul. I'd just started working as a chef, so it fell to me to gut and clean them. It was a cold day, but I rolled up my trousers, took off my top and lodged myself among the rocks of a tiny inlet 50 yards or so away from where the rest of the group were lighting a fire. I gripped my penknife tightly and knuckled down to the task, getting colder and wetter by the second as the wind whipped the waves and spray around me. What was extraordinary about that solitary and rather primal moment was the gore – the blood from the four or five fish spread out and coloured the waves for yards around me. It felt wild – the mackerel, the sea – as though I'd formed some sort of primeval bond. Slightly dazed, I clambered back across the rocks to join my friends. By now the fire was hot, so we cooked them with nothing more than salt and pepper. That was the moment, as I ate those flakes of just-cooked, fresh-as-you-like, smoky mackerel, that I finally got it. It's very easy to overcook fish, especially mackerel, but these were perfect. Even my sister, who can be quite fussy, wolfed them down. Afterwards, we all just looked at each other with awed and happy faces – the silent knowing of the just initiated.

Getting to grips with the fish seasons in the UK can be tricky. Although native oysters have a distinct season – from September to April – very few fish do. Fish farming muddies the waters and makes it even more confusing for consumers. Another factor is that the temperatures of our seas are so diverse because Britain marks the division between the Gulf Stream and the slightly colder North Sea. Fish are very sensitive to even fractional changes in temperature, which means the fish seasons on one side of the British Isles can be quite different to those on the other. Some catches are more localised than others, and with these it's easier to get a bearing. Sprat, which used to be abundant in the North Sea but are much less so now, don't crop up nearly as much on the Atlantic side of the British Isles, which makes their winter season pretty predictable. However, mackerel are all over the place, so although their main season runs through the summer they are available to a certain degree for most of the year. It's only in the late winter that they really tail off.

All in all it can be a bit confusing, so I always turn to Ben Woodcraft from Ben's Fish on Mersea Island to guide me when I get lost. His understanding of fish runs deep, and even though I've been known to ask the most irritating of questions he never tires of sharing his knowledge with me. When it comes to freshwater fish my encyclopedia is my cousin, Howard Sooley, an avid angler, as well as a wonderful photographer. He's a great advocate of the grayling, a freshwater fish from the salmon family, which is abundant in the rivers of England, Scotland and Wales and, according to Howard, cooks a lot like bass. I'm constantly asking him to fish me some, but he always eats them all so I'm still none the wiser. The coarse fishing season starts on 16 June and carries on until March, so this is when the first fishing opportunities arise in England, but in Scotland the grayling season never closes.

As we turn the page on June summer gets underway and the weather gets hotter. This isn't always the case, but hopefully we have sunny days to look forward to. Though life is now easier in the seasonal calendar the equinox has passed – June presents us with the first real sense of liberation in the kitchen, but the days have started shortening so we need to start enjoying it, as it won't last forever.

JULY

—

Picnics

Redcurrants

Raspberries

Lavender

Flour

Barley

Samphire

Turnips

Apricots

Dab

Tomatoes

Cucumber

Garlic

Garlic scapes

Scallops

Green elderberries

Answer July—
Where is the Bee—
Where is the Blush—
Where is the Hay?

Ah, said July—
Where is the Seed—
Where is the Bud—
Where is the May—
Answer Thee—Me—

Emily Dickinson, 'Answer July' (1863)

July can be a confusing month. It feels like it should be exciting: it's the height of summer – usually the warmest month in the year – and schools break for the holidays at some point; Ramadan, which started in June, trundles on for the first couple of weeks, but other than that there aren't many major landmarks. Some years it isn't even that hot. July feels slightly smooth, unblemished, without much in the way of peaks or troughs.

Perhaps this blank canvas is a good thing – it leaves us the freedom to roam, to change our habits from year to year. One reason that July has become significant to me is picnics. July is a good time to picnic because of the weather, but it's also a great time of year because of all the produce available – not only are there lots of different vegetables but the fruit crops are starting to pick up too.

I never feel a picnic is complete without a good quiche. Quiche Lorraine is the absolute classic, but you can put pretty much anything into the asparagus tart recipe in the May chapter. Even though it's not a very seasonal combination I love leek, mushroom and either Norbury or Cashel Blue in my quiche, or broad beans, peas, sorrel, dill and goat's cheese. Braised chicory is a great one for the winter, again with a blue cheese and walnuts.

Quiche Lorraine

Use the method for making and blind baking the tart shell from the asparagus tart recipe on pages 209–11.

Makes 8–12 slices

For the filling:
6 rashers of unsmoked streaky bacon
1 large onion
4 eggs
250ml crème fraîche
250ml double cream
Salt and pepper
250g Gruyère
125g cheddar
1 tbsp chopped chives

Preheat the oven to 170°C. In a bowl, combine the eggs, crème fraîche, cream, chives and half the grated Gruyère and half the grated cheddar. Season with salt and pepper.

Fry the bacon in a saucepan until rendered and crispy. Remove from the pan with a slotted spoon, leaving the fat behind. Put the bacon into the cream mixture. Fry the onions in the bacon fat until translucent and golden brown, then add them to the cream mixture too. Mix gently and pour into the tart shell and grate the rest of the Gruyère and cheddar on top.

Bake in the oven for 30 minutes or so until golden brown and just set. Be careful not to overcook or the tart will lose its creamy texture. Leave to cool and set a little before serving.

Another of my favourite picnic foods takes a bit of effort to make, but it's worth it. Scotch eggs have enjoyed a resurgence in the last few years. Long gone are the days when a greasy sphere of tasteless, nondescript pork, coated with soggy breadcrumbs and enclosing a bullet-hard, greying, rubbery egg was an acceptable offering; nowadays it's relatively easy to find a runny-yolked Scotch egg with crispy-crumbed, well-seasoned moist pork. The name comes from the verb to scotch, which means to beat or chop, and refers to the minced pork. There are many variations on the theme – one of my favourites is made with haggis instead of pork mince, although I've never got round to making one myself. I've tried a few different options in the past – my best was a quail's egg and morcilla version, and I once made a good kedgeree egg too.

I was awakened to the potential of the Scotch egg at the Bull and Last on Highgate Road, back in the mid-2000s – the meat was well seasoned and moist, the coating was crispy and the yolk was runny. Having hitherto eaten only lesser versions, this was a revelation, but it took me a long time before I attempted one myself. A Scotch egg is essentially a peeled boiled egg, wrapped in pork mince or sausage meat, breaded and deep-fried. It sounds pretty simple, but there are various points at which it can go wrong.

Although you can cover it in whatever you like, getting the egg itself spot on is probably the most important thing. I like mine a little bit runny, but if they're too soft they can be difficult to eat. Boiling an egg with a runny yolk is easy, but soft-boiling, peeling and handling one without it falling apart is tricky. The pork mixture needs plenty of seasoning, and I like to add a little bit of minced pancetta or bacon. Thyme or sage in the mince is good too.

For the breading I'm now a convert to Panko Japanese breadcrumbs as they give a very crisp, even result. You can buy them in some shops now, but home-made ones do very well, just make sure they're not too fine or the breading will be soggy. Run fresh bread through a food processor and then spread the breadcrumbs out to dry, it's easier to get an even result than if you let the bread go stale first. If you don't have a food processor you can use a blender, or grate the bread. Some people bake the egg after deep-frying to make sure the pork is cooked through. If you don't do this, it can be difficult to cook the meat enough before the breadcrumbs burn. I try to keep the oil at a low enough heat to allow the first cooking process to do the job – 160–165°C should do it.

Scotch egg

For 4
275g free-range, fatty pork mince
50g minced or grated onion
75g minced pancetta or bacon
1 tsp chopped fresh thyme
¼ tsp ground fennel seed
¼ tsp ground juniper
1 pinch nutmeg or ground mace
Salt and pepper
6 medium eggs
Plain flour
250g Panko breadcrumbs
Vegetable oil for deep-frying

First make the mince. If you have a mincer attachment for your food processor and want to mince the meat yourself then use pork shoulder – make sure it's not too lean as you need the pork to be quite fatty. Then mince the bacon and onion, putting the onion through last to help bring any scraps of pork or bacon through. If you're buying the mince from your butcher, ask them to make sure it's fatty, and ask them to mince the bacon in with it. Either very finely chop the onion, or grate it, or blitz it in a food processor – if you use either of these last two techniques you will need to drain it a little in a sieve before using. Combine the pork, bacon, onion and spices and season. Fry a little bit of the mixture in some oil to check for salt. It should be quite highly seasoned as the pork has to carry seasoning for the egg too. When you have the seasoning right, divide the mixture into 4 and roll them into balls. They should weigh about 100g each. Cover and put in the fridge.

Boil 4 of the eggs. Getting this right has taken me a fair bit of experimentation, but I get consistently good results now. After a spot of playing around I found that 6½ minutes in boiling water and then straight into cold water until cool is a good balance. Peel the eggs carefully then rinse in cold water to remove any stray bits of shell. Put them onto a dry tea towel or kitchen paper to dry off.

Take the balls of mince from the fridge. Shape each one into a flat oval on the palm of your hand and then wrap it around the egg, pulling the edges together, teasing them until the mince covers the whole egg. Go over it, making sure the layer of mince is even and there are no cracks. Repeat with the other eggs. Return to the fridge.

Break the remaining 2 eggs into a bowl and beat them lightly. Tip about 150g of flour into another bowl, season it and then put the breadcrumbs into a third bowl. Take each Scotch egg ball, check that it's still round, giving it a final shape if necessary, and then dip it into the flour, rolling it to make sure it's all covered. Lift it out, gently shake off any excess and then drop it carefully into the beaten eggs, turning it over to ensure it's covered. Lift it out with a fork and let any extra egg drip off. Drop it carefully into the breadcrumbs and cover it all over, making sure the crumbs coat it evenly. Try not to touch the egg too much at any stage of this process. Lift it out of the breadcrumbs and place on a tray lined with parchment.

Half fill a medium saucepan with frying oil and bring up to 170°C. To know how hot this is, a 1-centimetre cube of bread will go brown in 1 minute at 180°C, so if it takes a little bit longer than that then it's about right. Or use a temperature probe. Cook two eggs at a time, keeping the heat up. When the coating is a deep orangey brown the pork should be done and you can take it out of the oil and let it drain on kitchen paper. If you're worried about the pork being cooked through you can finish them in a medium oven for a few minutes, but I think you run the risk of overcooking them like that.

Allow to cool before serving. They are delicious when freshly cooked, but it's nice to let them rest first.

I do love a good picnic, as you can tell. The main reason is that almost every July since the late 1990s I've held a big picnic on Hampstead Heath. Although the date varies, it's usually on the last Sunday of the month. We've almost always held it at the same tree[1] to the north of Parliament Hill, and on a good year it's attracted more than 200 people. It's an entirely open affair and everyone is free to invite as many friends as they like, or even arrange a separate party of their own to coincide with mine. I intend to be doing it for years to come, so do join us one day if you can.

My mum and dad are faithful picnic attendees, and my friend Sanchia Lovell has a particular penchant for picnics (so much so that she's written a book about them) and is always a partner in picnic crime. Now that she has a family she generally comes with an independent picnic, brandishing a hamper to rival all others. Sanchia and her husband, Jack, my oldest friend, actually met at one of the picnics. I usually press-gang one or two friends or family to come over to my house in the morning to help. It takes many hands to get everything to the Heath and up the hill to the tree.

1 51.561989, -0.161034 (tree co-ordinates)

There's a lot of work on the day, but I also spend a couple of months beforehand cajoling people and reminding them that it's going to happen, posting it on Facebook, dissuading them from going on summer holidays or having other picnics elsewhere. All in all, it's a bit of a palaver, albeit an enjoyable one, but the month can become quite preoccupied with it.

The eating of the food and tasting what everyone else has brought is immense fun, but my favourite part of a picnic is when the hurly-burly's done, the food's been eaten, most of the drink's been drunk, the Frisbee thrown and the shadows start to lengthen. The heat of the sun, should it have decided to bless you with its presence, starts to wane but you know you still have an hour or so left to sit talking, with a full belly and one last glass of warm Pimm's.

While the summer picnic is my stand-out event of July, there's a lot happening in the food calendar. Strawberries and cherries just keep getting better but there are new fruits joining the fray.

Redcurrants and raspberries – the two main ingredients for the most quintessential of the season's desserts, summer pudding – are getting ready to pick. We grew up with a redcurrant bush in the garden so I was always familiar with their sharp taste. It's an unusual fruit to have a preponderance of, and we perhaps didn't make the best of them but I'm glad I got to know them.

Raspberry is another sharp fruit and one of my favourites – they have a depth to their flavour that strawberries lack, so for me they always win that particular battle. Raspberries seem like a great luxury, so I was surprised to find huge banks of them growing wild on the island of Rùm off the west coast of Scotland. Apparently this is common across the country – having escaped from gardens they now thrive in its soil and climate. Scotland, and especially Tayside, around Perth, is well known for its raspberry growing. In the 1950s it was producing so many that it had a dedicated steam service called the Raspberry Special that chuffed its way down to London during the season.

—

Below is a recipe for summer pudding that I transcribed over
the phone from Emma Miles at the Clerkenwell Kitchen. I've
reproduced it below as I wrote it down – despite being vague,
they're the directions I always follow and it always comes out well.

The amount of fruit required depends on the size of your bowl. For
a 1.5 litre pudding bowl you'll need about 900g of fruit. And the
fruit you use depends on what you like and what's available. I like
a good slug of redcurrant acidity in my summer pudding, but there
are several fruits around now and for the next couple of months that
are perfect for this. I see blackberries as an early autumn fruit so I
generally turn my nose up at them, but redcurrants, raspberries,
blackcurrants, bilberries (also called blaeberries, whortleberries
and whinberries, and many other wonderful names besides),
loganberries, tayberries and white currants are all wonderful in
summer pudding and provide a selection of hues and flavours. I find
that cooked strawberries have an odd texture, so steer clear of them.
Gooseberry or rhubarb might be interesting to play with early in
the season, but they don't crop up in recipes that often.

The amount of sugar will vary with the acidity of the fruit used,
and you'll need to do a bit of tasting to get the right balance, but
for the amount of fruit mentioned above, around 200–250g should
serve well. And the fruit only need cooking for a couple of minutes,
otherwise they turn to mush.

Summer pudding

Pudding bowl lined with cling film
Sliced white organic bread, crust off, cut into triangles
Simmer fruit with sugar to taste – pudding-sweet
Dip bread in juice
Line bowl with bread – circle in bottom of bowl, triangles to just
above edge
Half fill with fruit
Layer of bread in middle for big ones – if necessary

Finish fruit
Cover with bread
Pull cling film over top
Snug fit plate on top
Weight
Leave in fridge overnight

I think raspberries and lavender go very well together so I often
serve this with lavender Chantilly or ice cream. Lavender ice cream
always divides people. Some, like myself, enjoy the floral taste, but
many find it reminds them of their grandma's underwear drawer
and can't stand it. Whether you like it or not, it's very important
not to overdo the lavender oil as too much will overpower the
creaminess of the ice cream base.

Lavender ice cream

I get my lavender oil from Castle Farm in Kent, which you can
order online. Food grade oil is best, but essential oil is fine, though
it can be a little stronger so use with caution.

Makes about 750ml
285ml whole milk
285ml double cream
1 bay leaf
125g caster sugar
5 egg yolks
A few drops of lavender oil
1½ teaspoons lavender flowers, stripped from the stems (dried flowers can
  be used but are less fragrant and their texture can be slightly chewy)

Whisk the egg yolks and sugar together in a big mixing bowl until
the sugar is dissolved.

Bring the milk and cream to the boil with the bay leaf in a saucepan
and remove from the heat. Stir 1 ladle of the hot milk mixture
into the eggs, then another, and then stir in the lot. Return to the

pan and cook over a low heat, stirring continuously with a wooden spoon until it coats the back of the spoon. Run a finger across the back of the spoon to leave a stripe – if the stripe holds then it's thickened enough. Remove from the heat and immediately pour into a jug. Allow to cool. Remove the bay leaf and add the lavender oil, a couple of drops at a time, tasting as you go. Don't let the taste of the lavender become overpowering, but do remember that the flavour dulls a little when frozen.

Add half a teaspoon of lavender flowers, then churn according to the instructions that came with your ice cream machine. Reserve the other flowers for serving.

To make without an ice cream machine, chill over an ice bath until cool, then freeze. When it starts to freeze around the edges, whisk to churn it – an electric whisk is ideal for this. Put it back in the fridge and repeat every half an hour until it freezes fully. This will take about 3 hours depending on your freezer.

Serve with a small pinch of lavender flowers on each scoop.

It can be hard to provide oneself with cereal crops of any type if working with a store cupboard that's strictly local to London, even if you widen it to include the UK. It's now becoming easier to find home-grown and milled flour, especially spelt flour, but a lot of the flours on sale in this country, even ones that appear to be milled locally, are made with a mixture of flours, some of which come from abroad. In most cases, and especially with bread flour, they come from Canada. Hard spring wheat from Canada produces very strong flour with a high protein and gluten content, so it's ideal for making bread. In the UK we struggle to get the same results. Pasta requires a very finely ground flour that is best produced in Italy and which we would struggle to create in this country – again for reasons of climate and soil. I've made a great deal of non-Italian pastas, such as pierogi and spätzle, from locally sourced flour, but pasta with a finer texture is impossible to make with British flour due to the high water content of our wheat.

Tackling this problem when opening Konstam led me to the doors of Wright's Mill in Ponders End on the banks of the River Lee. This is a mill with a long history – an entry in the Domesday Book, written in 1086, for Enfield, Middlesex, states that, along with 57 inhabitants and six slaves, the village had a mill. I made contact with David Wright, who runs the mill now, and he was very enthusiastic about producing a truly local flour. Unfortunately, although they mill with grain from nearby in Barnet and Mill Hill, it didn't appear possible for them to provide me with local flour as this is blended, in huge batches, with grain grown elsewhere. The problem was keeping them separate without causing massive disruption to their manufacturing process. We looked at various options and, after some discussion, I was over the moon to learn that he had worked out a way of doing it that didn't compromise the running of the mill. This was a real coup and took us a big step closer to a restaurant with a genuinely local pedigree.

Although we didn't bake our own bread we did find a baker in London who would use this flour to make local bread for us. It took some experimentation as the flour was quite soft compared with blended flours made using hard Canadian wheat, but in the end it worked very well and we were always proud to be able to serve high-quality bread grown, milled and baked in London. It was Troels Bendix, the maker of the splendid rye bread we used for Eggs Konstam in the café, who first took on the job, and when he was no longer able to provide bread for such a small operation the baton was passed to my friend Sophie Taylor and her team of bakers at The Flour Station in Hendon. Although Konstam, the restaurant that inspired it, is no longer there, the London Loaf – still made with Wright's local flour – has become a good seller for them and I often see it at The Flour Station's market stalls.

The reason I bring this up in July is because I want to highlight barley, which the UK climate is perfectly suited to growing. It's our second most widely grown arable crop, covering over a million hectares and yielding 6.5 million tonnes each year. This crop is significant to Europe as a whole, with six of the world's top ten producers being European nations, if you include Russia. Almost all the barley we produce in the UK goes to animal feed and the brewing industry, but it's perfectly suitable for processing into edible forms such as pot or pearl barley, which are available in some shops. Despite this, a lot of the edible barley we consume comes from China. Like wheat, it has a spring crop and a winter crop, constituting approximately equal amounts of the annual yield. It's hardier than wheat but less productive and is often used as a break crop.

My mum always puts barley in her Irish stew, the dish I first had it in, but I've since found out that not every recipe includes it – Darina Allen was once quite scathing when I asked her about the barley in hers – and many would say it's a stew made only with mutton, potatoes, carrots and onions. A good lamb stock is acceptable – bay in the cooking and parsley to finish are acknowledged flourishes – but it's a frugal dish and any attempt to zhuzh it up just produces a lamb stew of some other national persuasion.

I've always liked the nutty taste of barley and its slightly chewy texture, but my professional regard for it began to blossom when I ran the café and started making barley risottos. In Italy they call it orzotto (from orzo, meaning barley), and it's traditionally found in the north of the country. One of my favourites is with roast Jerusalem artichoke and mushrooms, neither of which is in season now, so here is a basic recipe which you can adapt to feature whatever takes your fancy.

Basic orzotto

The technique for making orzotto is much the same as risotto, though barley doesn't have as much starch as rice so you don't tend to get quite as rich a sauce as you do with rice. An extra drizzle of oil, or a knob of butter, and a bit more Parmesan will make up for it. Add in almost any vegetable you like – wild mushrooms, roast squash, roast Jerusalem artichoke, grilled courgette, aubergine and beetroot are all excellent – and it goes with any meat or fish as an accompaniment.

Serves 4
2 small onions
3 tbsp olive oil
3 garlic cloves
250g pearl barley
1 glass white wine
1 litre seasoned vegetable or chicken stock
50g goat's butter
1 tbsp mascarpone
½ small bunch parsley
Salt and pepper

The onions should be very finely diced. Heat the olive oil in a generous saucepan and cook the onions gently until soft and light golden brown. Chop and add the garlic and cook over a medium heat for 3 or 4 minutes.

Add the barley and cook everything together for a minute or two and then raise the heat. Add the white wine. When it's absorbed lower the heat to medium and add a quarter of the stock. Stir frequently, and when it's absorbed keep adding the stock a ladle at a time. When all the stock has been incorporated taste the barley, and if it's still too firm add water and keep stirring frequently until it's done – it should have a tender, nutty bite to it. Stir in the butter and the mascarpone, and a dash more water if needed. It should be glossy and rich, not stiff or soupy. Check for seasoning. Chop the parsley and add just before serving.

Barley really came into its own for me when I decided to commit to local ingredients. It can still be difficult to find locally produced barley and my best bet was health food shops and wholesalers. Once I'd got my hands on it I served it in many different ways, in stews and casseroles, soups, salads and tossed hot with any number of different vegetables. I particularly like it with broad beans, a good knob of butter and a generous handful of chopped fresh herbs such as dill, mint or tarragon, like the spätzle recipe in the May chapter.

My reason for talking about barley now is that June or July is when the winter barley is harvested, with the spring barley harvested in August. In July the heavy heads of barley swaying in the wind like waves spreading across the fields is one of the defining sights of the season. The feel of it in the hand, dry and prickly, comes to mind with visions of tractor tracks baked dry in the sun. Ever present on country walks, we would pop a few of the grains out of their little golden shells and bite down on them, floury and tasting of bran in our mouths. Little did I realise that it would become a kitchen staple for me further down the line. That my tight culinary brief gave barley such an elevated position in my kitchen is another demonstration of how reliance on unexpected ingredients can be rewarding, and is another reason why I enjoy embracing the seasonal food calendar so much.

Some of my favourite barley recipes are for salads, and one that used to be something of a signature at Konstam was mackerel with barley and bacon. I think this started out as a Hugh Fearnley-Whittingstall recipe – a cook who has inspired me a lot over the years – but it became our own and in the end we were using local ingredients and bacon we'd cured ourselves.

Grilled mackerel, bacon, barley, chicory and chervil salad

This recipe calls for a lemon dressing, which lightens the dish, but I make it with all sorts of dressings. Cider vinegar dressing works particularly well.

Serves 4

4 mackerel, filleted and pin-boned

100g barley

6 slices unsmoked streaky bacon

2 heads chicory

½ bunch of chervil

4 spring onions

Olive oil

1 lemon

Salt and freshly ground pepper

Rinse the barley and bring to the boil in a saucepan with plenty of salted water, reduce to a simmer and cook until tender but not soft – a little resistance to the tooth but no bite.

Cut the bacon into matchsticks and fry them off in a medium-hot frying pan with just a tiny touch of oil until crispy. Lift them onto kitchen paper on a plate to drain and cool.

In a small bowl sieve and season the juice of half the lemon with Maldon salt. Mix with enough oil that it no longer catches the back of the throat – 3 or 4 times as much oil as juice. Pick any damaged leaves off the chicory and cut in 1-centimetre slices crosswise. Slice the spring onions finely and pick the chervil off the stems.

When the barley is done, drain in a sieve, rinse thoroughly with cold water, drain again and then toss in a bowl with a few drops of oil.

You need a really hot grill for mackerel or it will stick, so if using charcoal, light it and continue when the flames have died down and the coals are hot and going grey. If you're using a griddle pan make sure it's blisteringly hot before putting the mackerel in.

Assemble the salad with the chicory, barley, bacon, chervil and dressing. Divide this between your plates ready to serve, reserving some of the chervil.

Season the mackerel fillets with salt and pepper on a plate and rub a smidgeon of oil on the skin side. Place the mackerel on the smoking-hot grill skin-side down, and cook until the flesh is cooked about halfway through, then turn them very carefully. The skin should be nicely crispy and a little charred in places. After about 10 to 20 seconds on the flesh side put them on the plate with a few wafts of chervil, a couple of drips of lemon dressing and a generous grind of black pepper. It is vital not to overcook the mackerel. The flesh should still be dusky pink in the middle when you take them off the grill – they'll finish cooking to perfection on the way to the table.

We were always told by our parents and grandparents that you could actually eat the funny-looking, knobbly sea grass we found growing on beaches, salt marshes and estuaries as we ran around exploring the coast in the summer. For years I thought it was called 'samfa' and despite its otherworldly appearance and tendency to grow in inhospitable environments, we would try it occasionally, screwing up our faces at the intense saltiness.

When I first encountered it as a chef, about 15 years ago, samphire wasn't as sought after as it is now. I hadn't thought about it for a long time when my fishmonger said he had some, and I knew straight away, when I had it before me in the kitchen, freshly washed and beautifully tender, that I was dealing with a very different ingredient from the hastily foraged version I'd experienced as a child, all twiggy and covered in mud. We served it with halibut, new potatoes and beurre blanc, and I still didn't take to its unapologetic saltiness, but it was the start of a journey we've taken together. These days I love it, having become more tolerant and understanding of its salinity.

There are several plants that go by the name of samphire but they aren't necessarily related. The two most common types are rock samphire and marsh samphire. Both are edible but the one we encounter most frequently on our plates is the latter. Samphire is one of the most pre-eminently foragable foods in the UK. Being surrounded by water we have a great deal of coastline and a fair amount of the saline mudflats and estuaries that it likes to live in. It has a very highly evolved system of photosynthesis that gives it the energy it requires to keep all the sodium ions out. When burned, samphire is a rich source of sodium carbonate, one of the chemicals needed in the production of glass and soap, which is how it got the names glasswort and soapwort. As far back as the 11th century glassworks have sprung up wherever samphire grew and, once it was understood that the ash from the plant worked as a replacement for lye, soap was made on beaches and in estuaries across the land. These seaside industries peaked in the 16th century, but it was the development of industrially synthesised sodium carbonate in the 18th and 19th centuries that brought them to an end. Now the only uses we have for these plants are culinary.

I've found that tender, young samphire needs very little cooking. Two or three minutes should be enough in boiling water, then toss it with melted butter – and obviously it doesn't need any salt adding to it. Although Richard Mabey's cooking times for samphire in *Food for Free* are, in my opinion, far too long, he makes the nice suggestion of serving it with spaghetti, the shapes echoing each other to form a culinary pun. I like to melt an anchovy and chop half a chilli into the butter before tossing them all together. Both Mabey and Roger Phillips, in *Wild Food*, suggest boiling it whole with the roots attached and then stripping the buttery flesh from the stalks with your teeth, as opposed to painstakingly picking away at its fronds, removing all but the most tender stems.

I like this gutsy approach but I think it's more suited to home consumption than in a restaurant where folk can get a bit funny about table manners.

You can grow samphire, but the water you use needs to be salted. I have heard of this being done inland on an agricultural scale to provide London's swankier restaurants with a year-round supply of micro-samphire. This horrifies me as I can't imagine it does anything but destroy the soil, and for this reason I prefer to keep it as an occasional, seasonal and often unexpected treat when I find it at the fishmonger's or happen to be near an estuary at the right time of year. Like so many of the best seasonal ingredients, it comes and goes quite quickly – the plants don't have to be very old before they become woody and inedible. Despite my calls for foraging, I've heard it said that marsh samphire is now being cropped so hard that our natural resources are being depleted, so bear this in mind – forage with care and do so responsibly, never taking more than you need, or more than a particular location can support.

Rock samphire – oft quoted from Act 4, scene vi of *King Lear* – is also edible, despite being completely unrelated to marsh samphire or glasswort. Although it also lives on seawater, it thrives some way back from the shoreline in warmer coastal areas. It has an even more distinctive flavour than marsh samphire, and used to be sold in London, having been salted in big barrels of brine and then hawked by street traders as 'marine crest', due to its passing resemblance to a cock's comb. It's less fleshy and therefore a tad less sexy than marsh samphire, with the result that it's less popular and less likely to be over-foraged.

Another edible salt marsh plant is sea arrowgrass. There are vast tracts of marshland on the Kentish coast that are covered in a combination of all three. The land they inhabit is an odd one: the salt makes it hard for vegetation to survive unless well adapted, and no trees are happy there, so the eroding, salt-drenched soil is covered with a blanket of low-lying shrubs and grasses. The wind skims across them unobstructed and the sun beats down, scouring the salty sand of anything other than these unusual plants. I went there with Howard a couple of years back, and we found just enough shelter to set up a little barbecue I'd brought with me. We stuffed our sea bass with the salty shrubs growing all around us, and despite the inhospitable landscape we managed to have ourselves a small feast.

One of the most humble vegetables we encounter as the year goes by is the turnip, a vegetable forever associated with peasantry. Later on they can become unwieldy and rather bitter, but in summer they're young – small and sweet – and come in bunches with their leaves. Turnip soup, though frugal, is delicious and glazed turnips are divine. To glaze them, cook them like Vichy carrots, steamed under a cartouche with a little water, lots of butter, some sugar and a good pinch of salt until tender with a brown sheen. Turnip leaves are good too – baby ones give a mustardy kick to salads, and later in the year they can be steamed or braised like greens or chard.

In my opinion, all these dishes pale into comparison when compared with the king of turnip dishes. Chinese grilled turnip paste is one of the least appealing sounding dishes I've come across, but I would go so far as to say that it's one of my favourite foods. These ignominious-looking squares of white paste seared on a grill and served with soy sauce and chilli oil are simply magical. Crispy on the outside and soft inside, when steaming hot they impart a massive hit of pure savoury boom. Clearly it's not only the turnip that's responsible for this palate happiness; it's the sausage, pork fat and stock which goes into making them that really does the job. Chinese turnip, or daikon, isn't quite the same as the vegetable we call turnip, but you can make them with European ones too.

Like many root vegetables, mature turnips store well and for this reason we associate them more with the colder months, but the summer is when the first crops are pulled. Young turnips are a different proposition altogether and this is the time when they can still be eaten raw. I wouldn't suggest eating them like a radish, but when very thinly sliced with a sharp knife or on a mandolin they make a nice addition to summer salads, or served with tarragon and good white wine vinegar dressing they go well with fish or almost any meat.

There is an intriguing linguistic connection between apricots, which are flourishing now, and the word precocious. Although they stem from the same Latin root, *praecoquere*, 'precocious' reached us from Latin directly through French, but 'apricot' took a far more circuitous route around the Mediterranean, taking in *abrecock* from the Catalan *abercoc*, the Portuguese *albricoque*, the Arabic *al-birquq* and the Byzantine Greek *berikokkia* before we get back to its Latin root.

This seems to show that words for thoughts and concepts are often taken straight from the Classics but that words we use to describe food tend to have a more meandering journey, picking up something from each culture they pass through, giving them a romance and richness I feel is entirely appropriate to the sensuality and intimacy inherent in the act of eating and sharing food.

Having taken the moral high ground in my earlier discussion of fish, I must be careful which ones I talk about. Another fish on the sustainable list is in season now but isn't widely known. Dabs are almost never caught commercially, but they should be. I've never seen very big ones on offer but a small one makes a delicious starter. Quickly pan roast them whole and top with a generous knob of chervil butter.

There's more in the idea of this following recipe than in the ingredients. Apart from the butter, they can all be substituted for something else. I've made more flavoured butters than I can say, with almost any herb you care to mention, various spices, mustard seed, garlic, bone marrow (a little time-consuming but perfect with steak), anchovy (see page 180), nasturtium flowers, red onion, the list goes on. It's an excellent way to deliver last-minute flavour that penetrates meat or fish quickly, moistening as it goes. It's also good stuffed under the skin of chicken before roasting.

Chervil butter

This will make more than enough butter for a decent meal, but it keeps in the fridge for at least a week and goes well with almost anything, even just spread on toast.

125g unsalted butter
½ bunch chervil
Zest of ½ a lemon
1 banana shallot
Maldon sea salt

Dice the butter and leave it in a bowl to come to room temperature. In the meantime, pick only the biggest stems from the chervil and refresh it in cold water for 10 minutes or so. Drain and leave in the colander for a minute or two, then spin in a salad spinner or gently pat dry with a tea towel. Very finely dice the shallot using a sharp knife.

When the butter is soft, chop the chervil and add this to the butter with the shallot. Zest the lemon into the bowl and lightly mash it all together with a fork. Fold in a good pinch of Maldon sea salt and taste. The salt should stay in crystals and all the other flavours should be present in gentle but equal amounts. Add more of anything that isn't coming through enough. Put the bowl in the fridge for a few minutes to firm up the butter a little, and then scrape it onto parchment. Roll it into a smooth cylinder about 3–4 centimetres in diameter and return it to the fridge.

Ten minutes before serving, cut it into little circles half a
centimetre thick, then put on top of the hot fish as soon as you
plate it up – it will melt onto the fish and soften as it goes to the
table. Alternatively you can let people help themselves by serving
it in a small bowl.

On a hot summer's day there is nothing quite like the smell that
hits you when you walk into a greenhouse where tomatoes are
growing. The dusty green smell of the plants is unique. It makes
me think of salads, compost, plastic hoses and old men pottering
around their allotments. Many people grow them in their gardens,
and if we have a good summer and they have enough light you can
get a good crop. But if you want to be sure to get the most out of
your tomatoes a greenhouse is the thing.

In the UK we're growing more and more tomatoes on a commercial
scale, but this is still only about a fifth of the 100,000 tonnes we
eat. Almost all these are grown in glasshouses or polytunnels.
While this is amazing and a decade or two ago you would have been
hard pushed to find a British tomato in the shops, let alone a good
one, the use of polytunnels has led to tomatoes being grown out
of season, which means the tunnels need heating. Although there
are various ways farmers can go about reducing the environmental
impact, it's still very difficult to be sure that this doesn't outweigh
the energy consumed in transporting them from warmer countries.
So, although I applaud supermarkets shouting about British
produce and focusing on local ingredients, I'm as appalled when
I see UK tomatoes available in January as I am about so much
of the unseasonal imported produce available throughout the
winter, like mange-tout, green beans, peas, asparagus, tomatoes,
strawberries and blueberries. The whole idea of focusing on local
food is that it should push us to be more seasonal, as this is when
the environmental and financial benefits can be seen. I'm not an
environmental scientist so I won't get too embroiled in the debate

about the real costs of producing food intensively out of season, other than to say that I've heard and read enough to be convinced that we are steadily borrowing against the future.

I also want to touch briefly on the idea of consumer choice. I read a comment recently at the bottom of an online article about local food and energy consumption that said the reader was sympathetic but also worried that it would be boring to stick too much to local food. There seems to be an assumption that keeping to a local diet, and therefore a seasonal one, is limiting. My experience is that it's the other way round. I see the same ingredients cropping up time after time in recipes that have no sense of seasonality, and it's the chefs exploiting what the year has to offer who are embracing a wider palette of flavours. When consumers buy asparagus from Peru in November they may be exercising their right to choose, but surely this is a case of choice to the detriment of variety.

It would be foolish not to acknowledge and understand the pressure that supermarkets are under to provide this year-round produce, but it would be interesting to see them make a genuine commitment to seasonality and locality. To do so would take a huge shift in corporate and consumer culture. Fifty years ago we spent 24 per cent of our disposable income on food; now that figure is well below 10 per cent. It is decades of developing agricultural, political and logistical infrastructures geared up to providing cheap food based on a thriving, carbon-based energy industry that makes it possible for supermarkets to provide food as cheaply as they do and still make a profit. It will take a similar amount of work to alter the trajectory of our local, national and international mechanisms and adjust the process so that it sustains itself. Perhaps we can do something about this, or perhaps it is simply an insurmountable task and it will take some sort of rupture before we really start to pay attention.

When I was little I liked cooked tomatoes but I didn't like them raw at all. I was given amazing tomatoes in France and Italy, and pressed to try numerous rapture-inducing tomato salads, but I never seemed to get it. As time went by I began to feel like I was missing out, and as a teenager started to wean myself onto them. Eventually I found I didn't hate them quite as much, but it wasn't until the summer of 1998 – my first summer working at Moro – when we received a delivery of beautiful mixed cherry tomatoes, grown by Sunnyfields in Hampshire, that I really understood. They were firm, juicy and had a punchy balance of sharp and sweet in equal proportions. That was the moment I finally saw the light, and I can still remember the taste when I think about it now. Since then I've eaten lots of fantastic tomatoes and have made some rather good tomato salads in my own right, but very few have equalled the eureka moment I had back then.

We spend £175 million on tomatoes each year, and although some of these are full of flavour and grown with care, the vast majority are pretty tasteless, imported from Holland or Spain, having been grown hydroponically in plastic tunnels under factory conditions. It fills me with horror to think of all the tasteless red discs of pappy nothingness dutifully plonked into lunches in all the sandwich shops across the land. Although the technology may have improved over the years and something that tastes a bit like a tomato is more easily available now than it used to be, I sadly suspect there are many people who rarely, if ever, get to eat a good tomato. Personally, I think we could quite easily do without all these boring tomatoes, using other ingredients instead, but getting people to make a sandwich without one seems to be an issue.

Most importantly, these methods of year-round growing remove the tomato's seasonality, encouraging us to forget that there is a time of year when they're naturally spectacular.

There are more tomato recipes than you can count, but the one I want to share the most is a simple tomato sauce, and it's the one my mum cooks. The key to this sauce is to cook it really quickly – no more than 20 minutes – which keeps the freshness of the flavour and makes it lighter than slower cooked sauces. You should also have plenty of oil in it, a good two millimetres in the bottom of the pan. One more important thing to remember is not to have too much juice going in at the start, so there's less need for reduction. You can make this with pretty much any type of tomato, including tinned, but my favourite is cherry tomatoes. If you make it with tinned tomatoes then put them into a colander first to strain, crushing them up with your hands if they're whole. And season the sauce at the end, not at the beginning, as it will necessarily reduce a bit and therefore the flavours will intensify with cooking.

Tomato sauce

This sauce goes with almost anything savoury, and is a delicious and fresh way to enjoy one of the best crops the summer can produce.

Serves 4
2 medium onions
12 tbsp extra virgin olive oil
1kg ripe cherry tomatoes
6 small garlic cloves, finely sliced
Salt and black pepper

Heat 4 tablespoons of oil in a medium saucepan and add the chopped onion and a good pinch of salt. Fry over a medium heat until translucent and turning golden brown. Thinly slice the garlic and add to the pan. Fry together for 3–4 minutes, until the garlic starts to colour, then turn up the heat and add the tomatoes. Cook hard until the tomatoes burst and then let it bubble away at a vigorous simmer for 20 minutes. Add extra olive oil five minutes before the end. It should be rich and unctuous. Remove from heat and season well. This gets better after two or three days in the fridge, so make extra.

In the UK we don't generally talk about green tomatoes very much, which is strange because we invariably end up with a great deal of them. It seems that the spiritual home of green tomatoes is Alabama, but this doesn't mean we can't enjoy them over here. For the classic American dish of fried green tomatoes you dip slices in cornmeal or polenta and then fry them in bacon fat. I tend to dredge them in seasoned flour, give them a shake and shallow fry them.

Green tomatoes make great chutney. The recipe below is one I've used a few times. The ingredients need chopping up quite small, so get your knife skills out – it's worth the effort.

Green tomato chutney

Makes four 500ml jars
1kg chopped green tomatoes
500g roughly diced onion
2 chopped sticks celery
2 bay leaf
1 sprig thyme
1 chopped green chilli
1 tsp coriander seed
1 tsp white peppercorns
1 tsp fennel seeds
1 blade mace
1 small stick cinnamon
5 juniper berries
3 cloves
350ml white wine vinegar
250g caster sugar
2 tsp Maldon salt

Wrap the spices in muslin and put all the ingredients, except for the tomatoes and the sugar, into a wide, heavy-bottomed saucepan. Bring to a simmer over a medium heat, stirring occasionally.

Reduce the heat to low and cook, stirring often, until the onions start to soften and turn translucent, for about 15–20 minutes. Add the tomatoes and cook until they start to break up, for another 15–20 minutes.

Add the sugar and taste for vinegar and salt, adding more of them all if necessary, bring to a boil and simmer until the chutney has lost its watery feel, stirring frequently. Your spoon should leave a trail behind it. This will take another 15 minutes or so. Check the seasoning again and remove from the heat.

Transfer to sterilised jars and store in a cool, dark place for up to a year. Best eaten after a month or two.

I have also made very nice bottled green tomatoes in the past. I can't remember the exact recipe we used but my memory of how we made them is as follows. Rinse the tomatoes well under cold water, removing any crowns, then prick them deeply with a needle. Clean your bottling jar scrupulously and dry it in the oven at 90–110°C for about 10 minutes. In the meantime, make a pickling liquor. I would suggest trying one cup of white wine vinegar to one cup of sugar and half a cup of water – you can get the balance of flavours right just by tasting it. Bear in mind that the tomatoes are quite tart so the liquid needs to be a tiny bit sweeter than you might think, but don't make it too sweet – you want a bit of a kick and it will sweeten a little over time.

Loosely pack your jar with the whole tomatoes and some onions, roughly sliced and quickly blanched, and then pour over the hot liquor. Seal the jar and submerge in a pan of hot water, bring to the boil and boil gently for about 10–15 minutes. Leave to cool in the pan, remove, clean the jar and leave it for several months. Taste it and then tweak the recipe the next year if it isn't quite right.

Much cheaper to build and easy to construct, the polytunnel has now supplanted the greenhouse in most situations. However, I can't move on from thoughts of greenhouses until I've mentioned a vegetable, or rather a fruit, that does grow outside but which really thrives under glass. This is, of course, the eponymous ingredient of that most quintessential of English foods, the cucumber sandwich. Cucumbers are for many people a bit of a non-event. They're around 96 per cent water and not exactly packed with either nutrients or flavour, but I love them dearly as they were always my refuge in place of the dreaded tomatoes.

Cucumbers originated in South Asia and have been cultivated for 3,000 years, but didn't appear in England until the 14th century. They were a favourite of the Roman emperor Tiberius, who is said to have eaten them all year round. His gardeners constructed frames with wheels to move them around with the sun in the summer, and built greenhouses glazed with crystal for the winter.

Despite their seemingly meagre qualities the taste of cucumber is distinct and unmistakable. Thinly sliced and lightly salted they make a delicate salad, and chilled cucumber soup is about as refreshing as a soup can get. The combination of cucumber, fresh herbs, such as dill, mint or coriander, and yoghurt or sour cream crops up in recipes from all over the world, including India, Bangladesh, Pakistan, Turkey, Greece, Poland and Ukraine.

Cucumber is also a good addition to many drinks. Sliced cucumber in iced water makes it even more thirst quenching, especially with a sprig of mint. Hendrick's recommend their gin with tonic and a ribbon or two, and the fruit salad in Pimm's should always contain cucumber.

Below are a couple of cucumber recipes, one for soup and one for a salad I made almost by accident. I happened to have cucumbers and pistachios on my chopping board and tried them together. The warm flavour of the pistachios marries beautifully with the coolness of the cucumber. The other ingredients just fell into place when I was thinking about how to make it work as a salad.

Cucumber soup

Serves 4

2 large cucumbers
2 medium onions
4 tbsp olive oil
1 medium potato
½ cup fresh podded or frozen peas
About 1 litre vegetable stock
½ cup yoghurt
2 garlic cloves
2 sprigs mint
2 sprigs tarragon
1 gherkin
Salt and freshly ground black pepper

Dice the onion and heat the oil in a medium saucepan. Gently fry the onions with a pinch of salt, stirring frequently until soft and light golden brown.

Peel and dice the potato. Add to the onions and cook together for 2 minutes on a medium heat. Add the stock and the peas, if fresh, and cook until the potatoes crush against the side of the pan easily.

In the meantime, grate 1 of the cucumbers. Add to the pan with the yoghurt and peas, if frozen, and bring to a simmer. Remove from heat, blitz – adding more stock, water or milk if required – season and chill.

To serve, grate the other cucumber and stir into the cold soup. Crush the garlic and stir this in too. Pick and chop the herbs. Finely dice the gherkin. Ladle the soup into bowls and garnish with the herbs, gherkin, a drizzle of olive oil and some fresh black pepper.

Cucumber, pistachio, mint and orange blossom water salad

Serves 6

6 small cucumbers or 2 large

1 lemon

3 sprigs mint

100g pistachios

1 tbsp orange blossom water

½ cup extra virgin olive oil

½ tsp caster sugar or honey

Salt and pepper

Toast the pistachio nuts in the oven for 8 minutes at 160°C and leave to cool. Very roughly chop them.

Peel the cucumbers in stripes lengthwise, halve and deseed them. Slice into half-moons about ½ centimetre thick.

Squeeze the lemon and add the orange blossom water to the juice, add the sugar and season with salt to balance the flavours. Whisk in the olive oil and taste. Add more seasoning if needed.

Roughly chop three-quarters of the mint and add to the cucumbers, add three-quarters of the pistachios, add the dressing and toss. Serve, sprinkling the rest of the pistachios and mint over the top.

It took me a long time to see garlic as an ally and a friend. I got there pretty quickly once I started cooking professionally, but it always felt like a particularly tricky customer when I was growing up and making occasional forays into cooking. In the 1970s, and even 1980s, there was still a general mistrust of garlic. I didn't share this mistrust but it left me with no tutelage on the matter. My mum and dad both cooked with it, but even for them it was a half-learned art.

I remember my dad rubbing garlic on warm terracotta dishes before serving us spaghetti al burro. One of the simplest pasta dishes to make but it's perfect – the garlic rubbed on the plate giving it just the lift it needs. My parents still have some of these plates; flat-bottomed with straight rims, and beautifully worn now. In his twenties, my dad carried about ten of them back from Valladolid in northern Spain, jettisoning the rest of his luggage to make space. The village was filled with terracotta workshops and their kilns. He watched the plates being fired and bought them as soon as they were cool enough. He came home with the plates and a huge plant pot stuffed in his bags and two big milk jugs tied around his neck, nearly breaking the lot getting off the boat, but luckily made it back with everything intact.

I played around with garlic for some years, never quite learning how to approach it, but slowly I came to understand its language and what it could do in its different states. Even now it sometimes says something I don't quite get, but we mostly communicate well.

There are numerous ways of bringing out the multitude of notes and characteristics that garlic has to offer, but the key ones are crushed, chopped, warmed, cooked and browned. Crushed has the most potency as the crushing process releases allicin, the sulphuric compound responsible for garlic's heat, and it's used in dressings, marinades and rubs. Chopped garlic is easier going but still has a strong raw flavour – I most often use it like this in relishes or gremolata. By warmed garlic I mean the flavour you get when you dress hot new potatoes or rub it on toast for bruschetta. Cooked garlic is mildest as the cooking process breaks down the allicin, leaving a mellower, less astringent flavour, and is often found in dishes when the flavour will be allowed to dissipate, such as stews and casseroles. Browned garlic goes through some lovely transformations, from creamy and aromatic to nutty and deeply spiced. Romesco sauce is a really good example of this, and these are the flavours that a lot of quick-fried Asian food will use. However, be careful not to take it too far as the flavour will become bitter.

Garlic has been cultivated for culinary and medicinal use for thousands of years, and is particularly high in phosphorous and manganese and vitamins B and C. Historically it has been used to treat all manner of ailments, including smallpox, sunburn, parasites, respiratory problems, poor digestion, low energy and as an antiseptic. It's currently thought to have a particularly good effect on high cholesterol levels and certain types of cancer.

Garlic is an indispensible ingredient in cuisines across the globe and it would be hard to imagine life in the kitchen without it. For the most part, we use it in a partly dried form, the flavour concentrated and intense, but for a brief period of the year we can find it in its fresh state. When it's first pulled from the ground it has a milder, sweeter taste. The soft skin on the bulbs is usually a mauve colour and the cloves are nice and plump.

New season garlic from abroad will have been available for some time, but July is the month when domestic garlic is pulled. There isn't a huge amount of garlic production in the UK as we struggle to compete commercially with the big hitters, the biggest of which is China, but it does grow well here and is mostly cultivated on a smallholding scale. Cooking with it at this time of year is a delight, and you can do a few things with it that dried garlic would find hard to deliver.

One of my favourite dishes is new season garlic soup. It barely has any other ingredients so you can really appreciate the subtle sweetness of the fresh garlic.

New season garlic soup

Many recipes for this soup have potato, but I like it when the texture comes from the puréed garlic, so this calls for a lot of it.

Serves 4
6 heads new season garlic
50g butter
1 onion
1 celery stick
About 700ml whole milk
2 bay leaves
1 sprig thyme
50ml double cream
50g crème fraîche
Salt
2 tbsp good olive oil
Black pepper
A few chives

Trim the stalks off the garlic and cut the bulbs in half crosswise. Break them up and put them in a saucepan with the roughly chopped stalks, the celery cut into chunks, the bay leaves and the thyme and enough milk to cover. Bring to a gentle simmer and cook, without boiling, for about 20–30 minutes, until the garlic is very soft. Strain, reserving the milk, and pick out the bay leaves and thyme.

If you have one, pass the strained garlic, celery and garlic stalks through the fine screen of a mouli-legumes, or vegetable mill. If not, pulse a few times in a food processor and pass through a sieve with the back of a wooden spoon or ladle, scraping off as much of the precious purée from the bottom of the sieve as you can. Reserve separately from the milk.

Rinse the saucepan and return to the heat with the butter. Dice the onion and add to the pan with a good pinch of salt when the butter has melted. Cook over a low heat until soft and sweet but not coloured.

Tip the onion into a blender with the garlic purée and a cup of the reserved milk. Blend until really smooth. Return to the pan with the cream, the crème fraîche and enough of the milk to give a smooth silky consistency. Season with salt (but not pepper). Bring to a simmer and remove immediately from the heat. Check for consistency and add a dash of milk if needed.

Serve with crusty buttered toast and a small drizzle of olive oil, some chopped chives and black pepper on top.

New season garlic and marjoram sauce

I love this with roast lamb and roast beetroot. Rosemary is also wonderful instead of marjoram.

    4 heads new season garlic
    400ml milk
    8–10 marjoram stems
    1 bay leaf
    100ml chicken stock

100ml white wine
100ml cream
Salt and pepper

Cut the garlic bulbs in half crossways and poach (with all the skin, any trimmings, the bay leaf and half the marjoram) gently in the milk until very soft. Strain, reserving the milk, and pulse the garlic and garlic skins a couple of times in a food processor, then work through a sieve with a wooden spoon, reserving the pulp separately to the milk and scraping it off the bottom of the sieve. Alternatively you can pass it through the fine mesh of a mouli-legumes.

Boil the wine in a saucepan and add the stock, reduce by half. Add the garlic purée and the cream and cook until thick and silky. Add some of the poaching milk if you need to thin it at any point.

Remove from the heat, season and leave to cool a bit. Strip the rest of the marjoram from the stalks, chop them a little bit and add to the sauce. Double-check for pouring consistency and seasoning, and serve with lamb, beef or chicken and roast vegetables.

When garlic is growing it sends up a shoot that will eventually form a flower. These are called scapes and are normally removed to allow the plant to focus its energy on the bulb, but they can be harvested as an ingredient in their own right. They have a lovely texture, a bit like a bean but with a garlic flavour.

King scallops don't have a season, they're good all year round, though many of them are dredged, which is a horrific and unsustainable way of fishing. But if you do get your hands on some of Guy Grieves's lovely diver-caught ones, and happen to see garlic scapes at the market, then you can give this recipe a go.

Seared scallops with garlic scapes and vermouth

I like cooking with Noilly Prat, partly out of habit, but any brand of dry vermouth will do.

Serves 4
12 diver-caught scallops
1 sprig fresh thyme
Zest of ½ a lemon
2 tbsp olive oil
2 bunches garlic scapes
50g butter
1 glass dry vermouth
1 sprig parsley
A handful of rocket leaves
Salt and pepper

Check over the scallops, carefully trimming any of the bits of firmer white flesh that are sometimes left around the edges. Be careful not to cut the corals off. Put the stripped thyme leaves and the olive oil in a bowl and very gently toss the scallops in it. Leave for half an hour or so to marinate.

Trim the garlic scapes and blanch them in plenty of salted boiling water for just a few seconds, refresh them in cold water and drain. Cut into 4-inch lengths.

Wash and rehydrate the rocket in plenty of cold water, drain and gently spin-dry.

Take the scallops out of the marinade and pat dry on kitchen paper. Heat half the butter over a medium heat in a non-stick or well-seasoned frying pan. When it foams, add half the scallops and colour on both sides. Season them with salt in the pan. Be careful not to overcook them – this is more important than getting enough colour – they only need a couple of minutes on each side. Lift them out onto a warm plate and fry the rest in the butter. If you're worried about the butter burning then deglaze the pan with the vermouth between batches and set aside, then wipe the pan clean. When you've cooked all the scallops, deglaze the pan with the vermouth again and reduce until thickened and a little sticky – toss the garlic scapes in this.

Arrange a few leaves of rocket on each plate, then the scapes and the scallops on top. Chop the parsley and sprinkle this over the lot, then the lemon zest, some more olive oil and freshly ground black pepper.

Although it's not long since we made cordial with the blooms of the elderflower it is now that the berries make their appearance. Their time, in the main, is still to come, and we'll discuss the mature berries later in the book, but when they first form on the bush – small, green and very unripe – they can be used to make a caper-like pickle. One of the foragers I've worked with over the years, the ever enthusiastic Anton, gave me this recipe: 'For elderberry capers, pick through the green berries and discard any stems. Lightly season them with salt and transfer to a sterilised jar. Keep in the fridge for four weeks. Remove from the jar and rinse well, cover with vinegar and leave for a couple of months.'

It's hard to do justice to everything that comes into season in July; it starts to get really busy and there just isn't enough time. But try to do something with as much of it as you can, as most of the produce is only here for a little while. We mustn't dally though, summer is in full swing, the handkerchiefs are knotted and the trousers are rolled up, but this little picnic is coming to an end, so we're going to get up, brush ourselves down, have a good slug of water, and head on into my favourite month, August.

AUGUST

—

Nasturtium

Capers

Courgettes

Kohlrabi

Blackberries

Plums

Greengages

Aubergines

Grapes

Wine

Game

Sardines

Haddock

*In August, the large masses of berries, which, when
in flower, had attracted many wild bees, gradually
assumed their bright velvety crimson hue, and by their
weight again bent down and broke their tender limbs.*

Henry David Thoreau

ugust is a heady time of year – make no bones about it;
heat and holidays are the theme, and everything else just
has to work around them. London's parks begin to look
bleached and hazy and melted ice cream seems stickier than ever.

In the countryside corn and barley turn gold in the sunshine and
there's a tremendous buzzing as bees, along with every other flying
insect nature can throw at us, go on the rampage. There are times
on summer walks when you see a butterfly and suddenly everything
seems to go quiet for a few seconds as you watch it flit around you,
and then you take your eyes off it and the buzz and the heat come
back. When I think of August, I imagine it with sun-flares and
Super 8-style bands of magenta across my mind's eye.

August is the month of my birthday, but as everyone is on holiday –
and we were often away ourselves – I rarely got to celebrate it with
my friends, leaving me a little ambivalent about it. I've reached a
compromise – making a non-event out of my birthday by having a
big non-birthday summer picnic the month before – I get to mark
the time of year without actually celebrating it.

Like July, August is a busy time in the seasonal calendar, though
there aren't as many new ingredients as in early summer or early

—

autumn. It's also a good time to catch up with anything we missed last month. The vegetables now available are similar to those that grow in the Mediterranean. Courgettes are a dead cert and the tomato season is in full swing. Cucumbers are ripening in the vegetable patch and peppers and aubergines in the greenhouse. It's a good time of year for fish as the season continues for many species, including lobster, sea trout, sardines and haddock.

One of my personal favourites of the summer is the nasturtium. As well as providing a fantastic splash of red, orange and yellow across a flowerbed, all the constituent parts of the plant are edible. I've eaten the leaves many times and enjoyed them, but when I was first offered nasturtium flowers as a crop, a couple of months after opening the restaurant, I couldn't get images of naff 1980s cooking out of my head – horrific salads with raisins, garishly garnished with bright orange flowers. Then I was told that the seedpods were great as a caper replacement, which made me curious. It took me a while to get my hands on them and my head around the idea of using the flowers. I still have a few prejudices and always think twice before garnishing a salad with them, even though they're very pretty and taste great. Nasturtium flowers have a distinctive flavour – creamy horseradish with a hint of sweetness. The leaves are more peppery and the pods taste distinctly of capers. One of my favourite nasturtium memories is staying at a friend's house in California, where we made pizzas topped with prosciutto and loads of nasturtiums, both leaves and flowers, that we'd gathered on our morning walk up the hill.

Nasturtiums bloom throughout August, with the pods appearing after the flowers. They can be used when mature, but after a while the seeds inside become hard and woody, so I suggest using them while they're still small and young. Although they have a great deal of similarity to capers in shape, size and taste, these are very different parts of the plant. Capers are buds of the flowers of *Capparis spinosa*, a rather pretty, low-growing plant found wild around the Mediterranean. At Konstam we salted the nasturtium pods: rinsing them, picking through them for detritus and tossing them with lots of coarse salt before packing them with extra salt to cover, putting them in the back of the fridge and forgetting about them for a week or so. They last for months, and a clean jam jar is ideal if you're doing this at home.

Mrs Beeton liked to pickle hers in vinegar and used this recipe:

> To each pint of vinegar
> 25g (1oz) Salt
> 6 Peppercorns
> Nasturtiums
>
> Gather the nasturtium pods on a dry day and wipe them clean with a cloth.
>
> Put them in a dry sterilised glass bottle, with vinegar, salt and pepper in the above proportion.
>
> If you cannot find enough ripe to fill a bottle, cap it with what you have got until you have some more fit, they may be added from day to day.
>
> Seal the bottles with airtight caps.
>
> They will be fit for use in 10 or 12 months and the best way is to make them one season for the next.

I love that nasturtium pods are a lost ingredient, one that people would have been familiar with in her day, and that we are rediscovering.

These nasturtium capers can be used in a multitude of sauces and dressings, scattered over salads and sprinkled into stews or casseroles, but one of my favourite ways of using both the flowers and the pods is with fish. If using the flowers, chop them up and mix them into softened butter that has been mashed with garlic or shallots, salt, pepper, a little lightly crushed mustard seed or mustard powder, and some lemon or orange zest, and then roll in greaseproof paper and leave to chill. The more flowers you use the better – when perched on top of a piece of delicious fish and just starting to melt it looks very pretty.

The pods can be used in much the same way, but make sure you pick out any hard ones. Soak the salted nasturtium capers in cold water (changing it if necessary) until not face-curlingly salty, chop them finely and mix with the same ingredients as above.

Like many vegetables, and the rest of the gourd family, courgettes are actually a fruit. Originating in the Americas, what we now know as a courgette was bred in Italy in the late 19th century and is now a staple of Mediterranean cooking. The Italians and Americans call them zucchini; both names are lovely, but in the UK we've adopted the French, which comes from their word for squash, *courge*. They're high in folates, potassium and vitamin A and are very low in calories. This low calorie count and low carbohydrate level makes courgette fritti an excellent alternative to fries.

Courgette is a main ingredient in ratatouille, one of the most classic of southern French dishes, which can be either served as a side dish or on its own. They grow well here but are so much cheaper from abroad that the main crops we buy are from Spain, Italy and France.

Like cucumbers and marrows, they have a high water content, so many recipes start with salting them. This draws out some of the liquid, which can be quite bitter, and also brings out the flavour. Many recipes also call for the seeds to be removed, which will make them less soggy and faster to cook. One of my favourite ways to cook them is to slice them, salt them for a few minutes, then sauté them quickly with finely chopped garlic, which should brown nicely in the time it takes for the courgettes to gently cook. You can eat them on their own like this, let them cool and squeeze in some lemon for a salad, or toss them through pasta with Parmesan and lots of chopped parsley or basil to make a really good summer lunch dish.

Courgettes make excellent fritters. The Turkish call them *mücver* and serve them with mint and yoghurt.

Courgette fritters

These are great for brunch, served with poached or fried eggs and spicy tomato sauce – try the recipe on page 291, with the addition of a few chopped red chillies and a sliced red pepper cooked with the onions. A spoonful of yoghurt lightly seamed with crushed garlic and lemon juice wouldn't go amiss either.

Serves 4
2 large courgettes
1 small red onion
1 red chilli
2 eggs – one of them separated
1 heaped tbsp gram flour
¼ tsp baking powder
75g feta
½ bunch fresh dill
Butter or olive oil for frying
Sea salt

Grate the courgettes and the onion. Squeeze as much of the liquid from them as possible by putting them in a tea towel and twisting the corners as hard as you can. Deseed and chop the chilli. In a mixing bowl, beat one egg and the yolk of the other egg with a pinch of salt and add the flour and the baking powder. Fold in the courgette, onion, chilli, crumbled feta and roughly chopped dill. Check for seasoning.

Beat the remaining white to firm but not stiff peaks, and fold into the batter mix.

Melt some butter or olive oil in a large frying pan. When it foams, drop large spoonfuls of the mix into the pan. When golden brown on the bottom, flip carefully and repeat. Drain on kitchen paper and serve quickly.

The herb that perhaps goes best with courgettes is mint, and a great
many recipes I've used them in makes use of this combination,
but they go well with most of the key European herbs – dill, basil,
parsley, oregano. A very summery dish that really shows them off
is chargrilled and tossed with a honey and lemon zest dressing and
scattered with feta and mint.

Chargrilled courgette salad with ricotta, mint, honey and lemon dressing

Serves 4

2 or 3 courgettes – more if they're small. It's nice if you can get a mixture
   of green and yellow

5–6 tbsp olive oil

Salt

1 garlic clove

1 tbsp lemon juice

Zest of ½ a lemon

100g good ricotta

1–2 tsp honey to drizzle

25g flaked almonds

A good pinch of black onion or nigella seeds

1 small handful of mint leaves

Thinly slice the courgettes lengthwise. When your charcoal or
griddle pan is hot toss the courgette slices in a tablespoon or so of
oil and season them with salt. Grill them to colour on each side and
remove to a bowl.

As they're cooling, crush the garlic and put it in a bowl with the
lemon juice and zest. Season with salt, check the balance and then
add 4 tablespoons of olive oil. A dash of muscatel vinegar is a nice
addition if you have it. Check for acidity, adding a squeeze of lemon
or a dash of oil if needed.

Toast the almonds in the oven at 160°C until light golden brown
(about 10 minutes) or in a dry frying pan over a medium heat.
Don't let them burn.

Toss the courgettes with the dressing while still warm, but
not piping hot, leave to cool and serve on a platter with the
ricotta dotted over the courgettes, the honey drizzled on top,
the almonds and nigella seeds sprinkled over, and the torn mint
scattered around.

I came across this recipe for pickled courgettes a few years ago, and
it makes the courgette taste a bit like a really classy burger gherkin.
It's delicious with fatty charcuterie such as rillettes, and has been a
crucial part of many a late-night snack.

Pickled courgettes

Makes four 250ml jam jars of pickle (or 1 litre)
500g courgettes
2 tbsp fine salt
1 onion

Pickling mix:
500ml cider vinegar
120g sugar
½ tbsp yellow mustard seeds
½ tbsp black mustard seeds
1 tsp turmeric
1 tbsp flour

Slice the courgettes thinly into discs, either on a mandolin or by
hand. Slice the onion very thinly. Place together in a large bowl,
add salt and toss thoroughly. Cover with very cold water and stir to
dissolve the salt. After 1 hour, drain and dry thoroughly in small
batches in a salad spinner or by hand between kitchen paper.

Combine the ingredients for the pickling mix in a saucepan and
simmer for 3 minutes. Set aside until lukewarm.

Mix the courgettes and onion with the pickling mix in a bowl.
Transfer the pickle to sterilised jars. Leave for at least a day (but

preferably longer) before serving. This keeps for several weeks
in the fridge.

There is a vegetable that has made its way into our lives in a rather
innocuous way in recent years, but it's one we should take to our
hearts a bit more. Kohlrabi means cabbage root, from the Italian
cavolo rapa via the German word *Kohl*, which is quite an unusual
etymology. As the name suggests, it tastes largely of cabbage but
has a luscious, crisp, melony texture, a hint of sweetness and a touch
of mustardy heat. I don't know many recipes for it but it's lovely
when very thinly sliced and used in salads. You can also roast it,
pickle it and purée it. It occasionally crops up in Indian food too.
The Hungarians make a creamy soup with it, and I would suggest
trying this chilled, rather like a white and very light borscht. When
shredded it goes well in various slaws, and makes a nice alternative
to celeriac for remoulade.

Kohlrabi remoulade

Serves 6
1 large kohlrabi
2 tbsp crème fraîche
2 tbsp mayonnaise
1 tbsp wholegrain mustard
1 tbsp white wine vinegar
1 small bunch flat-leaf parsley
1-inch piece of fresh horseradish – more if desired
2 tbsp fine salt
Salt and pepper

Peel and matchstick the kohlrabi – do this on a mandolin on
a medium setting, or by cutting it into thin slices and then
slicing these into thin sticks. If you really want to save time (and
fingertips) you can grate it, but the texture won't be as nice. Toss
it in a bowl with two tablespoons of fine salt and leave to drain for

30 minutes in a colander over a bowl. Check for saltiness – if it's
not wincingly salty then use it as is, squeezing out any excess
liquid, as it will season the rest of the dish, otherwise, rinse, leave
to drain and squeeze dry in a tea towel. If grating then skip the
salting process and simply squeeze out excess water by hand and
adjust the seasoning as needed later.

Pick the parsley, wash and dry in a salad spinner, chop with a sharp
knife medium fine, grate the horseradish on the fine side of a box
grater or a microplane, and combine all the ingredients in a bowl.
Check for seasoning and serve.

Towards the end of August, as the temperature mellows, the
produce changes a little too – early apples start making an
appearance and the end of the berries is nigh. Raspberries carry on
until September but strawberries are in their last natural weeks.
Blackberries come to the fore to take their place, and they trail on
through to September to join up with the apples for a classic early
autumn crumble combo.

As the month progresses, as long as it isn't too dry, blackberries
crop up in almost every hedgerow. Although I can't say I was
brought up in a foraging household, blackberry picking was a
yearly event, but we wouldn't have seen it as foraging back then.
Richard Mabey talks about 'food for free', and that might be more
the phrase I would have used. A handful of sweet-sharp berries
from an obliging bramble would provide welcome relief on many
a long, hot walk.

One of the most lovely appearances of late August is that of the plum,
and a little later the damson. Sloes are from this same subgenus,
Prunus, but we'll come to them in time. Making plum jam marks
an early point in two great friendships of recent years. I was in my
old flat above the café in King's Cross, making jam with Walter
Donohue (the editor of this book), when Sanchia came round to

look at a room I was renting. It was the first time I'd met her, and although it was one of my earliest meetings with Walter, the jam-making had somehow flowed very naturally out of our book meeting. For Sanchia, a genuine lover of food, it had seemed idyllic, so she took the room and we've been friends ever since.

One of the nice things about making plum jam is that it's terribly easy. Even the fruit is quite easy to prepare – slicing around the stone, twisting the fruit and pulling the two halves apart, and using the tip of a small knife to cajole the stone from the flesh, a bit like a small avocado. Sometimes the stones are a bit stubborn, but it's very satisfying when they come out with ease. Weigh out the same amount of sugar as fruit – a bit less if the plums are very ripe – then put them into a large clean saucepan, bring it all to the boil and simmer vigorously until it's reached setting point. This is 105°C if you have a jamming thermometer or digital probe, but if not, a small stack of side plates in the fridge will help tell you when you've reached this point. Place a few drops of jam on the plate, put it back in the fridge for a minute or two and then draw your finger through it – if the jam wrinkles a bit then you're there.

If you don't mind avoiding the odd plum stone, leave them in – they have a lovely almondy taste that adds to the jam's flavour. Don't crack open the stones as the flavour of the kernels can be intense and rather bitter – they also contain compounds that break down into cyanide, so it's best not to use too many of them. You can put them in muslin if you have some, and then remove them before you put the jam in the jars. This gives you a little extra pectin too. I often put a squeeze of lemon juice in towards the end of the cooking, both for the flavour and for its pectin.

Once I've made this jam I don't just put it on toast, but also use it as a sauce for a variety of meats. Plum jam goes beautifully with duck and other game, or with pork. Not everyone likes such a sweet sauce with their meat, but I think pork and duck can take it. If you find jam too sweet you could make a compote, cooked less and with less sugar, so the texture remains rougher, and the sharper side of the plums comes through. Or try these pickled plums.

Pickled plums

This is a quick and very simple recipe I learned from my talented and passionate friend Nico Rilla, whom I'm lucky to have worked with on many occasions over the years, including in 2012 when he helped me style the second edition of *The Silver Spoon*, with Ed Park behind the lens. Nico taught me this recipe a couple of years later and I've used it many times since. It goes perfectly with duck, pigeon and pork. It's also great with smoked duck and grilled radicchio as a starter, and some toasted hazelnuts or fresh cobnuts make the dish.

    6–8 plums
    2–3 tbsp sugar
    2–3 tbsp good red wine vinegar
    1 or 2 star anise

A few peppercorns
4 cloves
A pinch of whole coriander seeds

Halve and stone the plums. Sprinkle the sugar in a heavy-bottomed frying pan and heat until caramelised. Deglaze with the vinegar and add the plums and spices. Toss around in the sugar and vinegar quickly and then cook for 4–5 minutes. Tip out carefully onto a plate.

This can be used straight away while warm, or left to cool and served with smoked duck as mentioned above.

The greengage, a cousin of the plum, is often overlooked, and I always think this is a shame. A cultivar of an Asian plum originating in France, they were brought here in 1724 by Sir William Gage, who lost the documentation they came with. There are several gages, but these are the best known and are cultivated mainly in western Europe. In French they're called *Reine Claude*, or Queen Claude, after the Duchess of Brittany, who became queen consort to King Francis I of France. Elsewhere they have taken the names *Reneklode* in Germany, *ringle* in Poland, *ringlo* in Hungary and *ringloty* in Slovakia. You can use them in pretty much the same ways you would use a plum, and they make a lovely jam too, but I've most often had them stewed, chilled and served with double cream.

Aubergines are a tenuous vegetable to include in a book about essentially British seasonal food – I've only seen them grown on a handful of farms in this country – so they effectively come under the same category as the Seville oranges and persimmons in January. On the Continent August is the height of their season, and no summer is complete without baba ganoush. I first learned how to make it at Moro and have loved the rich, smoky dip ever since. There are

certain dishes that take you somewhere new the first time you have
them, and baba ganoush was one of those dishes for me. I'd watched
it being made and felt there was no way that aubergines charred
to that extent could possibly be edible, but when the burned skin
was pulled away and the soft flesh beneath was mixed with tahini,
garlic, lemon juice and lots of olive oil, it was so unexpectedly
special that the first taste has stuck with me ever since.

Baba ganoush

This recipe tastes so much better when the aubergines are grilled
over wood or charcoal, but you can char them under a grill or over
a gas flame. They can be roasted in the oven but it's difficult to get
the same charring and flavour this way. You may want more lemon,
garlic or tahini – let your taste guide you – but you should be able
to taste all the ingredients, and remember that the garlic flavour
will continue to develop as the flavours mingle. Serve as part of a
mezze selection with freshly made flatbread – recipe below.

Generously serves 6
3 aubergines
2 tbsp tahini
2 garlic cloves
½ lemon
½ cup olive oil

Grill the aubergines until completely blackened on the outside and
collapsed. Remove from the heat, put in a bowl covered with cling
film and leave until cool enough to handle but still warm. Remove
the stem and the charred skin. Leave to cool completely.

Crush the garlic and juice the lemon. Crush the flesh of the
aubergines with your hands, checking for lumps, then add the
tahini and other ingredients. Mix thoroughly with a wooden spoon.
Season well and check for oil – it should be glossy and unctuous.

Flatbread

250g strong white flour
5g dried yeast
½ tsp sugar
1 tbsp olive oil
5g salt

Dissolve the yeast and sugar in 150ml of tepid water.

Put the flour in a bowl and add the salt and oil. Pour in the water
in increments, incorporating with a wooden spoon as you go. When
all the water is incorporated, tip onto your work surface and start
to knead. You may not need all the water, or you may need to add
more to incorporate all the flour. If you need more, just wet your
hands a little and knead it in.

Knead for 6–8 minutes to form a smooth, springy dough. Lightly
oil the dough and the bowl, then replace the dough and cover with
a tea towel. Leave to rise until it springs back slowly when indented
with a fingertip.

Knead a few times and divide into 4–6 balls. Leave to rest for a
couple of minutes, then roll out on a well-floured surface – they
should be pretty thin. Drizzle with a little oil and place on a hot
charcoal grill until bubbled and a little charred on both sides.

Probably the most local produce we ever had at Konstam was
grapes – a small harvest from the garden of a house up the road. We
served them with our cheese plate and put on the menu '… with
grapes from Number 11'. Eating grapes aren't commonly grown in
the UK, but grapes grown for wine are becoming more and more
prevalent. In the time it has taken me to write this book the acreage
planted has increased by over 140 per cent, and the sparkling wine
industry has gained a value of over £100 million.

Grapes are the largest global fruit crop and the vast majority of these are grown for winemaking, something we've been doing for quite some time now. Wine jars dating back to 6,000 BC have been discovered in Georgia and other parts of the Caucasus, which means we've been winemaking for about 8,000 years. The Romans brought viniculture to these shores, and remains of Roman vineyards have been found as far north as Lincolnshire. British winemaking has waxed and waned over the centuries but during Henry VIII's reign there were over 130 vineyards recorded in the country. It wasn't until the First World War and the rationing of sugar that winemaking ceased in Britain – for the first time in 2,000 years. Since then, although the number of vineyards has gone up and down, there has been a steady increase in production and there are now over 500 vineyards in England and Wales, and even a few in Scotland. Most of the wine we now produce is sparkling, some being of the very highest quality – in the last 15 years English wine has won 12 trophies in global wine competitions for best sparkling wines, both white and rosé – no other country has matched this.

I mention this now as it is in late summer that grapes are harvested. We served some very nice wines at Konstam – our house sparkling was Chapel Down Brut NV, and we always tried to have one or two non-sparkling English wines on our list at all times. The problem with English wine, and one that still persists, is that the size of production is so small in comparison with many other countries, meaning costs are higher and therefore the wine is more expensive to the consumer. So, although you can get good English wine, you're paying more than you would for wine from abroad of a similar standard. At the moment we produce about 1 per cent of the wine we consume, and as that figure rises and production increases we should be able to compete on a more level playing field. We have the soil for it – the chalk of the south-west is excellent for wine production; in fact, it's the same seam of chalk that runs under Burgundy – but our climate is still just a few degrees cooler than is ideal. There is conjecture that climate change will provide us with the warmth we need to overcome this. Several of the big champagne vineyards, Moët in particular, have bought large parts of arable land in Kent in the belief that this will be the case, but there doesn't seem to be much evidence of it just yet, and it isn't clear whether climate change will leave us warmer or colder.

So much for fruit and vegetables, but what do we find of meat and fish in our penultimate month? On the meat front, the hunting season for ptarmigan, red grouse, black grouse and common snipe all begin in August. Having been brought up in Camden Town I have yet to try my hand at much in the way of hunting. Beyond a few rabbits, a pigeon and a few fish, I've caught very little edible wildlife. Nonetheless I am a keen eater of game and particularly fond of pigeon. I love quail, but they're mostly reared these days so they barely count, and I've spent a little time with a partridge or two over the years in various kitchens.

With most game the trick is to only just cook it, keeping it pink so it breaks down but isn't dry. With whole game birds one of the main challenges is cooking the leg, which tends to be tougher, in the same length of time as the breast. Generous resting – about half the cooking time again, in a warm spot – is always required, along with lashings of redcurrant, apple or quince jelly. I remember a grouse I had at St John Bread and Wine – sister restaurant to the world-famous St John, and one of my favourite restaurants – that came with apple jelly and chicken liver parfait on bread fried in dripping. It was outstanding – the grouse perfectly done, the apple jelly tart and the parfait light.

On the fish front, sea bass are dipping – spring and autumn are their seasons – but sardines are present in abundance. A sardine is really a small pilchard, *Sardina pilchardus*, and these days they're mostly eaten fresh, often grilled in the Mediterranean style. But when it comes to canning and the global sardine community, there are 21 different species all canned under the name sardine. Pilchards are an oily fish that form part of the herring family, but they have a different cycle to their cousins that swarm our waters at the other end of the year.

Tinned sardines were a regular lunchtime feature when I was a child, though I wasn't keen on them as I was very pernickety about all the little bones. They don't crop up so much anymore, probably because fresh fish are more easily available now, which is rather ironic considering the decline of the local fishmonger who is powerless in the face of the supermarket fish counter. Over the years I've developed quite a penchant for a variety of tinned fish products – octopus in ink sauce, smoked mussels and pilchards in tomato sauce, all on toast, are favourite lunchtime standbys and my cupboard is rarely without one of them.

Despite the allure of tinned sardines, I'll always go for the fresh version given the choice. One of the nicest ways to serve sardines is grilled quickly with gremolata. Simply clean and gut the sardines, wash and season them and throw them under the grill or on a barbecue. While they're cooking – and they don't need very long so move quickly – grate lemon and orange zest, peel and finely chop a clove or two of garlic and toss them all together with a tablespoon or so of chopped flat-leaf parsley. Put the sardines on a plate, drizzle with the best olive oil you can find, sprinkle the gremolata on top and finish with a pinch of Maldon salt and a hefty twist of black pepper.

The haddock season started a month or two back, but they're really on form in August. When I think of haddock I firstly remember it poached in milk with mashed potato and peas, then I think of adding a poached egg, and I usually ponder for quite some time on the subject of kedgeree, but ultimately my thoughts end up with a man called Iain Spink, who smokes the meanest Arbroath smokie in the land. I first met him some years ago in Dorset. He'd brought his smoker down from Arbroath on the east coast of Scotland and was serving up the freshest of the freshest smokies. We ate them straight from the barrel and I fell in love with them there and then.

I met Iain again a few years later, when I was catering for the wedding of my friends Katherine and Duncan near Aberdeen. We served three meals a day for 80 people for nearly five days, sourcing as much as we could from the local area. As soon as I realised the venue was within striking distance of Iain's beach I got on the phone to ask if he could provide us with smokies. Not only was he able to deliver 40 freshly smoked and absolutely delicious Arbroath smokies, but he also supplied us with the rest of the seafood we needed, all landed locally and fresh as could be.

An Arbroath smokie can only be made within five miles of Arbroath and consists of gutted, headed and salted haddock, hung on struts in pairs in a whisky barrel fitted over a pit fire. They're smoked with hessian covering them for 30–40 minutes, and when they come out you want to eat them fresh and still warm. They really are special. It's said that Iain's are the best, and although I've never tried a smokie by any other hand, I can believe it. He's very passionate about what he does and I've seen first hand how hard he works. I found it an honour to work with someone who does what they do with such good grace and finesse.

Now I've sated my thoughts of Arbroath smokies I can turn to kedgeree. This is one of my favourite dishes and I don't think you can get a better breakfast, or lunch or supper for that matter. Having mentioned earlier in the book that haddock is now on the endangered list, I must add that if you can't get responsibly fished haddock then smoked mackerel or almost any other smoked fish will make a good kedgeree too.

Kedgeree is an Anglo-Indian dish with both its linguistic and culinary origins in *khichri*, a rice and lentil dish brought back by

British colonials in the 19th century. Although similar dishes are sometimes accompanied by fish or an omelette, especially in Bengal, the boiled egg and smoked haddock (or fish of some sort) were probably added in Britain. It can be served quite wet, like a risotto, but I prefer to make it like a buttery pilaf, folded with fish, onions and parsley and topped with slightly soft-boiled eggs.

I've seen many recipes for kedgeree over the years, from risotto-type dishes with smoked haddock and poached eggs balanced on top to much more rough and ready versions with everything folded into steamed or boiled rice. My mum's is superb, so mine is based on hers but with a few subtle tweaks. I make a light pilaf with the rice – which she doesn't – fold in the onions and haddock and then scatter the eggs on top. I like a few spring onions as well as the parsley, so these are a personalised addition too. Fresh coriander goes well, though I usually favour parsley. I used to very soft-boil the eggs and perch them, oozing, on top, but these days I like semi-soft-boiled eggs which can be cut up and distributed. Very few recipes will tell you this but a spot of chutney on the side really sets the whole thing off, bringing another taste of the Raj to the plate.

Kedgeree

Serves 4–6

400g undyed, sustainably sourced smoked haddock fillet

320g basmati rice

3–4 medium, free-range eggs

50g butter

2 onions

1 tsp coriander seeds or ground coriander

3 cardamom pods

2 tsp curry powder

1 tsp turmeric

1 pint of milk

2 bay leaves

½ tsp black peppercorns

½ tsp fennel seed

A good handful of parsley

4 or 5 spring onions

Salt and black pepper

Slice the onions and sauté in half the butter with the coriander seeds and a good pinch of salt until translucent and golden brown. Remove from the heat and set aside.

Boil the eggs for 7 minutes and then immediately put them in cold water – 6½ minutes will leave them a bit runnier.

Rinse the rice until the water runs clear. The traditional instruction is to use 3 changes of water, but don't let it soak as it can become soft and break easily. Melt the rest of the butter in a saucepan with a close-fitting lid over a medium heat and add the cardamom pods, and about a minute later add the turmeric and curry powder. Let them cook for a minute or so more until fragrant, add a good pinch of salt and then add the rice. Stir and cook together for a minute then raise the heat and add 640ml of boiling water from the kettle. Shake the pan a bit to make sure the rice has settled evenly, then spread a piece of crumpled-up and dampened parchment over the top of the rice and water. Put the lid on the saucepan and lower the heat. Cook for 10 minutes and then leave to stand with the lid on for at least 10 minutes – don't take the lid off.

While the rice is cooking, pin-bone the haddock and put it into a saucepan with the milk. If it doesn't quite cover it add a little water. Add the bay leaves, the whole peppercorns and the fennel seed. Bring to a simmer and cook very gently for 7 minutes, then remove from the heat and leave for another 5 minutes – it should be just opaque and easy to flake. Remove from the milk and flake into chunky pieces.

Chop the parsley and slice the spring onions. Peel the eggs. Take the lid off the rice, separate the grains a little with a fork – taste for seasoning. Gently fold in the onions, the fish, most of the herbs, half the eggs – cut in quarters – and some more salt if needed. Put into a serving platter or bowl and quarter the rest of the eggs, scatter them on top with some black pepper and the rest of the herbs. Serve while still hot.

I opened the café in January, and closed it in the same month three years later so I could focus my over-stretched resources on the restaurant. Konstam opened in April, but that too came to an end, in early August just over four years later. It wasn't quite as sharp as closing the café, but the blow to my ego was much more powerful. The process of winding it up was far more convoluted, as by then it was a limited company. Insolvency is a tricky process and you have to be careful who you tell about it before it happens. Obviously the board, shareholders and the solicitors dealing with it need to know, but you can't tell anyone you owe money to, which included the bank, the staff and most of my suppliers, many of whom were passionate farmers I'd been working with for the last four or five years. This meant there was a period of a few weeks when I knew what was going on but the people working around me didn't. That was very difficult to manage. It wasn't until the last day that I was allowed to tell them they didn't have a job anymore. I ended up not owing much money to the staff – I did my best to make sure they weren't left out of pocket – and did what I could to level things with my suppliers before pulling the plug, but nonetheless I felt pretty atrocious about the situation. Not only that, but I couldn't let on to the customers who had supported us through the years, many of whom had become friends.

The last day was a Sunday, and as well as a quiet service we had an engagement party that lunchtime. At the end of service I started to tell the staff and some of the customers who were in. The couple who were engaged overheard the conversation and asked me what was going on. When I explained to them that this was the last day they were devastated. The reason they'd had the party here in the first place was because it was where they'd had their first date a year or so before; for them the restaurant was a significant part of their story. On the spot they asked me to cook for them at their wedding – it was at this incredible wedding in Scotland that we had Iain Spink's Arbroath smokies.

I rang everyone who had booked to explain the situation, and made sure all the staff and suppliers were up to speed over the next couple of days. The staff were amazing, I think they knew something was up, even if they didn't realise it was so imminent, and all my suppliers were incredible, taking it in their stride and appreciating that these things happen. The bank was less understanding, and I was left paying them money for some time to come. By the time I'd taken care of the most pressing arrangements I was crushed, and I remember sitting in the empty restaurant a few days later, after the insolvency company had taken everything away. Part of me was relieved that it was over, but the rest of me was just gutted, and very, very ashamed – the sense of failure, and such a well-publicised failure at that, was deep and stuck with me for years.

But some years have passed now, and although the business didn't
work as a commercial concern it was an extraordinary project that
had set out to achieve a difficult and demanding task, but one
that provided me and the many people who worked with me the
opportunity to become really immersed in the seasonal year in a way
we would never otherwise have been able to do. It brought with it
some big puzzles to solve, but it also gave great depth and richness
to the food we were making and to the lives of the people who were
involved in it. Of course there are some things I would change, but
would I do it again? In a heartbeat.

So August draws to a close. We slowly say goodbye to the summer.
The hopeful freshness of May and June is long gone and a more
sombre coolness is in the air – replacing the warmth and goodness
of summer. There is still much to look forward to, with harvest
festival just around the corner and the flood of produce it celebrates,
but, Indian summers aside, the end of August brings a sense of the
inevitable – autumn is coming and winter will follow.

SEPTEMBER

—

Elderberries

Mushrooms

Ceps

Marrows

Leeks

Damsons

Sloes

Hazelnuts

Cobnuts

Figs

Peaches

Oysters

Today I walked on the lion-coloured hills
with only cypresses for company,
until the sunset caught me, turned the brush
to copper
set the clouds
to one great roof of flame
above the earth,
so that I walk through fire, beneath fire,
and all in beauty.

Elizabeth Coatsworth, 'On the Hills' (1924)

I started cooking in September. Really cooking, that is. A year out of college, still tanned from a summer spent abroad in Italy and Greece, my hair shaved and wearing a faded black T-shirt and ripped jeans, I wandered into Moro in Clerkenwell, with my friend Lucy in tow, feeling thoroughly out of my depth, and asked if they had any jobs in the kitchen. I was told to 'Go and speak to Samantha,' so I walked to the open kitchen at the back of the restaurant and asked for her. A very busy-looking woman peered over the pass and gave me a quizzical and rather withering look, and I was surprised when she told me to come in and do a trial shift a few days later. So I did, on the 6th. Although my memories of that shift are hazy, one of the things I remember well was putting on my uniform for the first time. Crisp and white, I loved it straight away – it made me feel very special, very grown up and part of something. I made the decision to leave one of the buttons on my chef's jacket undone at the top, and I've worn it like that ever since, like a superstition.

I'd like to say that first shift went swimmingly, but I just felt
very slow and in the way all the time. It took me most of the prep
section of the shift to pick through a few lamb shanks, taking out
the sinews and mincing the meat to make *kibbeh nayeh*. All too soon
service began. My memory tells me that they put me on the cold
section, on my first day, on my own, but I'm not sure – Samuel
might have been doing it with me. I remember it slowly occurring
to me what was going on and a general sense of blind panic setting
in. I really didn't have a clue what I was doing – and there was
an endless stream of tickets and a sea of people waiting to be fed.
Despite my ineptitude they gave me a job, and a few weeks later
my dad took me to buy my first knife at a kitchen shop in Soho.
I tried out several and the man said to go with whichever one felt
right, so I did; it was a 27cm drop-forged Global chef's knife.
It was beautiful. And it was very, very sharp.

Those first weeks passed in a flurry, I was working harder than I ever
had before, so it took me a few days to figure out who was who. It
transpired that Samuel and Samantha were husband and wife, and
co-owned the restaurant with their friends Mark Sainsbury and Jake
Hodges. After I'd been there a couple of months, I asked Samuel if
I could have a chat. I told him that I didn't want to waste months
or years of my life trying to do something I wasn't any good at, and
did he think it was worth me persevering? At that point he said
one of the nicest things anyone has ever said to me – he said that he
thought I could possibly become one of the best. Although he was
being a little over-optimistic, it was a nice thing for someone in his
position to say, and looking back I feel it was a significant moment
in my career.

Time went on and I eventually became Sam and Sam's deputy.
I was at Moro for three and a half years; it was hard work, and
very stressful, but it was an amazing place, and to this day I feel
pushed by the standards it set.

As summer decays into autumn we come full circle. By the end of September we will have navigated a full food year. Some of the crops available now have already been covered in the October and August chapters, but there are still a few more that I feel define this time of year in a different way.

In recent years, as I've immersed myself more and more in the seasons, it's the elderberry that most tells me autumn has arrived. As may be clear by now, the elder holds a certain fascination for me, both the berries and the blooms – if I were so inclined I would weave them into stories of magic and mystery. The flowers and fruit of the elder lead a double life – on the one hand, they warn of turmoil and unease but they also open our eyes to a world of pleasure. There is power coursing through them; they help treat a variety of human ills, but their place in the kitchen is also assured, and with simple preparation they provide us with a window into an otherworldly landscape of unexpected flavour all year round.

By now, as the remains of the elderflower cordial are mixed into one last refreshing jug of iced water, any upturned sprays of ivory flowers we missed back in May have been replaced with heavy-hanging hands of small, dark purple berries. I mostly stew or make a syrup with them, which can be used in various ways, and they are exceptional in apple compote to go with roast pork. Pick out and discard any unripe ones and they are delicious raw sprinkled over a smoked duck salad or with cheese. I've been told raw berries can be mildly poisonous when unripe, so it's probably best to avoid them, but I've eaten them many times with no ill effects.

There is a darkness to the taste of elderberries that's almost gothic; on one level it's in the same vein as many other soft fruits, such as blackcurrants and blueberries, but underneath this the flavour sums up something of the time they come to fruition. It is now, as we reach the cusp of the season, that the first hint of the year's mortality rises in the east. Winter is on its way – the rain, the cold, the mulchy leaves and soggy soil. None of that has yet arrived, but the taste of elderberries gives you an inkling.

We made lots of excellent elderberry ice cream at Konstam, which strangely tastes a bit like old-school chocolate-flavour yoghurt. I'm not sure they make them any more, but my grandma used to get them for us. They had a distinctive flavour, which was, as Douglas Adams might have said, almost, but not quite, entirely unlike chocolate.

Elderberry syrup is simple to make and keeps for a long time in the fridge or in sterilised bottles. Put the berries in a saucepan and boil them until they start to fall apart (add a little water so they don't stick), then hang them up in muslin to drain. Return the liquid to the saucepan, then add the appropriate amount of sugar – not quite 1:1, pounds to pints – bring it to the boil again and bottle it. The juice of berries and dark fruit usually contains a fair amount of pectin, but elderberries have very little and won't produce a jelly. If you want to make elderberry jelly then boil them with some chopped cooking apples – peel, pips, cores and all – and the combined juice will set.

For me elderberries are the quintessential autumn fruit and can be found in hedgerows across the British Isles, but another potent symbol of autumn is wild mushrooms. They can be foraged in all sorts of places, but there's an art to finding them, and people who know where they're growing in quantity will often go to great lengths to keep it to themselves. I know an Italian man called Enrico who used to forage ceps for me when I ran Konstam. I knew he hunted for them somewhere west of London, but when I asked for more detail – to make sure they were within our sourcing area – I saw him stiffen and I realised I'd made a faux pas. All he would say was that they were from somewhere near Henley; his caginess was unsurprising as ceps are very valuable and his livelihood depended on them. Henley was a little outside our remit but the mushrooms were so fine I wasn't going to turn him away for the sake of a few miles.

Mushrooms like woodlands because the loam is ideal and the decaying leaves keep the earth very moist. They don't like extended spells of dry weather, nor do they like too much rain as they become waterlogged and will rot. As for poisonous mushrooms, the general rule of thumb when foraging is: if you're not 100 per cent sure, don't eat it. That's why it's a good idea to take an expert with you, or at the very least a mushroom book. Even if you have a book, some edible ones can be easily confused with poisonous ones. Although very few mushrooms will kill you – and they're almost never found in towns or cities – there are several that cause serious illness. The most toxic mushroom found in the UK is known as the death cap, and eating it can lead to liver failure and death. Others, such as the beechwood sickener, may cause vomiting or diarrhoea but aren't usually fatal. Some notable species, such as the liberty cap (magic mushroom) and fly agaric, have hallucinogenic effects. This may be desirable in some instances, but can cause problems if taken unwittingly or in the wrong quantities, so once again, unless you know what you're doing, steer clear. Despite these words of warning, there are lots of lovely mushrooms that can be gathered safely and used for culinary purposes.

There are thousands of ways to cook wild mushrooms, but I think it's hard to beat them served on toast. Fry a little garlic in olive oil or butter until it turns light brown and smells nutty, add freshly picked and cleaned mushrooms, such as chanterelle, pied de mouton, horn of plenty or girolle, and cook them over a high heat with a dash of vermouth or fino. Serve them on toasted sourdough with the sticky liquid left in the pan. Puffball mushrooms are stunning cooked this way, but need to be picked before they form spores and soften. Check that they aren't immature agarics or amanitas, which will have gills inside – a good puffball is solid white all the way through. Giant puffballs not only taste amazing and have a wonderful texture but they look very striking on the plate.

Ceps (*cèpes* in French, *porcini* in Italian) are a real feature of the British mushroom season, as Enrico would testify. They flourish on the Continent but also grow well here. However, wet weather is bad for them as they absorb water like sponges and aren't much good for anything once waterlogged. They have a powerful nutty smell, like an unrefined truffle. Again, I like them cut in thick slices and fried in butter to get a hint of colour on each side, with some chopped garlic thrown in towards the end. The texture is very sensual and they go really well with chicken, steak, game, fish, risottos and pastas. I sometimes make a potato gratin with any odds and ends left over from making other dishes; they have just enough flavour to permeate the dish, perfuming the potatoes and cream.

One of the best mushroom dishes I've ever had was at a trattoria in Tuscany, when I visited in autumn 2008 with a group of chefs and various other people involved in the food industry. We'd been to the two Slow Food biennial events – Salone del Gusto and Terra Madre – which take place on the site of the old Fiat factory in Turin. Afterwards, some of us went on to a friend's farm near Florence for a few of days cooking, eating and drinking. We ate some wonderful food on that trip but the meal that really stood out was a fungi feast served at the unassuming Trattoria Montalbino, where every dish contained either porcini or truffles. The one that stood out for me consisted of grilled fillet steak topped with the cap of a large porcini mushroom. I'm not sure what else they did with it, if anything, but it was absolutely stunning.

Talking about this meal reminds me of something else we ate on that visit. We went to a restaurant in the Piedmont region called Osteria del Boccondivino, where we had an excellent meal, but

what stood out this time was the dessert. It was a very simple
panna cotta, but what was most striking was that it was allegedly
made without gelatin. It was easily the best I've ever had, and the
gelatin debate has generated much discussion among my friends
over the years. The restaurant is near the Slow Food headquarters
and its panna cotta is legendary. *Ricette delle Osterie di Langa*, a
book of recipes from the region compiled by Slow Food, gives a
recipe for this panna cotta and lists fish glue, or *colla di pesce*, in the
ingredients, along with a tablespoon of flour. While I was there
I was struck by the consistency and suggested it was simply the
natural setting of the cream that occurs when you bring it to room
temperature or a little above and then chill it. This is the process
the chefs at Boccondivino claim they use, but no one believes them.
I've never come across fish glue myself, but in Italy it's used to set
dishes such as budino. It's also a traditional woodworking glue and
is made from the air bladders of sturgeon. Seeing as there aren't too
many sturgeon left, I'm not going to make the switch just now and
I'm not sure that Slow Food should be promoting its use. Maybe we
should start a vigil.

Even after all these years, I am still a little confused as to what
marrows are. They appear to be overgrown courgettes, but some
articles I've read seem to imply they're a separate species. There
are always lots of marrows at harvest festival and marrow-growing
competitions at village fetes, but nobody seems to eat them much.

Although the marrow is a rather unassuming vegetable to look
at, the crops themselves are fascinating. The broad leaves seem
unremarkable, but crouch down and look beneath the canopy and
you'll see a green-tinged chapel populated by elegant bright yellow
flowers that look like miniature triffids. Similar to courgette flowers
only bigger, and perhaps a little less refined in texture, they can be
cooked in much the same ways (see recipe in June).

At Konstam I was always very gung-ho about new produce as it came into season, and the first autumn after we opened I ordered boxes of marrow, before realising we weren't quite sure what to do with them. We tried roasting them, but because they have such a high water content this brought limited success. Traditionally they ought to be stuffed, but I've never really managed to make this taste particularly exciting. Perhaps I'm revealing a failing as a chef, but the blandness of the vegetable always seems to let the dish down. In the end, we decided the best thing that could be done with marrow was to make it into soup.

We roasted it first, cut in half lengthwise, laid skin-side down on a baking tray, drizzled with a lot of oil and put in a very hot oven until some colour was achieved on the flesh, which is no mean feat. In the time it takes for the flesh to roast the skin gets very burned where it comes in contact with the baking tray, but that doesn't matter as you then scrape out the flesh and combine it with a base of onions, garlic and leeks, which you've been cooking in the meantime. You can finish it with either chicken or vegetable stock and blitz thoroughly as this soup needs to be smooth. We added a little cream to make it richer, and the end result was much sexier than anything you'd expect from a marrow.

That said, it doesn't matter how good the soup is, you can only eat so much marrow, and we always felt a certain relief when the marrow season came to a close. Unfortunately they store so well we were using them all the way through to November, and sometimes even December.

Having felt we'd achieved all there was to achieve with a marrow, my mum cooked me steamed marrow covered in white sauce. It was an unexpected hit. White sauce, or béchamel, is one of the reasons I became a chef. I remember my mum cooking it when I was little, and then adding masses of grated cheddar to make what I thought was the most delicious thing on the planet. Naturally, I wanted to learn how to make it, and from the age of about nine I tried, but whatever I did, I couldn't make it without it being lumpy. The strange thing is that I now find it hard to make it anything other than smooth, even if I break all my own rules. Even in its most complicated forms, it's one of the easiest and quickest sauces to make from scratch.

Béchamel

First, infuse the milk, a pint or so. Just bring it to a simmer with some onion, celery, parsley stalk, leek, carrot, bay leaf, thyme, fennel seed and black peppercorns – a clove or two won't go amiss either. Once it's simmered, remove it from the heat and leave to cool with all the aromatics in, transferring it first to a new container in case the bottom has caught a little as it warmed up. You can use milk straight from the fridge, and although the flavour will be a bit lacking the sauce will be fine, but I do recommend taking the time if you can. The classic béchamel has equal parts butter and flour, so 50g of each is a good starting point. I usually use 40g flour and 45–50g butter, as it makes it a bit softer and it sets a tiny bit less after. If you're going to make something like a croquette or fritter, which demands that the cooled sauce holds its shape, then you'll need to add a little more flour, so 50g butter and 60–70g flour. Chop the butter up and put it in a smallish saucepan over a medium heat. When it starts to melt, add the flour and mix together. Once the butter has melted properly the two will have combined, so give it another stir and turn the heat down to cook out the flour. The mixture should bubble like molten lava. Let it cook for 2 or 3 minutes and then start adding the strained milk. A whisk helps at this point. I add it in 3 or 4 goes, making sure it's smooth each time. You've added enough milk when it's about the thickness of single cream. Then cook it out again until it reaches the required thickness. This will take 3 to 5 minutes. If it's too thin you can cook it a bit longer to reduce it. I add salt to taste at this point and pepper just before using. Béchamel keeps in the fridge for a couple of days at least, so if you don't use it all you can keep it for another time. It will set, so just warm it up, adding a little more milk if required.

I love béchamel made with finely chopped leeks added to it for the last five minutes of cooking. The leeks you find at this time of year are very different to the baby leeks you get in the summer, and although they crop up at various points in this book, I feel they warrant another mention. We used to have leeks in blankets when we were little – steamed or boiled leeks covered in white sauce. I think it was a ploy to get us to eat vegetables at a time when we might not have been quite so excited by them as we are now.

A few years ago September took me to the South of France. Not the dry, post-August Provençal south but the greener, more familiar landscape of Cantal. It was a short break, to celebrate Sanchia's mother's 60th birthday. We were staying in a tiny hamlet called Inchivala, little more than a huddle of houses on top of a small hill.

The house is of the type where the animals would have been kept on the ground floor below the main room to provide heat during the cold winters. The ceilings are all heavy wooden beams and the rock of the outside walls lines the inside too. In keeping with the agrarian history of the area it had a kitchen garden filled with autumnal bounty. Just a week before our own harvest festival it had pumpkins, courgettes, aubergines, several types of basil, beans, mint, rosehips, artichokes, onions, leeks, tomatoes – the list goes on. Nearly all the fresh produce we used that weekend came from the garden. Apart from being a legacy to untiring and constant gardening, it was a haven for those of us from London, where such produce is less easy to come by so close to the source.

There were several of us who in various ways spend our lives immersed in cooking, so it was very exciting to cook together while surrounded by such incredible produce. For the birthday feast we had fish stew, aubergine caviar, duck rillettes, walnut bread, merguez, frittata, bean stew made with local haricots, and tomatoes from the garden. We worked softly but incessantly to put it all together, fuelled by lunches of cheese, wine and dauphinoise.

The region is known for many things, not least its eponymous cheese. Enjoyed in many stages of its ripening, that weekend we had some Cantal fermier vieux, which was so ripe it defeated all but the brave. When we were there the leeks had just been harvested, and Melinda, Sanchia's mother, wrote a poem about them that really captures this time of year.

'Summer Leeks'

Their last day. A few leeks
about to send up seed pods
hover in the attacking sun
wanting not to be forgotten

Later in the day they're seen
propped up in a watering can
with a bunch of sloping shadows
waiting nonchalantly

for earth to be hosed off –
the same earth that fed them all along.
Iron can judders and clangs
leeks glitter in star-spray

water juts off them
all roots now un-matted
loosened from their gritty element
done with growing.

I felt there was a seasonal disparity between the title and the autumnal tone, and when I asked Melinda about it she explained it was a late-season poem about summer leeks, which are named after their growing period and pulled as the autumn draws in, unlike winter leeks, which are pulled earlier in the year. These are harvested from December and can be left in the ground for longer than the more delicate summer ones. Summer leeks are planted in April and you can eat them from any time they look edible to when they flower in October, hence baby leeks being around from May or June.

By the time we get to September the main crop is ready and will be happy in the ground over winter, providing us with a source of fresh green veg throughout the darker months. They are a key ingredient in some of the most comforting foods around – chicken and leek pie, leek and bacon quiche, leek and potato soup – and the winter months would be starker without them.

The story goes that the Welsh wore them into battle to distinguish themselves from their Saxon foe. Leeks don't have the same legendary status in England, though they're one of our favourite vegetables and we use them in all kinds of dishes – a mild, sweet allium that gives an unobtrusive hint of the potency of onion and garlic. Despite our fondness for them, I feel the deliciousness of leek in its own right is sometimes overlooked. I've always liked the way the French celebrate this vegetable with the simple and classic dish, leeks vinaigrette.

Leeks vinaigrette

You can dress the leeks with just about anything – try different vinegars, mustards, herbs or oils. You can toss them with yoghurt, ayran, crème fraîche or lemon dressing. If you have a barbecue on the go you can char them and peel off the burned layers instead of blanching them. Even blanched, a few minutes on a blistering griddle wouldn't hurt.

Serves 4
4 or 5 whole leeks
1 tbsp white wine vinegar
1 tsp wholegrain mustard
1 garlic clove
4 or 5 tbsp olive oil
1 handful chervil or parsley leaves
Salt and pepper

Trim the leeks, peeling off any damaged or tough layers and cutting off the roots and dark green ends, leaving the white and the light green parts. I'm generally against leek fascism but the darker green leaves take longer to cook and the tenderness of the leek is important in this recipe.

Crush the garlic with a pinch of salt and mix it with the mustard and vinegar. Check the balance of the seasoning, adding more salt if needed. Stir in the oil and check again.

Bring a pan of salted water to the boil and cook the leeks until tender but not soft. Lift them out of the water and plunge them for a few seconds into cold water – you don't want to chill them, you just want to stop them cooking.

Chop the chervil and add half of it to the dressing. Slice the leeks in half lengthwise. You can leave them whole if you prefer but I like the dressing to penetrate the layers. Gently toss them in the vinaigrette while still warm and leave them to marinate until cool. Serve with the rest of the chervil chopped or picked on top and some black pepper. Taste them before serving as they may need a few extra salt flakes.

Leeks go well with lovage, and a chopped sprig stirred into braised leeks brings any fish dish to life. You can also put them into a tart.

Leek, Cashel Blue and lovage tart

This is another great seasonal tart. Follow the pastry and blind baking recipe on page 209 for asparagus tart.

35g butter
1 onion
2 or 3 large leeks
1 or 2 sprigs lovage
100ml cream
1½ cups crème fraîche
1 tbsp wholegrain mustard
4 whole eggs
Salt and pepper
150g Cashel Blue

Peel and dice the onion. Trim the leeks, leaving some of the greener parts on, and carefully wash them, making sure to get between the layers, then slice into 1cm thick rounds. Melt the butter in a medium saucepan, add the onion and a pinch of salt and cook until soft and golden brown. Add the leek and continue to cook until sweet and tender but still green. Remove the pan from the heat.

Preheat the oven to 165°C. Pick the lovage leaves off their stems and chop. Assemble the filling with the rest of the ingredients, lightly beating the eggs in the bowl first, and roughly crumbling the cheese. Lift the leeks and onions from the pan, leaving any excess butter behind, and add to the rest of the filling. Mix, season and tip into the tart shell. Bake until only just set, lightly puffed and golden brown. Remove from the oven and leave to cool before serving. I find reheating to serve hot is best as the cooling process lets the filling set and makes the tart easier to slice.

There's a lot of luxury at the height of summer, what with the strawberries, raspberries, peaches and all. Everything starts to change when the autumn comes around. It's not that autumn produce isn't delicious and seductive, but it tends to ask more of us than some of the floozies you get in the summer months. Plums are quite sophisticated, but damsons are the plum's dark alter ego, sexier and more alluring: they're what plums want to be when they grow up. Sharp in taste and deep in colour, traces of *Prunus domestica* subsp. *insititia* have been found in the remains of Roman camps throughout Britain. The Romans brought them to us from Syria and they knew them as *prunum Damascenum*, which is why they're sometimes called Damascus plums, and where the name damson comes from. Plums hint of the must at the end of the year, and a good one should have an almondy sharpness alongside the sweetness of the yellow flesh, but the breathtaking drop into the underworld that the tartness of a damson provides is one of the defining moments of the food year.

I think damsons go better with meringues than almost any other fruit. They're so singularly lacking in naivety that they match up beautifully with the fluffy innocence of meringue – the combination of sharp and intensely sweet provides a serious punch, and a good dollop of high-quality crème fraîche helps to level it all out.

Some of the most exciting foods I've eaten were exciting because they demanded the decision as to whether I liked them or not. Damsons offer this opportunity, and sweetening them too much can be a crime. Not everyone likes their food to challenge them in this way, and I've landed myself in trouble by serving some of the tarter fruits with a little too much sharpness than the diner was expecting. However, when offering something seriously delicious it's important to take this risk. Of course, you can't please everyone, but there have been times when I wanted a flavour that almost crossed the line. I've served rhubarb ice cream that made one diner wince but drew sighs of delight from another. As they say in France, *A chacun son goût* – one of the most amazing things about food is that we all taste in different ways. Although I would never seek to alienate, there are times when I like the questions I can ask of those eating my food, encourage them to think about what it is that the person next to them is enjoying.

There are many different types of meringue but the two main varieties are the soft one with a thin, crispy shell and the drier, crunchier one with powdery bits and chewy bits. This recipe, which is my adapted version of Angela Nilsen's from *The Ultimate Recipe Book*, works perfectly for either; it all comes down to preference. If you want a crisp outside with a soft centre, cook for about 50 minutes; the longer you cook it, the dryer and chewier it will be.

Damson meringue

4 large egg whites
115g caster sugar
115g icing sugar

Preheat the oven to 100°C. Line 2 baking sheets with parchment.

Separate the eggs. In a large mixing bowl with an electric whisk at medium speed beat the egg whites to stiff peaks. Now turn the speed up and start to add the caster sugar, a dessertspoonful at a time. Continue beating for 3–4 seconds between each addition. It's important to add the sugar slowly at this stage as it helps prevent the meringue from weeping later. However, don't overbeat. When ready, the mixture should be thick and glossy.

Sift the icing sugar into the eggs in 3 stages, folding it in carefully with a metal spoon or spatula each time.

Use a couple of tablespoons to form rough quenelles and drop them gently on the baking sheet. Bake for around 50 minutes if you want crispy shells and squidgy middles, or for an hour and a half if you want a drier, crisper meringue.

For the damson compote:
Pick through them, discarding any that aren't up to the job, then give them a quick rinse, drain and put in a big saucepan with a little cold water to get them started and to stop them sticking. It's important to add sugar to taste and not to measure, but you'll need a fair bit, so put a few handfuls in at the start. Gently bring them up to heat, not stirring too much, until the sugar is fully dissolved. It's nice if the damsons aren't too crushed, so be gentle, they won't need much cooking. I always leave the stones in, partly because they slowly release a subtle almond flavour into the compote, and because they're a bit of a pain to remove beforehand, but mainly because it's fun playing 'Tinker, Tailor, Soldier, Sailor' with them as you eat the compote.

Make the compote the day before – it will be better the next day,
and on subsequent days, and it should be chilled when served,
mostly to the side of the meringue with a good tablespoon of crème
fraîche next to them both.

Another member of the plum subgenus, *Prunus spinosa*, known to us
as blackthorn or sloe, is the origin of a true delight of the seasonal
year. Since it's extremely hard, the wood of the blackthorn is used
to make walking sticks and tools, but it is for its small, dark-blue
berry that it is best known, and this mainly for the gin we make
with it. Making sloe gin is very easy but it should be left to steep
for at least two months, which fortunately coincides nicely with
Christmas – there are very few drinks that strike the festive note
quite as well as sloe gin.

The taste is deep and layered. Not only do you benefit from the
skill of the gin maker but the sloe also brings warm notes that
comfort alongside medicinal ones that pique the palate and
imagination. I remember the first time I had it, aged about 25,
at the house of a friend who was living in Islington. Her mum
came round and produced a small bottle of deep-pink elixir, which
we were only allowed the smallest sip of due to its short supply.
It was bright and delicious, not too sweet, with the sloe dancing
around the bite of the alcohol.

All you need is gin, sloes, sugar and a sterilised bottle or jar.
Most recipes agree on just under half fruit to gin. Some do this by
weight, some by eye, putting the sloes nearly halfway up the jar or
bottle and topping up with gin; I'm of the latter persuasion. Almost
everyone agrees that a good quality gin will produce a good quality
sloe gin, which stands to reason, but using the highest quality gin
you can buy is probably an unnecessary extravagance as the sloes and
sugar will put its delicate balance out of kilter and mask some of
the more subtle botanicals you're paying good money for. The sloes

should be picked when ripe; it doesn't matter whether the frost has come as you can recreate this effect in the freezer. Freezing them splits the skin and does away with the need to prick each one with a pin – this allows the gin to infuse the berries more effectively. Where there seems to be a point of debate among gin recipes is in how much sugar, but this comes down to taste, and on this count I'm with the advice from the London gin makers Sipsmith – they suggest sweetening it after it's infused. This means you can adapt the drink to the sweetness of the crop. They also suggest using a syrup so you don't have to dissolve the sugar, but if you're worried about the time this process will take then you're looking at the wrong drink. I also think the water in the syrup is an undesirable addition to the end result. I've had gin that's been aged on the sloes for six months or so and then kept for three or four years before drinking. The vital thing when it comes to sloe gin is to take it slow – it gets better with time.

Few varieties of nut grow well in the UK, certainly not cashews or almonds, but one that does is the hazelnut. There is evidence of hazelnuts being cultivated in the British Isles for millennia, and as recently as 1913 there were around 7,000 acres of them growing in the home counties alone, most of which were in Kent. The majority were a variety called Kentish Cob and this is still the case. Unfortunately, only around 250 acres are now set aside for cobnut production, but there has been a great deal of interest in them in recent years and hopefully production will increase in years to come.

Whereas the hazelnut you find in your local wholefood shop is usually round and dry, the Kentish Cob is oval and will most likely be sold fresher and still in its shell. Extracting them requires a bit of patience, but persevere and you'll be presented with a sweet, creamy kernel that is very well suited to autumnal salads. Make a dressing with Dijon mustard, cider vinegar, cobnut oil, salt and a pinch of sugar, toss in freshly shelled and roughly chopped cobnuts, bits of fried streaky bacon, frisée, chopped apple, some blackberries or elderberries and a good scattering of crumbled Stichelton or other blue cheese. Cobnut oil is great in salads and can be used as a substitute for walnut oil in most cases.

If you've ever stumbled upon a fig tree while on holiday in the South of France, Italy or Greece, and eaten one of the ripe purple fruit still warm from the sun then you'll know it's an unforgettable experience. Fig trees like to have their roots confined so they grow well in containers, which is ideal for a small, inner city garden or patio, and they like lots of water – which is a given during the average British summer – but unfortunately they also need a lot of sun, so figs grown in the UK rarely rival those from abroad.

My parents have a huge fig tree in their garden, and for many years it barely produced anything. It now bears unripe, knobbly green figs in abundance and, scattered among these, 15 or so rather pale but more promising fruit, the final ripening of which must be done indoors. I like them cold, fresh from the fridge – they are to the luscious figs of the Mediterranean as a watermelon is to a cantaloupe, delicate and fragrant, and just sweet enough to make you want more.

I've experimented a little with green figs, thinking that maybe a chutney would be nice, but I wasn't particularly happy with the results. However, I found that boiling them in syrup and packing them in jam jars produced something pretty good. They take on the flavours of the spices you cook them with, and I recommend doing this to save for the winter months, when spiced fruit seem to take on a magic bereft of them in the summer.

Another fruit we don't grow here but associate with summer is the peach. Now running towards the end of its season, it deserves a mention nonetheless. Beyond memories of biting into juicy peaches on holidays in the South of France when I was a child, there are a few more recent recollections that the thought of peaches evokes.

A couple of years ago I went to a stag do in a yurt in the Lake District, and rather foolhardily agreed to organise the food for the weekend. We talked about all sorts of things like whole roast pigs and sheep and so on, but ended up with much less adventurous fare. I procured a fantastic sirloin from my local butcher, which we had one night with caponata and a potato salad. That went down well with the boys, but another surprise hit was something I thought of while I was shopping for the trip. I saw some of the lovely flat peaches that only appear in the shops very briefly. I knew we were going to have a barbecue and so I wanted to try grilling and serving them with honey and crème fraîche, which I'd never done before. I have to say they were absolutely stunning. The smokiness from the fire and the sweetness of the peaches and honey set off by the creamy sharpness of the cold crème fraîche left us all quiet and smiling with our mouths full.

The wonderful peach saw me through another difficult improvisational challenge in 2008, when I was in San Francisco, having been invited by Alice Waters to give a demonstration at her Green Kitchen as part of a Slow Food Nation event. I did a demo about blanching, using local produce, which went down really well. But there was a night when some of us ended up at the apartment of one of our friends. As the only professional chef among a group of devoted food lovers I was charged with conjuring up a midnight feast from the bits and pieces in the kitchen. The culinary calibre of the group was very high, so I was on my mettle and a little nervous. I ended up making a simple pasta dish with bacon and cashew nuts, but right in the middle of the kitchen was a big bowl of peaches, and as we didn't have any tomatoes I decided to substitute them. It worked a treat – the bacon and cashews combining with the peach to give that salt-sweet hit that sends the taste buds wild, and the peaches having just enough acidity to play the tomato role as well as I'd hoped. Everyone was very impressed with my on-the-spot cheffery, so I felt pretty good.

Peach, bacon and cashew pasta

I originally made this with penne rigate, but it goes well with any pasta shaped to hold a tomato sauce.

Serves 4
300–400g pasta
1 large red onion
2–3 garlic cloves
2–3 peaches
3 rashers of unsmoked streaky bacon
About 1 tbsp red wine vinegar – sweet Cabernet Sauvignon is ideal
75g cashew nuts
Olive oil
Salt and pepper
Parmesan to serve

Dice the onion and cook in 2 tablespoons of olive oil with a pinch of salt until sweet and a little caramelised. Matchstick the bacon and add to the pan. When it's fried and making a sticky, sweet mix with the onion, chop and add the garlic and cook for a further 1–2 minutes.

In the meantime, cut the peaches in half around the stone and twist them off. Roughly chop them, and when the onion and bacon mix is ready turn up the heat and add the peaches. Cook over a reasonably high heat for 5 minutes or so, but turn down if the sauce looks a little dry and is threatening to burn – you can add a dash of olive oil or a splash of water or white wine if you need to. Cook for about 15 minutes, stirring occasionally. Turn off the heat when it's nice and thick. The peaches should be falling apart and soft but not completely broken up. Add the vinegar a bit at a time, tasting as you go. The acidity of the sauce depends on the ripeness of the peaches, but they don't have the sharp edge of tomatoes so the vinegar does this for you. Season with salt and pepper.

While the sauce is cooking, toast the cashew nuts in a frying pan with a drop or two of olive oil and a pinch of salt. Be careful not to burn them. Tip them onto a plate and let them cool. Crush them roughly.

Cook the pasta according to the instructions on the packet. Make sure it has a little bite to it – this sauce won't be good with flaccid pasta. Drain and return to the pan, add the sauce and a third of the cashews, stir and divide it among the plates. Drizzle a little olive oil, sprinkle the remaining cashews and grate some Parmesan on top.

The rule of thumb that oysters shouldn't be eaten in the summer months is the result of an act of Parliament passed in the late 19th century when native oyster beds were in rapid decline. This is the time of year when native oysters spawn and harvesting them during this time can lead to a significant drop in the numbers of mature oysters in subsequent years. This means that September is the beginning of the new season. The native oyster (*Ostrea edulis*) is generally considered to be superior in flavour to rock or Pacific oysters, which are farmed all year round and therefore don't have an off season. There are many oyster festivals around the UK early in the month, including at Whitstable and Colchester, both significant towns in the oyster industry. As mentioned in February, oysters were a staple food for Londoners until the early 20th century when scarcity pushed the prices up and they became a luxury item.

I had my first oyster at the age of 21, at a party in a small town called Bellingham, when I was hitchhiking down the west coast of America. I remember a sense of trepidation before upending it and feeling a sensation in my mouth I couldn't have imagined up until that point. Extraordinary. It took me about a decade to really get my head around the texture, but now I'm sold.

You can buy all sorts of oysters reared in various ways from waters all around the British coast. Areas of particularly high production include Essex, Dorset, Cornwall and Ireland. They're also reared elsewhere, and it's worth trying different types to see which you like and how the different rearing styles affect the flavour. Native oysters tend to be stronger tasting, while oysters reared in a mixture of salt and freshwater are milder and sweeter. Mersea Island, where I've sourced a great deal of my fish over the years, is famous for its oysters and holds an annual festival.

The oyster is a bivalve mollusc that feeds on plankton and other nutrient particles in the water, filtering them through its gills at a rate of up to five litres an hour. They safely process the nitrogen that plankton feed on and therefore help to keep water pollution down. Oyster beds also increase the effective surface area of the seabed by up to 50 times, creating a rich biodiversity for all kinds of other marine life that either hide among or fasten themselves to the oysters. Like mussels, harvesting them causes very little secondary damage to the seabed, so they are a very sustainable source of seafood. Although there have been reports in recent years of an increase in norovirus levels in the UK oyster population, it seems that susceptibility is more a case of person-by-person than an overall increased health risk, so there's no reason to stop enjoying them if you've felt no ill effects in the past.

Oysters are enigmatic and the idea that a bad one can leave you sick as a dog only adds to the excitement of eating them. Throughout the ages oysters have been regarded as an aphrodisiac owing to their shape, taste and texture. There is certainly something very suggestive about the slithery mineral hit you get from them, but recent experiments conducted by a group of American and Italian scientists suggests there is scientific evidence to back this up. It seems that both oysters and mussels contain high levels of the amino acids that stimulate the production of various sex hormones, especially in spring.

Another mysterious element of the oyster is the age-old problem of how to get into them without leaving the shell full of shards. It's tricky at first, but with a little practice it's relatively easy. There is an element of danger to it, and the potential injuries can be gruesome, but again, this just adds to their allure. There are two types of oyster knife: short and blunt or longer and more pointed. I prefer the longer ones. Professional shuckers use chainmail gloves, but I use a folded tea towel to rest the oyster in and protect my hand in case the knife slips. The oyster has to be placed with the flatter half of the shell upwards. Sometimes this isn't immediately obvious, so another thing to look for is the 'nub' of the hinge, which needs to be facing up. The knack is to get the point of the blade deep into the hinge of the shell, then – when you have a bit of leverage – crack the hinge and slide the knife around the lip to release the oyster, slicing it away from the upper shell as you go. You need to clean the blade of any muck or shards and then use it to clear the oyster of its moorings on the lower shell. Make sure you don't spill the liquid in the shell as it's part of the whole experience and helps it go down easily. I've only injured myself shucking oysters once, and that was when I tried opening one with a small folding penknife. Predictably the penknife folded and I was lucky to get away with only a cut finger.

You can eat your oyster as it comes, savouring the salt and other minerals, letting it transport you off to sea, or have it with any one of several classic accompaniments, such as shallot and vinegar, Tabasco sauce or freshly squeezed lemon. I like them best with lemon, or unadulterated, and sometimes with shallot vinegar – also known as a mignonette – but I don't really like them with Tabasco as it masks too much of the flavour. I always chew my oysters, loving the creaminess you get when you give it a couple of quick bites, but some prefer the slithery feeling of it going down in one.

Allspice and shallot mignonette

Enough for a dozen oysters

5 tbsp good white wine vinegar

1 tsp ground allspice

1 large banana shallot

1 small strip lemon zest

1 small strip orange zest

Very finely dice the shallot and combine with the rest of the ingredients. Add more vinegar if required. Leave to infuse for half an hour before using. Spoon onto the shucked oyster just before you eat it.

Oysters can be cooked but it needs to be done with care and skill or it can result in a travesty. I once had a curried oyster soup in France that was an expensive disaster, but I had grilled oysters in California that were divine. I haven't done much with cooked oysters myself other than a slightly underdeveloped recipe for lamb with oysters, which I wrote for a demonstration a few years back. It was inspired by some delicious mutton and oyster sausages I bought at Borough Market, and the combination chimes with the classic lamb and anchovy pairing I love so much. Since then I've developed a dish of lamb stuffed with oysters. Autumn lamb is fuller in flavour than the lamb at the start of the year, and the belly is perhaps the most flavoursome cut of all.

Braised lamb belly with oysters and chervil

I like the idea of the rich lamb belly slow-cooked until melting, lightened gently with a little white wine, chervil and the subtle minerals in the oyster. This goes well with boiled potatoes and a fresh green salad. Later in the year try it with salsify, also known as the oyster plant.

Serves 4

2 lamb bellies

14 oysters

2 large shallots

2 sprigs thyme

50g lardo

2 carrots

1 celery stick

1 onion

2 garlic cloves

½ glass dry white wine

1 bay leaf

1 tbsp white wine vinegar

Olive oil for frying

½ bunch chervil

Salt and pepper

Butcher's twine

Finely dice the shallots and strip the thyme. Shuck 6 of the oysters, reserve the liquid and keep it in the fridge. Lay the bellies flat on your work surface or chopping board. Very thinly slice the lardo and place in a line down the middle of each belly. Arrange the thyme and shallot and the 6 shucked oysters on top of this, half on each belly. Season with salt and pepper. Roll the belly around the oysters and tie them with string, either using a running knot or with individual circles tied off.

Preheat the oven to 140°C. Dice the carrot, celery and onion and slice the garlic. Fry the lamb bellies with olive oil in a frying pan until well browned all over, and set aside. Wipe out the pan with kitchen paper. Add 2 tablespoons of olive oil and gently fry the diced vegetables with a good pinch of salt until softened and starting to take on a little colour (about 10 minutes). Add the garlic and cook for another 3 or 4 minutes. Meanwhile, arrange the lamb in an ovenproof dish or casserole, and when the vegetables are ready add them to the dish with the bay leaf. Pour in the white wine and add a little extra seasoning, cover tightly with foil or a lid and cook in the middle of the oven for 3–4 hours, or until the lamb is very soft.

Remove from the oven and let the lamb bellies cool in the liquid. When lukewarm, wrap each one in two layers of cling film to make two tight sausages and chill in the fridge. Reserve and chill the liquid separately.

To serve, remove any fat from the top of the liquid and put in a small saucepan, reduce by two-thirds, or until slightly sticky, then add the vinegar and remove from the heat.

Take the cling film off the lamb and slice into 1cm rounds. Fry these in a hot frying pan with a little olive oil until coloured on each side.

Shuck the remaining 8 oysters and add the combined liquid from these and the others to the lamb sauce. Heat gently until just simmering. Chop the chervil and add to the sauce, reserving a few fronds to garnish the plate. Serve the lamb and pour the sauce over, arranging the fresh oysters on the plate.

Since the start of October the year has been turning, crops have been planted, harvested and eaten, but this is when it all comes together and the traditional harvest celebrations begin. Harvest festival is celebrated on or near the Sunday of the harvest moon, which is the full moon that occurs closest to the autumn equinox. Most years the harvest moon is in late September, but one in three years it comes at the beginning of October. While the increasing availability of produce around the year dims our seasonal awareness, most of us know about harvest festival and, particularly if we have young children, celebrate it in some form or another. Although it's essentially a pagan ritual, the Church has always seen it as an opportunity to give thanks and so it especially resonates in parts of the country where the church is still central to the community.

This is the time of the year when all the hard work reaches its conclusion and the produce is at its most bountiful. A good deal of what's been in season over the summer is still around and there isn't much change in what's available now and in October, but it will start to thin out as winter sets in.

September is our final month, but there is no postscript, just a continuation of the cycle. As we come to the end, so we come back to the beginning, slowly building momentum to reach next year's harvest with all that comes in between. Everyone marks their years in different ways, and this is how I mark mine, with the changing seasons of food.

The more we immerse ourselves in the food year, the more we allow ourselves to be drawn into its sphere of influence – the growing and rearing, the harvesting and gathering, the preparing, cooking and eating. We are what we eat, but we are also our history, culture, commerce and environment. Food shapes us in so many ways, and a preoccupation with it need not be unhealthy. In fact, I feel it's the concerns that prevent us from engaging with food properly that lead to unhealthy choices. Eating seasonally enhances our engagement, opens us up to a story with food at the heart of it. And ultimately, for me, this is what's important – food and the enjoyment of it. So many of the best times in my life have been when food was the catalyst – a springboard for other good things. Time spent with friends making and eating food – the breaking of bread – means more time together, more conversation, more appreciation of each other and the world around us. It leads to journeys that wouldn't otherwise have been taken.

ACKNOWLEDGEMENTS

—

There are two men without whom this book would never have happened. To Walter Donohue I owe a gratitude I can hardly express, for nine years of nurturing, editing, support and friendship; an understanding yet firm source of unconditional belief in me and in my book. But it was Paul Godfrey who first suggested to Walter that he approach me, on behalf of Faber – without that nudge I probably never would have come into their sights. Thank you both.

I also owe a special debt of thanks to Howard Sooley, with whom I collaborated for many years on the book. Although its final form was without photographs, his knowledge, enthusiasm, unique eye and shared vision pushed me on, and helped me have greater conviction in my own work.

Since my manuscript was accepted, in 2015, and it went from being just words on a page to a book in the making, I keep having to stop and pinch myself; to be published by the same house as Eliot, Beckett, Armitage, Hughes, Plath, the Coen Brothers – so many great writers – is a boyhood dream. But then Faber is an extraordinary institution – there are few publishers who would have waited so long for a manuscript only one person had laid eyes on. Faber loves authors and their authors love them. So thank you, as a whole, to Stephen Page for showing a personal interest in an ephemeral and unpredictable project, and to the many people who have given of themselves to the book, Charlotte Robinson, Anne Owen, Donna Payne, Kate McQuaid, Sophie Portas, John Grindrod . . . thank you.

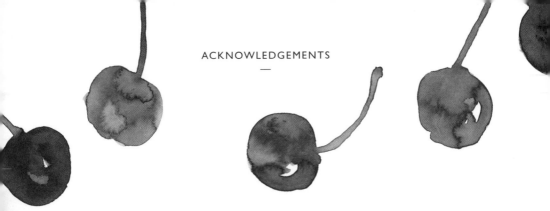

I'm extraordinarily lucky to have worked with Caz Hildebrand
and her team at Here Design. In particular Camille Blais, for her
patience, hard work and delicious illustrations, and Josh Shires.

I must also give a special thank you to Anna Swan, my copy editor,
for her additional voice and making my writing so much better; to
Robert Caskie – my agent for this book, and to Polly Robinson for
her endless help and friendship.

To all my recipe testers and contributers – Ella Tarn, Anna Koska,
Charlotte Jarman, Abi Zabron, Mark English, Danny Kingston, my
mum, Julian de Feral, Ellen Farqharson, Emma Miles, Nico Rilla.
Thank you Melinda Lovell for your words, and Elena Heatherwick
for your pictures. I must also thank Olia Hercules – she helped me
pick up my tired legs in my marathon's last hundred yards.

I had some amazing people with me at Konstam – I want to thank
them all for their hard work and dedication. Paul Thomas was my
rock for years; Luke Matthews, Tom Downer, Victor Hugo, Jack
Mitchell, Patrick George, Adam Laing, Roberta Jenkins, Stephane
Bechu, Prask Sutton, David Netherton, a much longer list than I
have space for here. Judith Rattenbury and my investors, for their
faith, and all of my customers from both the café and the restaurant.
Thank you to Caro Pickering for her unstinting work and support,
as a director of Konstam and as a friend. My sister Maisie for
many things, and for pulling me into shape when my café was
born. Frith Kerr and Amelia Noble for their extraordinary talent,
understanding and creativity – I loved our meetings. Thomas
Heatherwick for his mind and vision, and his entire studio for what
they managed to achieve, in particular Fergus Comer, Ingrid Hu

and Dandi Zhang. Semih Aslan and the team at Solmaz. Isobel
and Baroness Janet Cohen. Christopher Scott, Amy Williams and
the Sauce Communications team. Claire Banks for her friendship
and huge amounts of help with tax returns and other money
matters. Theresa Hickey, my agent for *The Urban Chef* and more.
Emma Bebb and the team at the London Cooking Project.
Everyone at Sustain and the London Foodlink.

I owe the farmers, growers, producers and suppliers who have
provided me with so much amazing produce over the years a
very special thanks. There are many but in particular, Keith and
Liz Bennett at Chiltern Farm Food, Peter and Joan Clark, Duncan
Mitchell at White Heath Farm, Toby Williams at Stanhill Farm,
Ben Woodcraft at Ben's Fish, Chris Frederick and Ian at S. J.
Frederick & Sons, David Wright at Wrights Mill, Paul at Cramers
Butchers, Michaela Edge at Norbury Blue, Chris Herald, Phil Guest,
Steve Benbow, Sam Fairs at Hill Farm, Troels Bendix, Dennis
Warrington at Bill Bean.

Sam and Sam Clark, my culinary mum and dad, much of this book
is because of you. Leila McCallister, my godmother of food, Jacob
Kenedy for helping turn my café food into restaurant food. Alice
Waters for inspiring us all and for having me at Chez Panisse.

Sanchia Lovell for being my partner in crime, gastronomic and
beyond – you have kept me sane so many times; and Jack Pickering,
for a lifetime of friendship. Adam Penny, my brother, for *The Urban
Chef*, for everything; without you I would be much less.

Julie Morris, George Mallory, Rosie Holtom, Laura Freeman, to all my
friends, everyone who shared my life during this time and supported
me through tantrums, tears and heavy workloads – it's appreciated
more than I can say.

Most of all, I want to thank my parents, for their faith and support,
not only in my culinary endeavors, but in everything I do; for being
who they are, and giving me what they have.

—

ABOUT THE AUTHOR

—

Oliver Rowe is a Londoner who first learned to cook in Tuscany. He trained and flourished at the award-winning Moro in Clerkenwell and was Head Chef at Maquis in Hammersmith. After a stint in Paris and the south of France he went on to open his café – called Konstam, after his grandmother – followed by his restaurant, Konstam at the Prince Albert, both in London's King's Cross. Oliver featured in BBC2's *The Urban Chef*, which followed his search for local suppliers to provide high quality, seasonal produce for his restaurant. More recently he has worked in kitchens in the UK and abroad, including Chez Panisse in Berkeley, California.

Photo: Elena Heatherwick

Recipe index

—

General index